The Bible Teaching Commentary on Romans

by

Paul J. Bucknell

Books by Paul J. Bucknell

Allowing the Bible to speak to our lives today!

Overcoming Anxiety: Finding Peace, Discovering God
Reaching Beyond Mediocrity: Being an Overcomer
The Life Core: Discovering the Heart of Great Training
The Godly Man: When God Touches a Man's Life
Redemption Through the Scriptures
Godly Beginnings for the Family
Principles and Practices of Biblical Parenting
Building a Great Marriage
3xE Discipleship
Christian Premarital Counseling Manual for Counselors
Relational Discipleship: Cross Training
Running the Race: Overcoming Lusts
The Bible Teaching Commentary on Genesis
The Bible Teaching Commentary on Romans
Book of Ephesians: Bible Studies
Book of Joel: Bible Studies
Book of Romans: Bible Studies
Life Transformation: A Monthly Devotional
Walking with Jesus: Abiding in Christ
Inductive Bible Studies in Titus
1 Peter Bible Study Questions: Living in a Fallen World
Satan's Four Stations: The Destroyer is Destroyed
Take Your Next Step into Ministry
Training Leaders for Ministry
Study Guide for Jonah: Understanding God's Heart

Check out these and other valuable resources like our digital online libraries at www.foundationsforfreedom.net.

The Bible Teaching Commentary on Romans

Laying a Solid Foundation

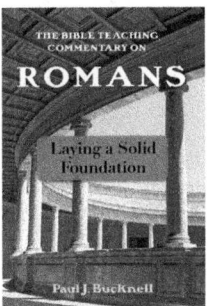

Paul J. Bucknell

The Bible Teaching Commentary

The Bible Teaching Commentary on Romans: Laying a Solid Foundation
Series: *The Bible Teaching Commentary*
Printed:
ISBN-10: 1619930323
ISBN-13: 978-1-61993-032-2
Copyright © 2015 Paul J. Bucknell

E-book:
ISBN-10: 1619930331
ISBN-13: 978-1-61993-033-9

www.foundationsforfreedom.net
Pittsburgh, PA 15212

The NASB version is used unless otherwise stated.
New American Standard Bible ©1960, 1995 used by permission, Lockman Foundation www.lockman.org.

All rights reserved. Limited production is acceptable without prior permission for home, educational and ministry use. For extensive reproduction contact the author at info@foundationsforfreedom.net.

Dedication

"Oh, the depth of the riches both of the wisdom and knowledge of God! How unsearchable are His judgments and unfathomable His ways! For who has known the mind of the Lord, or who became His counselor? Or who has first given to Him that it might be paid back to Him again? For from Him and through Him and to Him are all things. To Him be the glory forever. Amen."

Romans 11:33-36.

Appreciation

How exciting to have had so many opportunities to leading a team of teachers to work through the wonderful Book of Romans. Each chapter captures our mind and life as it seeks to conform us to the image of Christ.

My daughter, Allison Bucknell, has worked hard at helping shape this book. Her fascination with words and sentences simply amazes me!

Introduction

God's truth transforms lives. The Gospel of the Lord Jesus has crossed every border, bringing God's glorious redemptive message to millions around the globe. The Lord has used the apostle's letter to the Romans to lay a solid foundation for the believer's life.

The problem no longer is not having the Book of Romans in our language but understanding how to present its rich meaning to God's people so that they can be equipped to do God's work. Once the Christian is buttressed by the strong teaching in Romans, he or she can firmly stand against the cults and worldly philosophies that attack the Christian faith inside and outside the church. The secular world tells us to 'listen to our hearts.' Religious people falsely state that it 'doesn't matter what one believes, just so we believe.' These are rejections of the Gospel of Jesus Christ. We are damned if we trust our hearts and hopeless if our hope is not fixed on Christ.

In contrast to the world's message, The Book of Romans powerfully projects the truth of God that shapes our thoughts and allows the Spirit of God to touch our souls and draw us into a deeper relationship with Him. This results in a stronger commitment to love and serve God's people. The gospel, sin, redemption, justification, glorification, predestination, and global mission work are some of the themes presented in Romans that ought to drive us into God's marvelous presence, causing us to consider the ways He transform our lives.

The Bible Teaching Commentary series acts as a useful expository commentary designed to unlock the power of God's Word so that lives can be strengthened and deepened. This series is committed to the belief that the Word of God must shape the disciple's heart and mind (2 Tim 3:16-17) rather than only become an exchange of ideas. Empowered by the conviction that God's Word is true and relevant for every Christian no matter where they live, we want to step into the classroom so that each student understands the message of God in each passage.

In teaching Romans to local college students many times during the last two decades, I have searched for an effective way to convey the faith that God is trying to instill in them during the short time I have to explore His word with them. Teaching outlines, along with extensive summaries, keep the book as a whole in mind despite the apostle's deep digression into extended logical arguments. A careful balance is maintained between the explanation of difficult passages and the communication of Paul's main message of transformation in each passage.

The companion volume: _The Book of Romans: Study Questions_ provides extensive study questions that allow the teacher and student to dive deeper into the meaning and application of the Book of Romans. _BFF's New Testament Digital Library_[1] not only includes these two books on Romans, but all our New Testament teaching resources such as handouts, audio/video messages, and powerpoint slides that further equip the teacher to bring the amazing truth to others.

May our gracious God enable each of you to possess the solid foundation that is presented in the Book of Romans so that you can see Jesus Christ working effectively and powerfully in your life, and so that those from every nation will join Paul in declaring, "the only wise God, through Jesus Christ, be the glory forever. Amen" (Rom 16:27).

Rev. Paul J. Bucknell

September, 2015

---

[1] http://www.foundationsforfreedom.net/Help/Store/Intros/DLibrary-BibleNT.html

Reference Books on the Book of Romans

Ancient Christian Commentary on Scripture, Vol VI, (IVP).

Be Right by Warren W. Wiersbe (Victor).

Commentaries on The Epistle of Paul the Apostle to the Romans by John Calvin. Trans. by John Owen, Eerdmans 1955.

A Commentary on the Epistle to the Romans by Charles Hodge (Wm. B Eerdmans).

The Greek New Testament, 2nd ed, United Bible Societies.

The Greek New Testament According to the Majority Text, 2nd ed., by Hoges and Farstad.

Linguistic Key to the Greek New Testament by Fritz Rienecker (Regency).

Men & Women in Christian Perspective by Werner Neuer.

An Outline of New Testament Survey by Dr. Dunnett (Moody Press).

New Testament Survey by Robert Gromacki (Baker).

Paul's Letter to the Romans by John Ziegler (SCM Press).

Romans: A Shorter Commentary by Charles Cranfield (Wm. B Eerdmans).

Romans by Paul Achtemeir (John Knox Press).

Wycliffe Exegetical Commentary by Douglas Moo (Moody Press).

Contents

The Book of Romans   15
Purpose and Outline

The Book of Romans   17
An Extensive Summary

The Book of Romans   29
An Introduction

Romans 1:1-17   33
The Proclamation of the Gospel

Romans 1:18-32   51
The Evident Guilt of Mankind

Romans 2:1-11   67
The Prosecution of Mankind

Romans 2:12-29   81
Three Lousy Excuses

Romans 3:1-20   91
Total Depravity

Romans 3:21-31   99
Salvation by Faith

Romans 4:1-25   **109**
    The Nature of Saving Faith

Romans 5:1-11   **125**
    A Faith Worth Believing

Romans 5:12-21   **131**
    Further Proof of Justification by Faith

Romans 6-7   **141**
    Eliminate Misunderstandings

Romans 8:1-17   **161**
    The New Man

Romans 8:18-39   **171**
    Conquerors Through Christ

Election and Predestination   **183**
    Understanding and Appreciating Romans 8:29-30

Romans 9:1-13   **191**
    Great Hope for True Israel

Romans 9:14-22   **197**
    Questions About God's Elect

Romans 9:23-33   **201**
    Grace and Election

Romans 10:1-21   **207**
    Sharing the Gospel

Romans 11:1-36 217
Salvation's Great Plan

Romans 12:1-8 237
Our Heart Responses

Romans 12:9-21 247
Principles of Christian Growth

Romans 13:1-14 257
Living in the World

Romans 14:1-23 263
Judge Not Others

Romans 15:1-13 281
Living for Others

Romans 15:14-33 285
Our Will and God's Will

Romans 16:1-27 293
Community Spirit

Appendix 1: Author's Information 301

The Book of Romans
Purpose and Outline

Purpose of the Book of Romans
Proclaim and defend God's glorious redemptive plan to establish His righteousness through the gospel of Jesus Christ in all peoples, both Jew and Greek.

Outline of the Book of Romans

    A. Righteousness Revealed: Gospel   (Rom 1:1-17)

    B. Righteousness Obsolete: Sin   (Rom 1:18-3:20)

    C. Righteousness Made: Justification   (Rom 3:21-5:21)

    D. Righteousness Attained: Sanctification (Rom 6-8)

    E. Righteousness eNlarged: Worldwide   (Rom 9-11)

    F. Righteousness Spread: Service   (Rom 12-16)

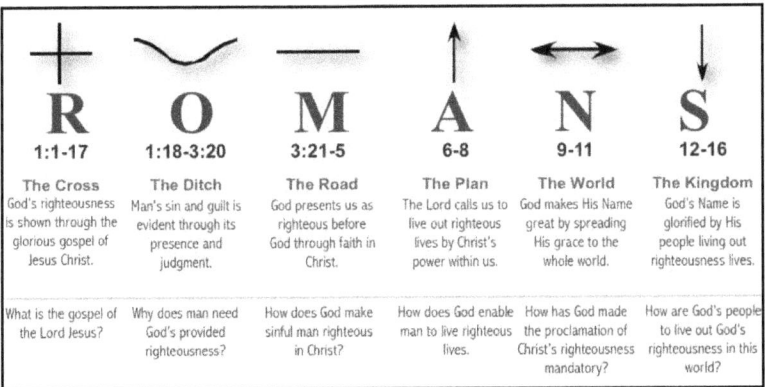

R	O	M	A	N	S
1:1-17	1:18-3:20	3:21-5	6-8	9-11	12-16
The Cross	The Ditch	The Road	The Plan	The World	The Kingdom
God's righteousness is shown through the glorious gospel of Jesus Christ.	Man's sin and guilt is evident through its presence and judgment.	God presents us as righteous before God through faith in Christ.	The Lord calls us to live out righteous lives by Christ's power within us.	God makes His Name great by spreading His grace to the whole world.	God's Name is glorified by His people living out righteousness lives.
What is the gospel of the Lord Jesus?	Why does man need God's provided righteousness?	How does God make sinful man righteous in Christ?	How does God enable man to live righteous lives?	How has God made the proclamation of Christ's righteousness mandatory?	How are God's people to live out God's righteousness in this world?

The Book of Romans
An Extensive Summary

Every Bible book including Romans has its specialized purposes. The Book of Romans was designed to lay a solid foundation for our Christian faith. If the foundation is built right, then the whole building (the Christian life) can withstand tremendous attacks, such that are coming against the Gospel in today's world. The Apostle Paul shows how the death and resurrection of Jesus Christ provides a perfect solution for man's problem, whether he be Jew or Gentile.

A Summary of the Book of Romans

The Book of Romans reveals God's great plan to establish His righteousness throughout the earth through the gospel of Christ. The 30 times the word 'righteousness' is used in Romans only partly reveals the importance of this theme. When we add the Greek root word for righteousness (*diakai*), including English words like 'justification' and 'justify,' the number of usages increase to over 50 times.[2]

God is ultimately concerned with restoring righteousness to man so that He can fellowship with man and work with Him in accomplishing His purposes. Man was unable to solve his sin problem so the Lord Himself carried out His redemptive plan known as the gospel (Is 63:5). God's powerful wrath like an ominous thunderstorm opposing mankind's sin and guilt became the backdrop of the revelation of God's great mercy and grace. God revealed His mysterious plan by sending His Son Jesus Christ to die for His people, both forgiving and recovering what the evil one had recklessly destroyed. Through the second Adam, Jesus Christ, God restored what the

---

[2] This list includes the word 'freed' from the Greek meaning acquitted or declared righteous (Rom 6:7).

first Adam lost and secured much more: an eternal display of love, wisdom and mercy is.

Man, being unrighteous and unable to become righteous on his own, still can secure God's righteousness through faith in Christ, securing both forgiveness and Christ's righteousness.

Purposes of the Book of Romans

Paul accomplishes his purposes for the Book of Romans through three chief ways.

(1) The Book of Romans is a Jewish evangelistic tract. Paul convinces the Jews that Jesus is the Messiah and should be believed in. His numerous arguments help convince the Jew that he should place his faith (or hold onto) in the Messiah. Paul's poignant questions and clear refutals dismiss the many false teachings that were causing confusion among the Jews.

(2) The Book of Romans presents the theology of redemption in Christ Jesus. Paul systematically presents the meaning and implication of our faith in our lives. Several key comprehensive salvation themes are given in Romans to help us understand the special place that Jesus' work has in God's overall eternal plan.

(3) The Book of Romans can also be seen as a personal letter to the Roman church to help the church of Rome understand why he had not yet visited them. He also wrote to help them properly handle a number of issues and questions that arose largely due to the mix of Jew and Gentile believers in the Roman churches.

These three underlying purposes will crop up in each of the six main portions of the Book of Romans as it is presented according to the outline. Each section presents a certain aspect of righteousness and marked by a key letter forming the word 'ROMANS.'

A. Righteousness Revealed: Gospel (Rom 1:1-17)

God's righteousness is revealed in the glorious gospel of Jesus Christ.
In this first section of Righteousness Revealed, Paul defines the gospel. He answers the question, "What is the gospel and how does it help us?" The gospel is clearly set out for us in 1:2-6. The word 'gospel' (lit. good tidings or news) is used 4 out of 10 times in this first section (1:1,9,15,16). In essence, the gospel is all about the life and work of Jesus Christ who died on our behalf and now has come alive and through the Holy Spirit lives and reigns in the life

of every one who believes in Christ. These believers are in communion with their Lord and are called 'saints', forming the corporate church (lit. called out ones, assembly) which Paul personally addresses in the closing (Rom 16:1, 4, 5, 16, 23).

Paul's preaching to the Gentiles caused much friction among the Jewish people. Because some Jewish people believed, their faith was strongly challenged by Paul's outspoken opponents. The validity of preaching the gospel to the Gentiles (non-Jews) becomes a major theme through Romans. The apostle does not merely defend his targeting of all peoples with the gospel, but convincingly shows that bringing the gospel to the nations was all along part of God's great plan (chapters 9-11)–the great mystery that is finally revealed to us. "I am under obligation both to Greeks and to barbarians, both to the wise and to the foolish" (Rom 1:14).

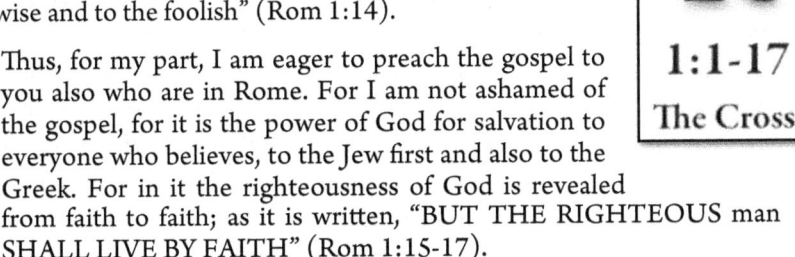

Thus, for my part, I am eager to preach the gospel to you also who are in Rome. For I am not ashamed of the gospel, for it is the power of God for salvation to everyone who believes, to the Jew first and also to the Greek. For in it the righteousness of God is revealed from faith to faith; as it is written, "BUT THE RIGHTEOUS man SHALL LIVE BY FAITH" (Rom 1:15-17).

The gospel, then, is the very power of God for salvation: the great news about what Jesus did in His person and work on the cross. It becomes the only means by which those who believe, whether Jew or Gentile, are saved and can live out their lives for the Lord. In verse 17 Paul articulates how our needed righteousness from God is found in Christ. In other words, those who come to God gain their needed righteousness through Christ so that they can live through His power in God's presence. God's righteous expression against our sins is satisfied through the death of His only Son, Christ Jesus.

"BUT THE RIGHTEOUS MAN SHALL LIVE BY FAITH."

This gospel, the offer of true righteousness, is freely offered to all. This is the place to discover the long lost righteousness that kept us from communing with God and participating in His good will. Paul is not ashamed of what gives life and liberty and neither should we.

B. Righteousness Obsolete: Sin (Rom 1:18-3:20)

Man's sin and guilt is evident through its presence and judgment.

Man is not righteous, and therefore innately opposes God's righteousness, which is increasingly evident in our post-modern culture. In Romans 1:18-3:20 Paul answers the question, "Why does man need God's provided righteousness?" If the gospel shows us the way that we are to find that needed righteousness, that is fine, but what if man does not believe obtaining God's righteousness is important? Without a firm conviction of his need before God regarding the heinousness of his sin, man will never find, search or discover the forgiveness that the Lord offers in the gospel. Mankind persistently holds to the erroneous assumption that he is not that bad to deserve judgment and that God's love will accommodate his sin.

Paul jumps in and forthrightly reveals man's evident guilt. He does not only make known mens' unrighteousness, but how they resist God's display of righteousness. Man suppresses the truth. He does not accept it. When human beings rejects the truth, it reveals his unwillingness to acquire the truth. Many argue that education and knowledge would make a difference. If man knew better then he would act better, but Paul shows the error of this argument. Both the Jews and Gentiles reject the knowledge of God whether revealed in nature, one's conscience or God's revealed Law. So whether we have general revelation (through nature or conscience) or special revelation (through scriptures or visions) from God, man will turn away, harden his heart and face God's ensuing judgment, depending on how much truth he has rejected.

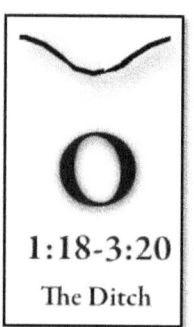

1:18-3:20
The Ditch

Those who are self-righteous, however, believe they are different from those categorized in chapter 1. They are better. Though they agree that the others should be judged, they excuse themselves. But it is here that Paul catches them: even the self–righteous are liable for their sins before God. Paul then presents argument after argument showing that man will be judged by their deeds and not by their religion, their connections, their circumcision, etc (compare the briefer John 1:12-13). Chapter one focuses on those with openly sinful lifestyles. Romans 2:1-11 catches those who exclude themselves from that first category due to their religiosity or morality.

In case they do not catch on, the apostle in 2:5-11 clarifies God's means of judgment. Man will reap what he has sown. Man has a will. All his actions have been recorded and will be accordingly rewarded dependent upon their pursuit of righteousness. Do you measure up? No one does but Jesus. God is just and will not use two different standards, and thus, eliminates the excuses the self-righteous often rely on. In the following verses Paul provides even more arguments on how their reliance on the Law will fail them.

Romans 2:12-29 reveals the weaknesses of three false confidences the Jews might place their hope in. They are not to depend on their knowledge of the Law, their heritage (their name) or their belonging to the covenant (marked by circumcision). Doing good works or belonging to the people of God cannot make a person righteous. Paul reveals their void of righteousness by revealing God's demand for upright living, which only Christ can provide.

Paul presses in by closing his powerful conclusion in 3:1-20 by asking and answering five questions. Paul systematically crushes any work or means apart from Christ that Jew or Gentile might depend upon for salvation. False ideas keep people from finding the Savior Jesus Christ. Lastly, he concludes with a description of human beings in their sinfulness. No one will find righteousness through the Law. The law only reveals our sin.

> **"Because by the works of the Law no flesh will be justified in His sight; for through the Law comes the knowledge of sin" (Rom 3:20).**

This section not only generally sweeps everyone into the category of a sinner and guilty before the righteous Judge, but proves to the self-righteous that they cannot depend on their religious heritage or possession of Law to find their needed righteousness. Paul moves on in his argument in the next section showing how one can obtain that much needed righteousness.

C. Righteousness Made: Justification (Rom 3:21-5:21)

God presents us as righteous before God through faith in Christ.

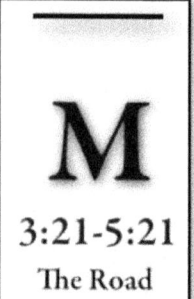

3:21-5:21
The Road

Romans 3:21-31 presents the means through which we secure that needed righteousness–through faith in Christ. Chapter 4 illustrates how salvation by faith is taught through the revered men and scriptures in the Old Testament. Chapter 5 goes one step further by demonstrating how both Jews and Gentiles are true children of Abraham because they received the blessings associated with righteousness.

Man will never obtain that needed righteousness through the Law for the Law only reveals our sin. Whether Jew or Gentile, people can find hope of salvation in Christ Jesus. We are sinners and need to find that righteousness (i.e. declared righteousness) through the redemptive work of Christ. Jesus died on our behalf. He suffered our penalty of death on our behalf so that we who have faith in Christ not only find forgiveness but also gain His righteousness which enables us to come before God's majestic presence (5:1-2).

> For all have sinned and fall short of the glory of God, being justified as a gift by His grace through the redemption which is in Christ Jesus (Rom 3:23-24).

Paul uses three illustrations in chapter 4 to prove 'salvation by faith' to the unbelieving Jews. Abraham was declared righteous before the Law (4:3). David greatly sinned and was guilty before the Law but found his sins covered (4:7). Abraham received acceptance before God through his faith before he was circumcised.

In Romans 4:13-25 he continues establishing how that same faith not only can save Jews but also those from any nation (i.e. the gentiles). "For the promise to Abraham or to his descendants that he would be heir of the world was not through the Law, but through the righteousness of faith" (Rom 4:13). People do not receive this righteousness through works but like Abraham through faith. God promised Him to be 'heir of the world.' Indeed, through his faith Abraham has become a 'father of many nations.'

In chapter 5 Paul expands on the blessing of that inheritance. The blessings are the proof of having obtained that justification by faith (5:1).

Romans 5:12-21 summarizes this section by highlighting our sinful dilemma through our joint guilt through Adam (pointing out again our unrighteousness) but also the common blessing of life found in Jesus Christ, the second Adam.

> **"That, as sin reigned in death, even so grace might reign through righteousness to eternal life through Jesus Christ our Lord" (Rom 5:21).**

Righteousness with all its blessings are for all who believe in Christ. Without Christ and His life, we are still bound to Adam and his judgment.

D. Righteousness Attained: Sanctification (Rom 6-8)

The Lord calls us to live out righteous lives by Christ's power within us.

Before going on in Romans 8 to positively state the Christian's relationship with God through Jesus Christ, Paul carefully eliminates the most dangerous misunderstandings (chapters 6-7) which arise from the biblical teaching of justification by faith. The apostle Paul needs to clear up this possible confusion before further developing the considerable impact the teaching of justification of faith brings to our lives.

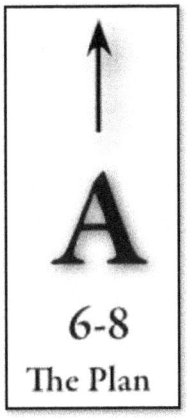

6-8
The Plan

Paul changes his focus as he comes to chapter 6 and beyond. He is no longer trying to prove that man is a sinner but guides the believer into deepening his knowledge and commitment to godly living largely by pointing to Christ's power within him. He does not mention any second experience to obtain God's full promises. Instead the apostle persistently presents counter arguments to keep the believer from being negatively affected through false teaching. Righteousness is an outgrowth of faith in Christ. This is not the righteous standing which one gains through salvation, but a righteous lifestyle resulting from salvation. These great blessings derive from the implanting of the Holy Spirit promised to every believer in chapter 5.

A genuine believer in Christ will increasingly live out a righteous life as he increases his or her understanding of the truth and applies those truths to his and her life. Falsehood, however, deviously surrounds God's people. The evil one constantly seeks for situations to deceive God's people through distorted teachings. The four repetitions of the phrase "May it never be!" in chapters 6 and 7 shape this section. Paul tries to eliminate the impact of each false interpretation before it has a chance to carry out its harmful influence, much like pulling a weed before it grows and bears its own seeds.

In chapter 8 Paul states and builds upon the declaration of our righteous standing in Christ through faith and begins to show its effect upon our lives. The Law could not make us righteous as we were devoid of the Spirit of God, but now that has all changed, having believed in Christ.

8:1-11 shows how one is freed from the power of the flesh (old nature) and empowered by the love, power and life of the Spirit of God. 8:12-17 displays how, having escaped the clutches of the flesh, we are now led by the Spirit of God as the children of God (blessing from chapter 5). Christ satisfied the law's claim on our lives, and so now, we are free to live under the principle or rule of the Spirit of life. We run by a different operating system (flesh in opposition to the Spirit).

8:18-39 continues on with a different focus on the question of suffering. Paul introduces suffering in 8:17, "And if children, heirs also, heirs of God and fellow heirs with Christ, if indeed we suffer with Him in order that we may also be glorified with Him." A question arises, "If we have become children of God and empowered by the Spirit of God, then why do we still suffer? Are we not to enjoy the blessings of new life (cf. chapter 5)?" Paul then sets before us, in this last part of chapter 8, an amazing ring of statements that assure us that having identified ourselves with Christ, we also will need to suffer with Him.

Paul closes this section by tackling three hard questions for those suffering:

"Can I endure (8:26-27)?"

"Is God really in control (8:28-30)?"

"Does He really love me (8:31-39)?"

By providing a picture of God's eternal redemptive plan, we find that God is eternally committed to our well-being despite our sinful past. If God spared His only Son for us so that we could gain life, will He not provide all that we need to endure the stresses and troubles of life (8:32)? Of course. Nothing shall separate us from God's eternal love.

> **"But in all these things we overwhelmingly conquer through Him who loved us" (Rom 8:37).**

As we avoid the false teachings that drag us into sin and doubt, we can through the power and love of the Holy Spirit increasingly live out a righteous life even in times of suffering. This is God's gift to us!

E. Righteousness eNlarged: Worldwide (Rom 9-11)

God makes His Name great by spreading His grace to the whole world.

Paul writes chapters 9-11 because of the critical need to biblically establish how God's redemptive plan encompasses not only the Jews but also the nations (i.e. Gentiles). Just as the teaching of justification by faith has raised many questions (6-8), so does this plan to reach the Gentiles. Did God make a mistake? Is God unfaithful to the Jews? How do the Jews fit into God's comprehensive program?

Through an intricate argument of election Paul shows how God's treatment of the children of God is fully consistent with the many promises given in His Word many centuries ago. There is no surprise; God's plan has not altered.

After this, he steps back and establishes that God can choose to bestow His grace on any that He desires. Grace is not deserved but, by definition, a voluntary extension of kindness. This is God's prerogative as Maker. God is just and faithful to those He called. "But it is not as though the word of God has failed. For they are not all Israel who are descended from Israel" (Rom 9:6).

Paul does not stop here, however. He continues on and proves through the Old Testament how the Lord has also elected many Gentiles to come to know Him through faith in Christ (9:24-33). Paul has a tender heart for the Jews but testifies to the truth, "For whoever will call upon the name of the Lord will be saved" (Rom 10:13). This offer is open to all, including the

Gentiles (10:15-21). If the Jews reject Christ, it shows that they do not have the necessary faith for salvation.

Paul closes this section in chapter 11 by establishing four truths about God's redemptive plan: 1) God has not rejected the chosen Israelites; 2) greater blessings will be upon the Jews who follow Christ; 3) Gentiles are being grafted onto the olive tree and 4) all Israel will be saved including many non-Jews.

> **"Oh, the depth of the riches both of the wisdom and knowledge of God! How unsearchable are His judgments and unfathomable His ways!" (Rom 11:33).**

The rebellion of the Jewish people could never frustrate God's eternal redemptive plan. God has not made any mistakes or major changes but simply carried out His awesome eternal plan of salvation through which He displays His great wisdom and compassion and gains all glory!

F. Righteousness Spread: Service (Rom 12-16)

God's Name is glorified by His people living out righteousness lives.

With the believer's relationship with God being restored (chapters 1-11), the apostle continues on to the end of the book (chapters 12-16), step by step, directing the believer to right living (i.e. righteousness).

In chapter 12, after he challenged God's people to fully dedicate their lives to God, he went on and shared the obligations of a righteous lifestyle among God's people (think of Jesus' two greatest commandments). In Romans 13 he clearly turns his focus through his many exhortations to right living with their contacts in the world, including their relationship with the government (13:1-7), further bolstered by general admonitions (13:8-14).

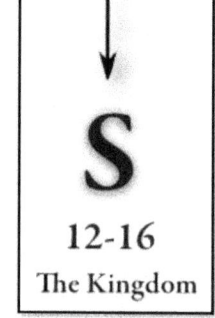

In chapter 14 the apostle begins to treat a specific issue that has become a problem between the Jewish and Gentile Christians. General principles were given in chapters 12-13, but they needed to be contextualized to become effective. In Romans 14 Paul specifically gives them instruction on what love and humility look like in this one given situation. These chapters are not about what is morally right or wrong but on how to work together with those having differing viewpoints and cultural values. He continues dealing with interrelationships between Jew and Gentile in chapter 15. The consistent practice of love brings glory to God who has called both Jews and Gentiles to establish the one church of God.

After sharing how God has led him to work with Gentiles and his specific reason for delay in going to Rome, Paul now shares how he plans to stop over in Rome in order to reach Spain. Paul was very knowledgeable of the churches there in Rome and showed his great affection for those in Rome. Paul was deeply committed to the community of God's people, composed both of Jews and non-Jews. This is God's mystery revealed (16:25), His kingdom here on earth. Although the church has many weaknesses, so we are to love God's people just as God loved them, so they in turn can awaken to devotedly give themselves to others, manifesting the grace and power of the kingdom of God.

The Book of Romans
An Introduction

Purposes of Romans
- Enable believers to be confident of what they believe.
- Help Christians to clearly communicate the gospel with others.
- Share with the Roman church that his visit will be delayed.

Paul, the Author
- Not many debate Paul's authorship of this book (Rom 1:1).
- Steeped in Old Testament teachings; Pharisee of Pharisees (Phil 3:5).
- Persistent logical thinking; from age 13 trained by Gamaliel according to law (Ac 22:3).
- Both parents were Jews and yet Roman citizens (Acts 22:25-29).
- Born in Tarsus of Cilicia but brought up in Jerusalem (Ac 22:3).
- Highly committed and motivated: Dramatic conversion (Ac 22:5-10).
- Suffered intensely for the gospel (2 Co 11:23-27).

The Church at Rome: the addressee
- 'Beloved of God' indicates their confession of Christ (Rom 1:7).
- They lived in Rome.
- The church was known for its strength and influence throughout the world (Rom 1:8).
- Composed of Jews (Rom 2:17, 4:12) and Gentiles (Rom 11, 15:15-16).
- Possessed characteristics of an urban setting (Gromacki, p. 179).
- They lived in a heathen, idolatrous, lust-oriented society.

The Time and Place of Writing
- Paul wrote Romans after he wrote the two Corinthian epistles (Rom 15:26).
- Paul wrote it during his brief stay at Corinth around 55-56 AD.[3]
- Phoebe probably carried it there.

The City of Rome
Rome's founding in 753 BC is a fanciful legend more than objective history. Rome was located on the Tiber river 15 miles in from the sea. Over time the swamps and mounds gradually were built up, and so Rome became known as 'The City of Seven Hills'. In New Testament (NT) times the population hovered over a million with some placing it about 4 million. There were about 420 temples to Roman gods and gods of conquered people. A sizable colony of Jews lived there.

Rome & Jews
Three hostile Roman rulings pressed against the Jews during Paul's life:
1) The expulsion of Jews under Tiberius in 19;
2) The withdrawal of the rights of assemble by Claudius in 41; and
3) The expulsion of Jews by Claudius in 54 A.D.

After Claudius died in 54 A.D., Nero took up the Roman throne. Each Jewish repulsion from Rome lost effect over time, and the Jews slowly returned. The Jews returned in the 30's as well as after Claudius' death in 54. So the Jewish Christians, Priscilla and Aquila (Rom 16), came back with many others. Only in the latter years of Nero's reign (AD 64) can we detect an awareness that Christians had become a distinct entity.

The Jews and the Church in Rome
Paul significantly does not mention Rome as a church because it had not fully come out of the synagogue at that point. The earliest Jewish Christians, in any given place, would attend the synagogue and only leave after they had been forced to. Christianity in Rome emerged from the Jewish community in Rome and therefore had passed on numerous teachings of the law along with the gospel. "... The best estimate of the number of Jews in Rome in the middle of

---

[3] Gromacki, p. 180.

the first century AD is about 40,000-50,000, most of them slaves and freedmen."[4]

An increasingly popular view in the second half of the twentieth century is that Paul wrote to counter (potential) divisions within Rome among the Christian house churches, particularly the danger of gentile believers despising less liberated Jewish believers.[5] (Rom 16:17-19)

The Christians in Rome

The Christians must have been well established and fairly numerous by the middle of the 50s. Paul had wanted to visit them "for many years" (1:10, 15:23). They had been sufficiently strong (or provocative) by AD 49 to provide the occasion for the "constant disturbances" with the Jewish community which resulted in the expulsion of many Jews. And in 64 they could be described as a new "sect" with a "a great multitude", "vast numbers", and indicted by those confessing to be Christians to provide many hours of "entertainment" by the varied deaths they suffered. The widespread use of such punishments suggests that few of the Christians had citizens' rights.[6]

From Romans 16 it can be deduced that a large proportion of the Christians in Rome were slaves or freedmen/women (at least 14 out of 24 names in Romans were commonly used slave names). Eight out of fourteen seem to be fairly well-to-do. The Christians met in house churches.

The Occasion and Purpose of Writing Romans

Paul had not established the church at Rome and had none of the original twelve apostles were there, and therefore he wanted to make sure they were on the right theological track. He gave them systematic teaching of the Christian faith.

- They lived under Caesar in the powerful Roman empire and often suffered persecution. Paul encouraged them to keep steadfast under the pressures and showed them the relationship they were to have with the empire.
- Easily accessible urban temptations flared up about them so he challenged them to live holy and dedicated lives to God.

---

[4] Classnotes.

[5] Ibid.

[6] Ibid.

- Paul wanted to give them proper theological perspectives on the problem between the Jews and the Gentiles.
- Romans was a letter in which he made preparation with the Roman believers for his fourth missionary journey to Rome and the West. He set Rome as a base for the northwest quadrant of the Mediterranean. Paul was returning from his third missionary journey to deliver a charity offering from the Gentiles to the poverty-stricken Jews at Jerusalem (15:25-28).

Romans 1:1-17

The Proclamation of the Gospel

Introduction to Romans 1:1-17

On May 24, 1738, a discouraged missionary went "very unwillingly" to a religious meeting in London. There, a miracle took place. "About a quarter before nine," he wrote in his journal, "I felt my heart strangely warmed. I felt I did trust in Christ, Christ alone, for salvation; and an assurance was given me that He had taken away my sins, even mine, and saved me from the law of sin and death." That missionary was John Wesley. The message he heard that evening was the preface to Martin Luther's commentary on Romans. Just a few months before, Wesley wrote in his journal: "I went to America to convert the Indians; but Oh! who shall convert me?"[7]

Have you experienced the power of the gospel? A lot of people have heard the word 'Gospel' but are not clear to its meaning. Through this study of Romans 1:1-17 we gain a better understanding of what the gospel is and how it is to affect our lives. The reason Paul goes from prison to prison and bears insult is to reveal the Gospel's message and power. It is in this introductory section that we actually get a good feel not only for the whole book of Romans but Paul's person. Just after this section, the apostle dives deep into his discussions.

A. The Gospel's Message (Rom 1:1-7)

Paul the writer, the believing Romans (the addressee), and the gospel of Jesus are the three interwoven topics discussed in these verses.

---

[7] *Be Right.* Warren Wiersbe, p. 7.

1. The Proclaimer of the gospel (1:1)

> ¹ Paul, a bond-servant of Christ Jesus, called as an apostle, set apart for the gospel of God (Rom 1:1).

Paul first designated himself as Christ's slave before further elaborating his position as an apostle. This humble approach characterizes his whole life. He sets before us a commendable example that we might join him in following Christ. The term slave has several implications, but they are rooted in his relationship with Christ. Later in this letter, Paul shows how he formerly was a slave of unrighteousness but now a slave to righteousness (of the Spirit). Paul probably was thinking of the million or so slaves there in Rome at that time. The ratio of slave to freeman was 2:1 or ever 3:1. In part he was identifying himself with his audience but also leading the way for all believers to rightly consider themselves as servants of their master Jesus Christ, the living Lord.

A slave has two characteristics. First, it speaks of ownership by another. Jesus Christ redeemed (literally 'bought') Paul and all the saints with his own blood (Rev 5:9). Positionally, he and all of us belong to Christ.

Second, being a slave means that one is occupied with doing the will of his master. Our only right is the right to serve our master. Whatever our master says, we do. Our task is not to question what our master asks but to accomplish for him what He asks, whether it be hard or easy. Unlike the epistle to the Philippians, Paul was not in prison (Rom 15:25), but the description well befitted him as it does every Christian. Chinese Christians call pastors, 'God's servants,' as if only they are so privileged, but all Christians can be properly called as God's servants.

Application

I am thankful along with Paul that our master is the Lord Jesus Christ. He purchased me. Do I loyally serve my Master? Do I first regard myself as his servant, and only later a missionary, a teacher, housewife or other profession? Do I delight in the fact that Jesus bought me with his own blood and gives me opportunity to serve such a great one as He?

1:1 Called as an apostle–set apart for the gospel

As important as his servant (the translation 'slave' is the same in the original Greek) relationship to Christ was, 'slave' does not fully describe who Paul is. Paul was also an apostle. If we really wanted to understand Paul's person and calling, we would need to fully understand his apostleship. He was not boasting but establishing his credentials before a church he had, up to this point, never visited. We have the same concerns today. We treat God's writings completely different from a book without divine authorship.

Some are concerned as to how Paul became an apostle. Our minds immediately turn to Acts 1:15-26 where the qualifications were set up to choose the twelfth apostle to substitute Judas Iscariot. That individual had to be with Jesus since the baptism of John. Paul obviously did not fit the early requirements that the other main apostles had.

The word 'apostle' literally means 'sent one.' We can more fully understand Paul's use of apostleship to describe the time when the Lord sent him to spread the gospel to the Gentiles. In other words, his calling was direct from the Lord Jesus. His call to ministry and to salvation were closely connected. Jesus at once qualified him by calling him. Man could not rescind that order even though he was a new Christian and not thoroughly tested.

Paul was appointed to preach the gospel. This appointment was recorded in Acts 9 and brought to our attention here through the use of the Greek aorist tense (punctiliar). The call was not something that happened again and again, but gains its power and thrust from its original point in time. Paul had his call from Jesus to go tell the Gentiles the gospel of Christ (Acts 9:15). He was to bear His name, the name of Jesus, which is the good news, the *euangellion* (ευαγγελιον literally 'good message').

Early on, many Christians doubted whether he was a true Christian and was secretly planning to trap all the Christians. Because Paul had an active role in the martyrdom of Steven in the early church (Acts 7:58), we can fully understand the other believers' concern.

We doubt whether Paul knew Jesus well because Paul does not often quote Jesus in his writings but copiously reuses Old Testament texts. Paul's unique situation of being an Old Testament scholar and yet not being heavily influenced by Jesus' teaching allows us to gain a much broader understanding of the gospel. Paul's view of the resurrected Jesus also was different from the other apostles.

Paul had no doubts regarding his apostleship. He knew the Lord's call for his life. Many a time he would defend himself as a true apostle (see Eph 4; Gal 1). He not only seriously took his place before Jesus Christ as a slave but also sought to fulfill the apostolic ministry which the Lord gave to him.

Application
- To what degree do I count my ministry as important? As a priority?

- Are you also appointed to spread the gospel? See Mt 28:19-20.
- What is it you are doing to spread the gospel of God?

2. The Promise of the Gospel (2)

> Which he promised beforehand through his prophets in the Holy Scriptures (1:2).

The gospel of God was a natural outcome of God's mercy and grace. Just as Christ was predestined to die to undergird the grace of the gospel, so the gospel's work–the spreading of the gospel–has been clearly cut out for His people. The word 'promised' rings with this truth; it was not an accident. This gospel age did not arrive because the Jews goofed up (e.g. classical dispensational thinking), but this promise was powerfully fulfilled according to the faithfulness of God's person, having been revealed long ago in the Old Testament (as we will later see in the Book of Romans). God's plan of salvation did not change but rather in time faithfully carried out.

The gospel was promised in the Old Testament and recorded in the writings of His prophets. Although the prophet is well known for messages of condemnation, he also offers promises of restoration and peace. God used 'His' prophets to speak to us. They spoke in God's name and accurately spoke the predicament of man and promises of God. These words came from God and were particularly shaped in the prophet's mind by the Holy Spirit.

> Seeking to know what person or time the Spirit of Christ within them was indicating as He predicted the sufferings of Christ and the glories to follow. It was revealed to them that they were not serving themselves, but you, in these things which now have been announced to you through those who preached the gospel to you by the Holy Spirit sent from heaven–things into which angels long to look (1 Pe 1:11-12).

The writings of these prophets came to be known as 'holy' writings. They perfectly reflected God's view. How easy to find man's view today on television, in the newspaper or on the smartphone. God's Word is recorded in the Bible, the Holy Scriptures (including both Old and New Testaments). It is worth the effort to translate God's truth into all the world's languages.

Application
- Praise God for His good will, sovereignty and ability to fulfill these good promises.

Romans 1:1-17 The Proclamation of the Gospel

- Trust the Holy Scriptures as God's voice in contrast to what we hear from men.
- Keep reading the Old Testament in light of the teaching of the New Testament.

3. The Person of the Gospel (1:3-5)

a. His entrance into the world (1:3)

> Concerning his son, who was born of the seed of David according to the flesh (1:3).

The gospel is very tersely but completely described in Romans 1:3-4. The center focus of the Gospel is 'His' Son. Just as the scriptures were declared His by the word 'holy' so God sets apart Christ as 'His' own Son. This phrase, and the later used 'God's Son', is not as easy to understand as we would normally think. Our thinking of a son is usually relegated to the male child of two parents. Verse 4 shakes our categories by calling Christ 'God's Son'. Several issues immediately arise, and it is easy to get them confused.

Verse 3 stresses the aspect of being a descendant of David as a person. He was 100% human. The genealogy is traced in Matthew 1 and Luke 3. One of the major tasks of the Bible was to establish this living chain of descendants. Although Joseph was Jesus' legal father, it was God's Holy Spirit that fertilized Mary's egg. Christ, as predicted, was born of a virgin (Isaiah 7:14). Jesus is the Christ, the one predicted in the Old Testament who would be the Savior. 2 Samuel 7 particularly enlightens us on God's future plans through David's descendants. This life that was promised was a physical heritage, which some might have hoped to be fulfilled in Solomon, but instead found the full fulfillment in Christ whose kingdom endures forever.

> When your days are complete and you lie down with your fathers, I will raise up your descendant after you, who will come forth from you, and I will establish his kingdom. he shall build a house for my name, and I will establish the throne of the His kingdom forever (2 Samuel 7:12-13).

One of the reasons for detailing the sins of the many great men of faith in the Old Testament is to help confirm our suspicions, whether he be Noah, David, Abraham or Isaiah, that they were not the Savior, the Christ.

b. His entrance into the heavens (1:4)

> Who was declared with power to be the Son of God by the resurrection from the dead according to the Spirit of holiness, Jesus Christ our Lord (Rom 1:4).

The divine side of Christ is set forth in verse 4. Verse 3 had the first descriptive aorist participle (who was born...) and now we have the second (who was declared...). Both of these clauses could be taken out and still the sentence would make complete sense. Their presence, however, does exactly what the author wishes–he elaborates upon the nature of Christ. This is somewhat explained through His supernatural birth where God impregnated Mary by the Holy Spirit, but this is only one clue out of many that provides an inkling of Christ's special role as God's son. Notice at His baptism that it was said, "This is my beloved son in who I am well pleased." Christ was begotten and yet eternal. His existence didn't begin at this time (Mic 5:2), but the way God would reveal Himself to Jesus did necessarily change.

This verse essentially discusses Christ as the heavenly ruler. He was first declared, or literally designated and appointed, as the Son of God. Since this is a participle, there is no focus on who did the appointing, but we know it to be God the Father. The Son came to do the Father's will. However, one can take the word 'power' to be one of agency: "By power" he was designated the Son of God. We do not need a special voice to confirm it. Christ's resurrection proves His divine nature beyond doubt. Dead man cannot talk let alone come alive. God's Son is not one only of declaration but one established by power.

c. His name (1:4b)

Before continuing on, we must more fully discuss the term the Son of God. We already looked at it from the perspective of his birth, but the term is much richer. By Son of God there is a great emphasis on His position of inheritance and authority. As the Son of God, He inherits all the authority and power from God (think of a monarch's son). As believers in Christ, we can by His grace share in this inheritance.

The Spirit of holiness had everything to do with displaying the power of the resurrection. This Spirit of holiness is the same Spirit that works in the lives of the believers. Jesus Christ is our Lord. If He is not our Lord then He is not our Savior. Those who make a distinction between accepting Christ as Savior and Lord completely confuse what it means to be a Christian. Christ's Lordship is relevant not only to Paul and the Roman Christians but to all believers.

d. His gifts (1:5)

> Through whom we have received grace and apostleship to bring about the obedience of faith among all the Gentiles, for His name's sake (Rom 1:5).

A three-fold description of grace is found in Romans 1:5.

(1) We receive abilities from the Lord

Only through the person of Jesus Christ our Lord has Paul and companions received the gifts of grace and apostleship. As to the word grace, we should at a minimum attach the whole notion of salvation. Only in Christ do we, Paul or anyone have salvation. The stress on that name of Christ is proper and needed. But we must go beyond this thought and see in this usage a greater concept of grace as shown in Ephesians 4:7-13.

Through Christ all sorts of gifts were given to the church. Along with the Holy Spirit, which is part of the grace given to us, we were given special abilities, better known as spiritual gifts. We were also particularly burdened to take part in different aspects of building up Christ's church. Our concept of grace must be broadened to include the way Christ works in and through us. We are not merely saved for heaven but for living out God's life now here on earth–for His Name's sake.

They received the authority of apostles. This plural usage of apostleship (we) seems to indicate Paul was using it broader than the original twelve apostles. Paul and his companions (Rom 16:21-23) were sent with a job to do. God's grace is not limited to the early church, but an essential part of salvation when we receive different anointings to complete God's spiritual work. The apostles which formed the foundation of Christianity remains the same. Many others are working on top of what the apostles have done. The gospel, however, is going to many new places even now. They need apostles to establish the church in those places, though the term apostle (best translated 'sent' like the word 'missionary') would not have the authority of the original twelve.

(2) We gain a vision

We are not gifted or saved without a clear purpose for our lives. God has much planned for our lives. We see this in the vision the Lord gave to Paul. He actually heard God's voice sound out His command to go to the Gentiles. Perhaps Paul, with his excessive Jewish pride, needed that loud voice and bright light.

We should not forget, however, that all believers to a certain degree must cooperate with God's goal of bringing about the obedience of faith among all the Gentiles (non-Jews). No one is to be left out because of bias, race, wealth or nationality. We are not to focus on our own needs but on how to give: just as Jesus Christ came from heaven to earth. God wants to use us. God's gifts are given to us to ultimately bless others.

(3) We obtain an ultimate purpose - 'for His name's sake'
This third point, 'for His name's sake' makes a lot of sense when we grasp God's greatness. Life doesn't rotate around our lives but ours around His. In connection to the gospel and the person of the gospel is the inherent grace which is meant to spread around the world. The gifts are received and the vision is gained for the greater purpose of honoring Christ's name (compare Rom 11:36).

4. The People of the Gospel (6-7)

> 6 Among whom you also are the called of Jesus Christ; 7 to all who are beloved of God in Rome, called as saints: Grace to you and peace from God our Father and the Lord Jesus Christ (Rom 1:6-7).

a. Participation in the calling (6-7a)

I wonder if anyone felt a bit funny when I kept using the word 'we' in the previous section. Christ equips Paul and his companions for that mission, but what is happening does not easily filter down to our own lives.

1) Paul was called (1:1), but so were the Roman Christians (1:6). The 'we' of the former verses melts away in light of the grand redemptive work God is doing all around the world. "You yourselves were called'. The stress is on the you, "To all who are beloved of God in Rome."

As we study this book of Romans, we must remember that it was written to the Romans. We can learn lots about the church there, but we must remember that we were not the Romans. We do, however, share a commonality with the Christians in Rome in Christ, equally being loved of God. We might live in different places and eras, but the many gifts and callings are the same. It is important to allow these truths to seep into our hearts to powerfully affect our lives. And yet, we must retain a distinction between the Romans and ourselves when making applications to our own lives so that we can maintain a greater degree of correct interpretation.

2) Paul further buttressed this argument by placing himself on the same level as the Christians in Rome ('you also'). Paul is the apostle, but he

includes himself as one of the many beloved ones in Christ. He, like the others, is a saint and shares a calling.

3) The Caller is the same. Just as God had been working in Paul and his companions, God is now working in His church worldwide, both back then and now. Christ is constantly forming His church. Christ is the head. We dare not separate God's love with His call. Salvation and service are uniquely joined together.

Application
What are you called to? How are you gifted? What are you doing about it?

b. Partakers of the benefits (7b)
Inside the salutation of verse 7, we can further discover the ways God has blessed His church. God doesn't capriciously distribute gifts or call His people but delivers the genuine grace needed to handle every difficulty they confront. They receive peace from God our Father and the Lord Jesus Christ. The derivation of this grace and peace make every bit of difference to their effectiveness. Grace is the favor God bestows on His unworthy creatures. Peace is the calm confidence within our hearts and minds even during tumultuous times.

Application
Are there any areas in which I think God's grace is insufficient? Do I fear that I do not have what I need to do what He leads me to do? Has He planned on giving what I need through another? God plans to distribute His grace and peace to others through our lives. How does God's calling practically work out in your own life?

Here is an illustration from India. One sister runs a tiny restaurant on a main road in northeast India. She says she has about 100 customers a day and is doing fairly well. She has been a believer for a few years. Her husband still does not believe, but she pays close attention to those that come to her place. If there are any needing consoling, she shares God's gospel with them. Her real burden is for the children who pick up plastic recycling items along the road, though. Many of them are addicted to drugs and have no parents. She hopes to start a little school for them if she can get the resources. She wants to not only educate them but share God's wonderful good news with them.

B. The Gospel's Mission (Rom 1:8-15)

1. His Concern For Service There (1:8-10)

> ⁸ First, I thank my God through Jesus Christ for you all, because your faith is being proclaimed throughout the whole world. ⁹ For God, whom I serve in my spirit in the preaching of the gospel of His Son, is my witness as to how unceasingly I make mention of you, ¹⁰ always in my prayers making request, if perhaps now at last by the will of God I may succeed in coming to you (Rom 1:8-10).

Paul often shares his prayer for those he is writing to in the introductory part of his letters. They are connected not by physically being in the same place but being spiritually joined together by God for His greater purposes.

a. Reason of Thanksgiving: Their proclaimed faith (1:8)

Paul begins the personal letter with thanks. He is sold to the vision God has for the church. He sees the Roman church carrying out her function as the called saints in Rome. Paul literally begins with a prayer. We can be assured that Paul practices what he preaches. Here are four points on giving thanks.

1) Give thanks. Don't forget to warmly respond to God's blessings.

2) Thanksgiving needs to be directed to God (the Father). He distributes all good things.

3) Be thankful when I see God accomplishing His great purpose of redemption.

4) Be observant on how God carries out His purpose in our hearts by pouring out gifts, unction and purpose.

Notice it is their faith being proclaimed (not just preached). It is not just a message but a life message. The gospel has been liberated within a group of Roman people, including both slaves and citizens.

Application

Is my life known for my faith? Do I have a faith to be proclaimed? How attentive am I of what God is doing around me? Am I thankful?

b. Outcome of Thanksgiving: Prayer (1:9-10)

Paul says, "For God is my witness," to demonstrate his sincerity. (This idiom stresses sincerity.) God watches what he does. The meaning of "In whom I serve by (or in) my spirit in the preaching of the gospel of His Son" is confusing in two places.

There are different translations for "in my spirit." Spirit (or spirit; πνεματι) can refer to the "inner life; self, disposition, state of mind." Paul meant that it was not only in his outward actions that he served others but also from his inner life. Another meaning suggests that because Paul was far away from the Romans he could not physically support them, but he could pray for them and this he did. He serves them in his spirit rather than through his physical presence.

Second, the phrase, "I serve ... in the gospel of His Son" refers to how he sees himself joining in the redemptive work of God. The NASB version adds the words 'preaching of the' gospel. These supplied words suggest that it is in a certain sphere or area of work that God has called Paul. Preaching is only one aspect of the gospel ministry, however, albeit an important one, that should never be forsaken. The gospel ministry embraces a broader area of work just as ordination papers affirm, 'Called unto the gospel ministry.' Any pastor or missionary or saint (Rom 15:30-31) would need to include the work of prayer as part of the gospel ministry.

Paul's thanks are spoken from sincerity. He has the authority to give thanks because it is genuine. Paul's thanks include bringing his points of thankfulness up to others (in this case even though he hadn't been there). Paul also gives thanks 'unceasingly'. This doesn't mean this is all Paul does, but it does mean he regularly does it.[8]

This has two practical applications: First, the Romans were upon Paul's heart. He thought about them and regularly prayed for them. Second, it means he was never so busy to neglect prayer. Prayer is an important aspect of ministry. Let's remember this calling is not just for Paul and his companions but for all of us.

His hope was to see them prosper as he prayed for them. He was trying to visit them and yet was frustrated. As long as he is not able to visit them (which was God's will for him), then he evidently must keep praying!

And yet, the burden to visit and minister to them is there. He needs to wait for God's timing. If God wants him to go, nothing will stop him. God's will not be hindered (Isaiah 46). And yet we must not forget Daniel's prayer which took a while before the angel could come and 'answer' a certain prayer of his. The message got through and yet God's action was being hindered

---

[8] The iterative present (present middle participle) shows how one can be constant in a certain activity and yet at different set times. Example: I was eating all day.

from being carried out. Paul did one clear thing: he prayed and hoped it was God's will. God has not only ordained the ends but also the means, and if the means includes prayer then I must do my part where I can.

Application

May God grant me a greater capacity to be concerned, not only for those I know and have seen, but also for those I have never seen.

2. His Hope For Ministry There (1:11-13)

> 11 For I long to see you in order that I may impart some spiritual gift to you, that you may be established; 12 that is, that I may be encouraged together with you while among you, each of us by the other's faith, both yours and mine. 13 And I do not want you to be unaware, brethren, that often I have planned to come to you (and have been prevented thus far) in order that I might obtain some fruit among you also, even as among the rest of the Gentiles (Rom 1:11-13).

Unless our requests can be scrutinized before God as to their motivation and purpose, then they stand to be shallow petitions. Many people run off to short term missions. Why don't they go into missions? Paul analyzes his specific desires and requests.

a. For sanctification (1:11-12)   Theirs (11) and his (12)

Paul's purpose is clear. He wants to build up the faith of the Roman Christians. He had something in the gospel that they could benefit from. It is important to ask if we are sending out mature enough individuals who have spiritual gifts to serve? Do they take up evangelistic and discipleship activities? We need to think of the type of missionaries we send forth.

Paul had a burden for them. This is a good indication that God might want him to go there but not firm confirmation. Paul saw the reason to visit was to build up that church. Yet God had not opened that door yet. As time progressed, we saw that the only way Paul got there was in chains. We don't pretend to understand God's ways but rejoice in them.

Paul had another purpose mentioned in verse 12. Paul needed encouragement from others. Although Paul was an apostle, he saw that they had gifts which God could use to benefit himself. Paul applied his theology! The greatest servant of Christ must have his faith encouraged by others. I hope we never underestimate the importance of missionary prayer meetings.

Our hearts should not underestimate what we can offer others nor underestimate what others can give to us.

Application

Evaluate potential and present missionaries in terms of what they offer their target groups and their effectiveness by both their attitudes toward the people and towards themselves. If they don't sense they can grow from national Christians, then they lack an important attitude needed for proper service.

b. For salvation (1:13)

Paul not only thought about the Christians there but was also convinced that he could find opportunity to share the gospel with unbelievers. "You" refers to the Romans generally rather than the Roman Christians. This is shown by the way he describes the fruit among other areas in which he has ministered as well as the following verses. Paul knew very clearly that God was using him as an instrument for many to hear God's salvation. He did not ignore his primary call even when he found himself in places which didn't look very strategic. Even though he hadn't yet received the 'okay', he planned a big missionary journey to Spain where the Roman church would provide the support he needed.

Paul has been put on hold right now. He has carefully examined his plans, hopes and motivations. God chooses to delay him. In fact, we can sense he had already planned to go at different times but was held back. Paul is not being finicky. God is delaying him.

3. His Basis For Ministry There (14-15)

> 14 I am under obligation both to Greeks and to barbarians, both to the wise and to the foolish. 15 Thus, for my part, I am eager to preach the gospel to you also who are in Rome (Rom 1:14-15).

Paul's theology, rather than the opportunities that lay before him, steered his decisions. He lists the reasons he believes it is probable that the Lord would open the way to Rome.

a. His debt (1:14)

Paul's main mission focused on the people that the Lord directed him to preach to: the Gentiles. This didn't stop him from preaching to the Jews when he went somewhere. The Jews served as a base from which God could reach out to the Gentiles. The lack of a synagogue didn't keep Paul from going to other places. When in Athens, he spoke out in the distinguished pagan pulpit.

Paul had a burden from the Lord; his charge, given by the Lord, led him to share the gospel to non-Jews, which he broke down into two categories: the Greeks and the barbarians, the civilized and the non-civilized.

Paul saw himself as a debtor to his people, the Jews. Many missionaries feel they don't have sufficient motivation to continue on. Maybe we need to emphasize this debtor concept more. Christ's great commission should continually challenge and direct us, and we ought to live to fulfill it. Dare we ignore this call? If God has called us to serve, then we are in obligation to go.

b. His desires (1:15)

It might have been odd that he had not gone to Rome, the capital of the Roman empire, earlier. Paul's ministry could have had a positive impact upon Rome, which is something he was eager to have a part in. When Paul eventually arrived in Rome though, the Lord never fully released him to public preaching. Instead he only could evangelize and disciple those that came to see him while on house arrest (which could easily hinder many people from seeing him). Part of God's purpose in this could have been to show how He could work without Paul; God wanted the believers to participate. The believers in Rome were also empowered by the Spirit to do a great job!

Waiting proves to be one of the most difficult tasks God puts before his servants. Paul was eager to see God accomplish His work in Rome, but he couldn't effectively help them beyond praying for them and sharing his hope to minister among them.

C. The Gospel's Power (Rom 1:16-17)

> [16] For I am not ashamed of the gospel, for it is the power of God for salvation to everyone who believes, to the Jew first and also to the Greek. [17] For in it the righteousness of God is revealed from faith to faith; as it is written, "But the righteous man shall live by faith" (Rom 1:16, 17).

Why is Paul so eager to preach the gospel? If we take a careful look at Paul's life, we can see that he believed both in the one who called him and the transforming power of the gospel. If necessary, Paul was willing to die preaching that gospel, which is exactly what happened.

1. The Gospel Creates Boldness (1:16a)

Paul is not ashamed of the gospel because it ushers in the power of salvation. Man cannot change himself, but God can change man's heart. When we see God's word change people, we are emboldened. This doesn't mean everybody is saved, but as it says: "To every one who believes, to the Jew first and also to the Greek." Though the gospel is freely proclaimed, it is not equally received. People reject God's good news in order to protect their sinful lives (whether they be immoral issues, pride, or other issues).

The phrase "to the Jew first" refers historically to how God first revealed himself to the Jews. The Jews can never say God did not favor them–they heard before anyone else. Instead of holding to the truth and spreading it around the world, the Jews as a whole rejected it, which left Paul, the lone statesmen, to trot the globe and address the Greeks. The Greeks are referred to instead of the Romans because of the wider Greek cultural and linguistic influences.

2. The Gospel Brings Salvation (1:16b-17)

There are several views of the phrase, 'faith to faith'. "For in it the righteousness of God is revealed from faith to faith; as it is written, 'BUT THE RIGHTEOUS man SHALL LIVE BY FAITH'" (Rom 1:17). Here are some:

(a) Faith begins at the Christian birth and continues to grow throughout life.

The first view of 'faith to faith,' as espoused from the Living Bible states that our faith begins at our Christian birth and develops through our entire Christian lives. Our faith is lived out by the righteous lifestyle we hold to. (See Wiersbe, Swindoll and William's translation). In favor of this view is the usage of the present tense of 'revealed'. This places a continuous focus on the growing process rather than a one time event (as in view c).

(b) "From faith to faith" is just a rhetorical means of saying it is faith which counts (Luther).

Luther's view states 'from faith to faith' was a rhetorical means of asserting the importance of faith. "It is **by faith** one is saved." Although somewhat similar to the first in meaning, it does not sufficiently develop the meaning of the two prepositions Paul uses.

(c) Faith in old gods and religions is forsaken (literally 'out of') and a new faith (into) of the living God is adopted.

Another view, garnered from my own study, treats 'from faith' as the faith non-christians had in their old gods and religions. The new faith, 'to faith' depicts our newfound Christian faith. The two prepositions 'out of' and 'into' favor this view.

(d) "God's righteousness arises from his faith(fulness)" (Zieler).

"It may be saying that God's righteousness arises from his faith(fulness), and is to be met by our faith."[9]

(e) The expansion of the community of faith.

"It could be saying that it begins with the faith of some (e.g. the Jews) but spreads to all who have such faith (e.g. Greeks)."[10]

From Faith to Faith

Whatever definition one holds, it must amplify and not contradict the quoted passage from the Old Testament, "But the righteous man shall live by faith." The preposition 'by' is literally 'out of' (ἐκ). The real issue hovers over the meaning of this preposition, which simply states that this salvation originates or is derived from faith. This is, no doubt, why some versions use 'by.' But there remains several unanswered questions at this point:

- Is the emphasis on righteousness one of ascribed (positional) righteousness or a practical righteousness?
- Is the focus on the righteousness that God has given to him by faith, or the righteousness received and lived out from the faith?

Both are, in a sense, correct. Perhaps the absolutism that it is one and excludes the other is the major problem with the reformed and unreformed perspectives. Both need to be true. The point that cannot be contested is that there is no righteousness apart from faith. Faith remains to be a true and vital issue of the Christian life and hope. If one said, "The crooked man will live by

---

[9] Ziesler, p. 71.

[10] Ibid.

(from) stealing," it follows that the crooked person is dependent on the stealing. So the righteousness of the person is dependent upon his faith and trust (πιστις).

Lastly, we must connect these separate thoughts. Notice the words 'righteous' and 'upright.' The righteousness of God is first revealed in the gospel, and is shown in the people's faith. Their beliefs and faith influence their lifestyle.

The emphasis seems to dwell on 'live by faith' (sanctification) rather than 'salvation by faith', which is often spoken of. Notice how the righteous life is rejected in the following section. In other words, this faith is going to be recognized because of the way a Christian's life is contrary to the world's way of life. Still, one must recognize that salvation by faith is the initial part of living by faith, so its meaning must be retained.

Summary

The gospel is the core of the Bible; it fits well as an introduction to the more heavily weighted theology presented in the rest of the Book of Romans. For Paul, Gospel belief is combined with Gospel life. Before Paul jumps into his theological treatise, it is good to see how the apostle and the church at Rome had been affected by the gospel. All of the believers are graced, gifted, and called–not just Paul. This is the message that the apostle had to be content to share with the Roman Christians, being removed far from them.

Application
- Are you ashamed of the gospel? Why or why not?
- How would things be different if you were not ashamed of the gospel?

Romans 1:18-32
The Evident Guilt of Mankind

The world has long argued that, since it is difficult for man to understand truth and God, he is not responsible for his sin. Man pleads "ignorant and innocent" regarding his knowledge of the invisible God and His standards. People often use the example of a remote, uncivilized tribe in an obscure part of the world without the Scripture as evidence that God will not judge them. Ignorance, however, is no excuse. In every case, man will seek a comfortable place to hide from the guilt of his sin and impending judgment (c.f. John 3:19-20) and will persist in His rebellion against God. God repeatedly warns that man is responsible for his sinful behavior.

> Although Calvin believes Paul is starting a new topic in verse 18, it seems fairly clear through the parallel language that Paul is continuing his discussion on the revelation of God and the accountability of mankind.

Paul identifies three stages of man's rejection in Romans 1:18-32, through which we can see God's great patience and wrath. Each stage is not only evident in segments of our society, but has unfortunately, for the most part, become accepted in wider society and treated as normal.

The biblical argument proceeds like this. In 1:18-19, the righteousness of God is revealed through the person and proclamation of Jesus Christ (as discussed in former verses). The great anger of God is revealed by observing God's judgment upon the lives of sinful men. God has not been hiding His truth from us, but kindly displays His ways, even His limited judgment, so that we might repent.

In verses 19-20, Paul expands this concept and shows man's spiritual tug-of-war with God. This struggle provides clearcut evidence that man inherently knows some things about God and therefore stands accountable before Him. Clear societal patterns are inextricably related to man's acceptance or rejection of God's truth. The more blatant the rejection of truth, the greater the immoral conditions within a given society will be. Each stage starts off with a certain understanding of truth and is given up or exchanged (see three stages 1:23-24; 25-26; 26-28), thus ushering them into further darkness.

> **An Alternative Outline**
> This outline centers on man's responsibility for his knowledge about God.
> A. The Confirmation of Knowing God (Rom 1:18-20)
> B. The Process of Scorning God (Rom 1:21-23)
> C. The Consequences of Rejecting God (Rom 1:24-32)
> An extended outline of this section is provided at the end of this section.

God does not want man to sin and rebel against Him, but if man refuses God's grace, then the Lord will give him over to his heart's desires. Man, by God's mercy, does not completely decline at once like the angels, although God could have made things that way. (He would have been perfectly right to judge man at the beginning.) Instead, God provides stages or holding patterns where He enables man to recover from his fall down the slippery immoral slope. The good news for us is that with the proper response, we can, by God's grace, return to proper living. This is the promise in Romans 1:16, "For I am not ashamed of the gospel, for it is the power of God for salvation to every one who believes." Note, we are not boasting of man's own power but of God's willingness to take man from one of his many depraved situations.

The three main stages of man's decline are carefully presented in Romans 1:18-32. At each stage, there is a departure from truth and a resulting consequence. There are two steps in the process of rejecting God: rejection and adoption. Man first rejects God's truth and then adopts false ideas. There is no neutral ground to stand. God's judgment upon man follows closely. Darkness necessarily follows a rejection of light.

The rejection of truth is a process that accelerates as greater amounts of truth are revealed. If a child does not like a certain vegetable in small quantities, there is no way he is going to be happy over a full platter of the same! A typical argument is that if the tribal people knew more truth, then they would more easily respond to the truth. This is inconsistent with man's sinful nature. Without God's intervening grace, their inclination to resist and reject truth grows stronger.

A. Desertion > Deception (Rom 1:18-21)

> ¹⁸ For the wrath of God is revealed from heaven against all ungodliness and unrighteousness of men, who suppress the truth in unrighteousness, ¹⁹ because that which is known about God is evident within them; for God made it evident to them. ²⁰ For since the creation of the world His invisible attributes, His eternal power and divine nature, have been clearly seen, being understood through what has been made, so that they are without excuse. ²¹ For even though they knew God, they did not honor Him as God, or give thanks; but they became futile in their speculations, and their foolish heart was darkened (Rom 1:18-21).

Man first refused to honor and thank God, which marked his desertion from God. It begins by disregarding His kindness. Futile speculations (deception) result. Desertion is the abandonment of a post or set of responsibilities. Deception refers to perspectives that are preferred and adopted, though they counter truth and reality (e.g. encouraging people to redetermine their sex).

Departure of Truth - Stage #1

Taking God out of politics, science, religion, and education

The concept that claims heathen people are ignorance or innocence is simply not documented well. Even those who are not exposed to mankind's great civilizations still have codes of conduct and belief systems. People can discover God from nature, which is God's miraculous display of His creative power (Rom 1:18-20). Mankind is not ignorant of truth. They have some light, but what they do with that is up to them. Rejection of that light is seen in all societies, which marks their guilt.

As the testimony of God and His truth becomes clearer through the teaching of His Word, the departure from truth and the antagonism against it grows. When He sent out 70 disciples, Jesus said that if the people do not receive the message, they were to wipe the dust from their feet for it "will be more tolerable in that day for Sodom, than for that city" (Luke 10:12). The nations that have heard the gospel and rejected it are worse off than those who have not heard the truth clearly explained. All will be judged, but some more seriously.[11]

---

[11] Never are we encouraged to stop spreading the gospel so to keep people in darkness and keep them from a greater judgment. For this keeps those ensnared in darkness there forever.

This departure from truth toward falsehood is evident all around us. If we think judgment was bad for a heathen city like Sodom, which didn't have God's Word, the severity of judgment will be worse for those who have God's Word but openly promote sinful living. God speaks about His clear judgment against these things!

The invisible characteristics of God are understood through what He has made (i.e. creation). Man strips God of His glory and demotes Him down to our own level, likening him to some kind of image that He originally created. God condemns these idolatrous acts because a form of something, that which was created, can never fully portray the Creator's glory. God must be dethroned in man's mind before they can openly reject his truth.

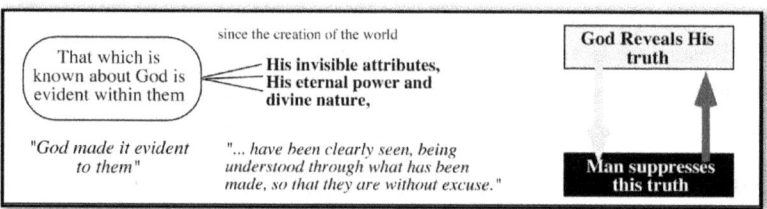

Certain aspects of God's invisible character are to some degree made known by the things that men can observe. The creation provides a vivid expression of God's truth (c.f. Psalm 19). Man, however, is looking for thoughts and philosophies, such as evolution, as a reason to reject God's authority over them. There is no excuse for man's apathy. The pictures of God's creation have become more evident, thanks to our telescopes and technological advances, but this means mankind's rejection will have increased consequences. Every man stands accused by the creation. The phrase 'clearly seen' (1:20) is a clever way of insinuating their knowledge of God's invisible attributes. The witness is so clear: one can even perceive invisible things! Let's look a bit closer at what these 'seen' things are.

Both eternal power and divine nature are the invisible attributes of God that can be 'seen' in creation. This eternal power belongs to God alone, and is a force that is commonly mentioned in today's world, a force that transcends our limited power. The word 'eternal' emphasizes the surpassing qualities of this power, which greatly differ from the gods attached to their passing cultures. The gods that man imagines are all subject to the great forces within the universe, but God's supreme power can only begin to be understood by the power and design from this creation. However, we must be sure not to equivocate God with this eternal power as many mistakenly do. Eternal power refers to the insight into creation that proves to man's heart that the might of this invisible God is greater than what is experienced on earth.

This divine nature reveals another conclusive insight into God's person. While eternal power brings thoughts of the greatness and unlimited scope of God to our minds, His divine nature speaks of His transcendence. The Creator is different from the creature; God is not a more advanced animal or man, but other worldly–God, who is not subject to earth's limitations as we are.

Reception of Evil - Station #1

Man first develops multiple substitute speculative theories (philosophical, moral, social, educational, and personal development). The first thing that happens once we cease acknowledging God's existence and involvement in their lives is futile thoughts, opinions, and motives. In 1:18 the scripture carefully uses the word 'suppress' to identify the presence of some form of truth about God and man's rejection of it. Sensing its upward surge, human beings respond by attempting to silence it.

Man's speculative thoughts quickly rise to fill the void. Scholars, carried away by their own thoughts and theories, find it as easy to discard the evident truth as cardboard boxes. Man carries on in his objections, false religions, and philosophies, and finally arrives at invalid conclusions. As these false theories are developed and accepted, their minds become further distorted. Darwin, Jung, Freud, and Marx are just a few of the more popular men from whom speculative theories have been developed in the interest of suppression of the truth.

This futile thinking displays itself in circulating theories, many of which are based on the assumption that God does not exist and that man can solve his own problems. Though people regularly blame God for not giving them enough miracles to believe in Him, the truth is that they have rejected God's general revelation. Let's go on to the next holding stage that God uses to keep man back from a total judgment.

B. Displacement > Decadence (Rom 1:22-24)

[22] Professing to be wise, they became fools, [23] and exchanged the glory of the incorruptible God for an image in the form of corruptible man and of birds and four-footed animals and crawling creatures. [24]

Therefore God gave them over in the lusts of their hearts to impurity, that their bodies might be dishonored among them (Rom 1:22-24).

They exchanged (displaced) the glory of God with created things. God gave them over to their lusts and impurity. Displacement is a defense mechanism in which repressed emotion or thoughts are transferred to a more acceptable object. Decadence is impure behavior, a departure from what is considered proper and moral. False thinking precedes immorality.

Departure of Truth - Stage #2 Worship of God is replaced (or exchanged) with worship of man and animals.

Instead of elevating God and delighting in His wisdom, man exalts the creature. Consider these two examples: (1) Humanism exalts man's contributions above God's, and (2) social evolution advocates man's godlike nature (e.g. even found in cults like Mormonism).

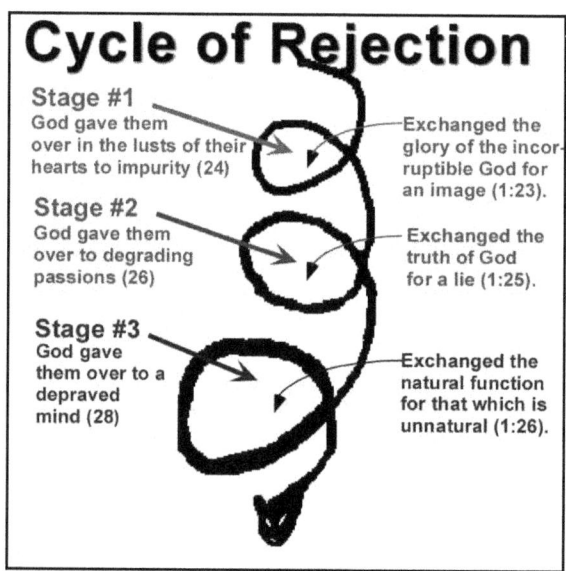

"Professing to be wise they became fools" (Rom 1:22). Man thinks all is going well. They make fortunes by selling books and programs based upon false ideas. Though they think themselves to be clever, they are foolish because they have rejected the truth and covered up their deceptive ways. We need to be wary of those who admit to any wisdom outside of God. The humanists have from early on professed to be a religion.

The phrases "God gave them over" reveals the key to understanding God's dealing with mankind. Paul shares quite openly the state of man's heart. The filthy impurities are already stored in man's heart, all of which lead to destruction. Yet God pulls back on the reins of our heart to prevent us from speedily moving down the path of destruction.

Reception of Evil - Station #2

Impurity of all sorts follows the exaltation of anything above God. Today's society is greatly influenced by humanism, whether it be capitalistic or socialistic in orientation. Adoption of relative ethics and the resulting immoral behavior: sensuous clothing, ads inducing covetousness, nudity, pornography, and abortion are now common.

The heart of society also becomes depraved. When man honors something other than the holy God, he finds himself rejecting God's holiness and replacing it with another philosophy to support his or her actions in order to ease guilt. Refraining from doing what is most natural brings on unnatural thoughts and affections. This affects the body. The mind makes excuses, the heart develops false affection, and then the body does what is improper. No wonder false religions and philosophies number in the hundreds of thousands! But if anyone captive to these lusts expresses a desire for truth, they could come right out of those darkened corridors.

The Greek word for 'lust' surprisingly has no inherent connotation of evil with it. Translated as 'desire,' the word could be bad or good. In this context, however, the strong desires are bad as they lead into impurity and therefore are translated as 'lusts.' The way people treat their bodies reveals much about how they perceive the truth.

The New Age Lie

The New Age promises a greater awareness and control of oneself, and even a greater freedom as a human. But humanism by definition rejects the creator and only accepts and worships the creature. This fosters a darkened mind, unnatural affections, and immoral life styles.

Worship

God expected worship and adoration to follow the revelation and knowledge He gave to man. In other words, the knowledge that God gave to man was of such clarity that He expected people to respond in worship. Instead, man-oriented religions developed, accompanied by worship reflecting themselves rather than the transcendent God for which they have plenty of evidence.

Only in this context can we begin to understand the sinfulness of 'missing church.' Our lack of enthusiasm for excited worship of the Creator God reveals adopted forms of idolatry or general secularism in our souls (see Paul's conclusion in Romans 3).

C. Delusion > Deviance and Darkening (Rom 1:25-32)

> [25] For they exchanged the truth of God for a lie, and worshiped and served the creature rather than the Creator, who is blessed forever. Amen. [26] For this reason God gave them over to degrading passions; for their women exchanged the natural function for that which is unnatural (Rom 1:25-26).

They exchanged the truth of God for a lie. As a result they became enslaved to degrading passions and received a depraved mind. Delusion is a false or firmly maintained distorted belief that is contradicted by social reality. Deviance is a marked divergence from society's accepted norms.

Departure of Truth - Stage #3: Stage of darkness and deviance

This third and apparent last stage is one of darkness. The truth that man is able to grasp at this stage is minimal. It is not that the truth of God is absent; they know it, but would rather believe a lie. They are not content to have the truth direct them how to live, but instead they favor living by lies so that they can live out their lusts. They become so enticed by the voices of these lies that they live out their false beliefs as if they are true. Reality is lost.

They exchanged the truth for something they desired more. They had their hands on what was good, but they swapped it for what they liked better, thus revealing their wicked hearts. They thought that once they put this knowledge of truth away, that God himself would be put away, but this was not true. The greater the truth that is rejected, the bigger the lie must become.

Abnormal behavior is treated as normal today. Divorce, sexual immorality, fraud, and deceit have become common place; not only does it happen, but people are encouraged to live likewise. Society today makes the Christians' values sound extreme. What God has stated as most deviant now prides itself in its own new 'morality.' The severe mark of judgment is pride, which signifies God's allowance of the degrading of thoughts and values, which soon becomes 'normal'.

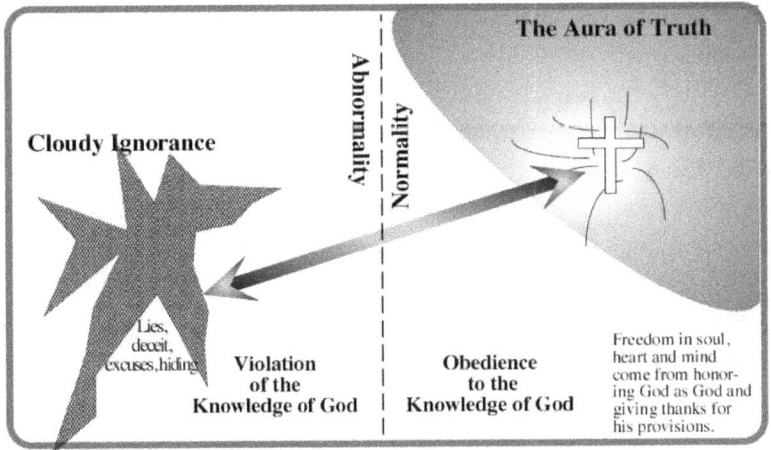

Reception of Evil - #3a

The way people treat their bodies says a lot about how they think of the truth (or, more accurately, don't think about it). God does not allow them to falsely profess to be wise without accumulating the associated evidence of judgment of rejecting him, which is most evident in the ways their bodies suffer from the perversions they are exposed to.

When a man's affections stray from worshiping God, his heart is said to have gone astray. Wayward affection ushers men and women into immorality, entertaining his (or her) unnatural functions as the most explicit statements to their folly. Even though they know others consider this abnormal behavior as perverse and illegal, they do not. They would rather hold on to a lie about God and enter further perilous conditions.

The above illustration shows how the truth is related to normality when a person responds in obedience. On the other hand, the further from the truth one removes himself, the more his mind is darkened, allowing him to live in violation of the knowledge of truth that he possesses. He believes all sorts of dark things.

Men and woman alike turn from good wholesome sexual desires within the marriage to deviant sexual behaviors. Instead of bearing children, mothers destroy children; instead of nurturing little ones, women choose 'self-fulfillment.' A woman's body was specifically designed to fulfill a beautiful part of God's design for creation, but this same body is now given over to public nudity, self-adoration, and profit-making. They have idolized themselves and their bodies.

God gave the responsibility to produce and protect life to the male, but they have turned to serve themselves through debased and defiling sexual behavior. The modern binge on porn is revealing. Instead of procreation, one ends with barrenness, bearing the marks of God's judgment seen in broken relationships, unmarried couples living together, and any resulting diseases. These serious abnormalities, once hidden and rare, are now common, public, and, in some cases, legalized.

Reception of Evil - Station #3b

The greater the truth rejected, the bigger the lie must become. The more one denies truth's advice and guidance, the greater he denies and resists God's ways. The swap is costly. One gains only the lie. The word for 'depraved' means a mind that is simply no good. It has failed the test and cannot be reliably used. The person's will is attached to all of these personal decisions and therefore incites aggravated guilt.

Perhaps here Paul is stating that when a mind has gone to such lengths in rejection of the truth, that the mind by itself cannot open itself up to reasoning. It cannot function as the mind should function. Arguments for some people are totally useless because their minds have fallen into such a useless state.[12]

Barriers and Doors

But God, in His great grace, has provided two significant ways in which He holds back man's waywardness.

- Barriers are provided to hinder man's rapid fall down toward judgment.
- Doors represent the way God enables mankind to reverse his wicked trends through repentance and the pursuit of godliness.

Let us briefly introduce both of them.

---

[12] Is this related to why believers give up on direct evangelism and only adopt friendship evangelism? Do they sense a lack of ability for the common man (or woman) to reason and understand the truth?

The Principle of Barriers

Upon rejection of God's truth, there are barriers that hinder a person or society from endlessly and effortlessly sliding down into degradation. At different stages, God slows man down, allowing him to observe his situation and to respond to His truth. If no positive response is made, then in God's timing, man is allowed to go down to another more degraded stage.

Application

The excuse, "I can't help it" is useless because of God's provision of the barriers. God allows extra time for man to evaluate his situation, thus human beings are fully responsible for their next step, whether up or down.

The Principle of Doors

Doors are meant to be passed through. God graciously makes it easy to positively respond to Him. Creation daily bears witness of Him. The conscience constantly convicts the soul. He sent His Son Jesus Christ into the world. His Word is being translated and spread throughout the world. Doors are truths show the rewarding result of our obedience to the Lord.

Application

Opportunities abound to positively respond to God. Are we opening our hearts to the Spirit's work or grieving His Spirit (Ep 4:30)?

D. Observing the Decay of a Society (Rom 1:28-32)

> 28 And just as they did not see fit to acknowledge God any longer, God gave them over to a depraved mind, to do those things which are not proper, 29 **being filled with all** unrighteousness, wickedness, greed, evil; **full of** envy, murder, strife, deceit, malice; they are gossips (Rom 1:28)-29.

The more a society allows or encourages this downward cycle, the quicker the decay degenerates into immorality, lawlessness, and despair. What we do in our spiritual lives has a great impact on our whole lives. If the society does not curb these evil tendencies, then the people will eventually mount a social revolution in which they hope to gain some stability and security or just fall into self-destruction. Oppression and ungodly behavior are inseparable.

The long list found in verses 29-32 can be separated into three sections: The first starts by describing things they are filled with; second, the things they are full of, and third, a long list of descriptive nouns. The list goes from general to more specific detail of evil behavior.

"being filled with all" (1:29)

This last stage is representative of those whose hearts are "filled with all" sorts of evil things (Rom 1:29). Their heart is not partially filled, but completely filled. The word "all" emphasizes the extreme degree of this evil and its effect on mankind. Each significant word is discussed below.

- unrighteousness: not righteous; improper action toward others; total lack of conformity against a standard of righteous.
- wickedness: a vicious and aggressive way of life.
- greed: "the insatiable desire to have more, even at the expense of harming others."[13]
- evil: malice, evil tendency, disposed to evil.

"full of" (1:29)

- envy: never content; focused on one's own accomplishments over others.
- murder: wanting and willing to destroy others who frustrate oneself or interfere with one's goals.
- strife: wrangling, always rubbing shoulders with an edge; prides oneself on the way to get one's way with words, etc.
- deceit: cunning, treachery, misguides to one's own advantage; breaking vows.
- malice: bad character; "The tendency to put the worst construction upon everything."[14]

"are" - being (1:29)

- gossips: tale-bearers, whisperers, pouring poison into a neighbor's ear, prideful destroyers.
- slanderers: speaking against another, tearing down, more blatant than gossip.
- haters of God: literally "hated of God" passive tense or "haters of God" in active tense. (the later preferred)

---

[13] Linguistic Key to the Greek New Testament, p. 350-351.
[14] Ibid.

- insolent: arrogant insolence and contempt for others displayed in cruelty for mere enjoyment.
- arrogant: proud, one who puts himself above others, self-sufficient, on a pedestal (higher than God)
- boastful: bragger, empty boasts, promises reward of gain and therefore deceit.
- inventors of evil: creative in destruction, malice and hurt.
- disobey parents: rebellious children, reject parents' words and requests.
- lack understanding: dull, senseless, the fool; ignores all warning signs and plows into foolish behavior.
- untrustworthy: faithless, disloyal, "covenant-breaker, faithless to an agreement."[15]
- unloving: "Without tenderness. It refers to the lack of the feelings of natural tenderness, as seen in a mother who exposes or kills her child, a father who abandons his family, or children who neglect their aged parents (Godet)."[16]
- unmerciful: without pity, harsh, abusive; abusing a person with needs.

Paul seems to take great strides to let us know that the epitome of the rejection of God's truth is the destruction of all morals. Individuals, families, societies, and even nations will collapse without the basic trust and support that sustains cooperative action. Evil worsens as people are filled with different sorts of evil. Sins grow in number, increasingly perverting relationships with deception and gross immoralities. There are such things as family degradation and the disintegration of societies, but they are always founded on the unrestrained evil behavior of men who have rejected the truth.

Application

First, we must accept God's judgment of His enemies. Some people have become so depraved that they cannot, and are unwilling to, think any good. This has great impact on evangelism. Proverbs says, "Do not cast your pearls upon the swine." The depraved of mind do not want to hear the gospel. Don't feel obligated to force-share it with them. Wait for God to prepare their hearts.

---

[15] Ibid.

[16] Ibid.

Second, we must reach out to those in moral free-falls. Remember, God designed those holding stages. Someone might be at the point of falling down another rung. Pray and share. God wants them to respond to His marvelous strength. There is no pit too deep for God's grace. The difference will be seen in their willingness to admit their problem and see God as their hope - not some counselor, experience, or philosophy, but in God's truth (1 Pe 4:3).

Third, we must detect how much we have been listening to the world. Has the world been so deceptive that we are convinced our way is better than God's? We need to know the overall pattern of decay so that we might, at least as far as our influence takes us, put a hold on it. Be salt!

Fourth, God is calling us to stop treating the abnormal as normal, even if it has become law. The secular life is not the less prejudiced position but the most rebellious one possible. Stop living passively among secularists, materialists, etc., but always act compassionately (truth with love). They are falling fast and are somewhere on the way down the path toward death. The more the wicked influence upon a society, the faster the society will decay, which, given the worldwide web network, is happening at an extraordinary rate.

Romans 1:18-32 Outline
THE EVIDENT GUILT OF MANKIND
Paul J. Bucknell

A. The Confirmation of Knowing God (Rom 1:18-20)
    1. The Wrath of God Later Revealed (18-19)
        a. The revelation of God's wrath (18)

        b. The target of God's wrath (18)

        c. The reason of God's wrath (19)

            1) The place: Within them (19a)

            2) The certainty: Very sure (19b)

    2. The Invisible Attributes of God Formerly Revealed (20)
        a. The time revealed: Since creation

        b. The characteristics revealed

            1) Eternal power

            2) Divine nature

        c. The means revealed

            1) He has been clearly seen

            2) He has been understood by creation

B. The Process of Scorning God (Rom 1:21-23)
    1. The Clear Knowledge of God is Abandoned (21a)

        a. They didn't honor Him as God

        b. They didn't give thanks to God

    2. The Cloudy Ignorance of Rejection (21b-23)

        a. Inwardly (21b)

            1) Their minds became speculative

            2) Their hearts became darkened

        b. Outwardly (22-23)

            1) Boasted to be wise (22)

            2) Dishonored God -took His glory away (23)

            3) Honored man and animals (23)

C. The Results of Rejecting God (Rom 1:24-32)
    1. God gave them over to the lusts to impurity (24-25)

        a. Result - dishonor their bodies (24)

        b. Reason (25)

        1) exchange truth of god for lie
        2) Worshiped and served creature than Creator
2. God gave them over to degrading passions (26-27)
    a. Women did unnatural things (26)
    b. Men (27)
        1) Forgot women
        2) Burned in desire for other men
        3) Committed indecent acts
        4) Justly rewarded with infliction of sorts
3. God gave them over to depraved mind (Rom 1:28-32)
    a. Reason - no room for God
    b. Purpose - to do what is improper
    c. Description of selves (29-32)
    d. Desperateness of their state (32)
        1) Know the ordinance of God
        2) Practicing those things receive death
        3) Do it just the same
        4) Encourage others in the acts of depravity

Romans 2:1-11
The Prosecution of Mankind

What is the Apostle Paul speaking about in Romans 2:1-11? If we are not careful to examine this passage, we will miss his point. Paul is continuing his train of thought from the previous passage, revealing man's great need of righteousness for both Gentiles and Jews. Paul's underlying argument is that all men need the righteousness of Jesus Christ. False teaching, however, corrupts one's understanding of the truth, enabling people to believe they are righteous and do not need the Savior.

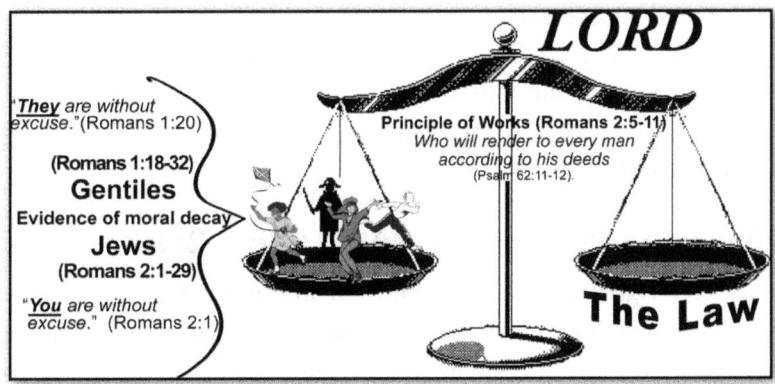

A careful analysis must be made on how Paul goes from generally describing mankind in the later part of Romans 1 to how he shows that man is specifically accountable for what he does in the beginning of chapter 2. This transition is evident through the use of the pronoun 'they' in chapter 1 to the use of the pronoun 'you,' second person singular, in chapter two.

Although Paul has not totally excluded the Gentiles from his arguments here, he definitely does include the self-righteous Jews who thought they would be treated significantly different from the Gentiles. The self-righteous would join Paul and condemn those in the later part of chapter 1. Paul, however, wants to bring the Gospel to those who fall into another category of sin and rebellion. Paul states that though the standards might be a bit different, the process of condemnation will be the same. People will be evaluated on whether they are righteous or not. Jews do not have special immunity from God's judgment. Here are some terms that need to be clarified.

- False teaching: Isolated, untrue instruction that creates false views toward God, self, and others.
- Cult: A systematic collection of teaching that bears a resemblance to Christian beliefs but holds at least one vital doctrine that consists of false teaching.
- False religion or philosophy: comprehensive answers for existence based on untrue tenets and thus oppose Christ's teaching.
- Occult: Those wrong teachings that would encourage people to investigate and manipulate the dark and hidden world ruled by Satan, the evil one.

Questions for Reflection
- Can a person be influenced by false teaching without belonging to a cult? Explain your answer.
- What popular false teachings around you keep people from believing that they need the Savior?

A. Everyone will be prosecuted (Rom 2:1-4)

Even the self-righteous are liable for their sins before God.

Paul makes sure he implicates the self-righteous person in these first verses. Observe how he traps the Jew by the way he rallies them in passing God's judgment against the pagans at the end of Romans 1. They would conveniently exclude themselves from this list as they point their finger, thinking, "We so clearly see the sins of those people." Paul presents two arguments in these first four verses.

Argument #1 Self-incrimination (2:1-3)

> ¹ Therefore you are without excuse, every man of you who passes judgment, for in that you judge another, you condemn yourself; for you who judge practice the same things. ² And we know that the judgment of God rightly falls upon those who practice such things. ³ And do you suppose this, O man, when you pass judgment upon

those who practice such things and do the same yourself, that you will escape the judgment of God (Rom 2:1-3)?

Paul first challenges those who exclude themselves from God's judgment (2:1) with a rhetorical question in verse 3. "And do you suppose this ...when you pass judgment ... that you will escape the judgment of God?"

Paul responds, "You verify you are liable to the same judgment, if not a worse one, because you do know the law but practice the same things." This perfectly captures the error of the self–righteous. The self-righteous consider themselves to be righteous in their own eyes, ignoring God's perspective. They feel as if they are righteous because they vehemently accuse others of sin. "Look what they do!" They believe that their self-appointment to the judgement seat excludes them from the possibility of being judged.

Paul cleverly challenges this deep-rooted assumption by treating their ability to judge as convincing testimony of their accountability to the same standard. They cannot say they did not know. They will be held to the same standards they use in their judgment of others. If they know it is wrong for a person to do something wrong, and judge that person, will they not be held to that standard too? They, then, will be more harshly condemned if they are found to violate the law by which they judge others.

Thought process of the self-righteous

- "What they are doing is horrible!" (Identifies the wrong action and judges it.)
- "They will get their share." (Passes judgment even though they have done the same.)
- "I am glad we are not like them!" (Separates themselves, but God doesn't separate that way! God looks at what they think and do.)
- "Stay away from them." (Prides themselves in not associating with them though they have the same sins).

Argument (Rom 2:1-3)	Counter argument #1 (Rom 2:1-3)
"We are above judgment because we can so clearly see their sins!"	But you verify your guilt because you prove you know the law and yet still disobey it!

Verse 3 identifies the fallaciousness of condemning one thing in a person and avoiding that same condemnation in another. In this case, they neglected to condemn themselves. This approach to others and self is quite predominant around the world.

> **Evidence of moral decay among the self-righteous.**

Everyone wants to point out the evil in the world but not at home in their own lives. They find excuses for neglecting to incriminate themselves because of their wealth, class, caste, race, religion, education, or family. Paul makes it very clear that God is not judging nationality or background but behavior. He delights in those from different cultures and languages. Prejudice judges people by race or economic scale. God judges people by their moral behavior, that is, the degree of their obedience.

Argument #2 Misuse of Privilege (2:4)

> Or do you think lightly of the riches of His kindness and forbearance and patience, not knowing that the kindness of God leads you to repentance (Rom 2:4)?

Verse 4 challenges those who might abuse God's patience. They are convinced God's favored treatment toward them (being Jews) places them beyond God's judgment. They say, "God's choice of us shows us that we are good and beyond judgment." Paul responds saying, "You are misusing God's kindness to cover up your sin!"

In a sense, they judge themselves. They define the law, set the penalty, and pass the sentence. The only problem is that they exclude themselves from the list of the accused. They believe their special relationship with God puts them in a better position. The converse, however, is true. Those having a greater portion of the truth are more responsible to live according to the truth.

Thought process

- "We are treated special by God." (God will not judge us.)
- "We are special." (They do not belong, but we do!)
- "They are different from us." (Are we really better?)
- "God loves us. (He doesn't love them, but us!)
- "We are better." (We take pride in ourselves despite falling short of our own standards.)

Romans 2:1-11 The Prosecution of Mankind

Argument #2 (Rom 2:4)	Counter argument #2 (Rom 2:4)
"We are above judgment because we are treated so special by God" (Rom 2:4)	But you verify you are to suffer the same judgment because you misuse God's kindness to cover up your sin! (Rom 2:4)

They excuse their behavior by stating that God is not very concerned with their behavior, because, if He did care, He would do something about it. Their mistake, a common one, is to misinterpret God by observing His patience.

Paul demolishes their protective argument by pointing out the truth that God's patience enables Him to put judgment off so that they have time to repent and find His grace, not to, as they erroneously concluded, excuse themselves from their sin. They are merely using an ancient device to shrug off their accountability to God for their immoral behavior. They treat God's kindness, forbearance and patience lightly. They misunderstand God's person and ways and are hardened rather than softened by God's beautiful grace. Self–righteousness horribly distorts both doctrine and the fact of a person's sin.

Summary

The self-righteous exclude themselves from God's judgment. They do not feel they are that 'bad' and therefore do not see any need of salvation for themselves. They are okay without a savior. They pride themselves on how good they are compared to others and have no time for standards in their lives. The apostle clearly implicates the self-righteous (i.e. Jews) by having them examine their own actions (rather than their words or claims) against what they claim is wrong in others (i.e. Gentiles).

Obviously there are many self-righteous among the Gentiles, but Paul targets his argument so that the Jews would seek Christ. The arguments and applications adequately reveal the sins of all mankind. Chapter 1 focuses on those with openly sinful lifestyles. Romans 2:1-11 catches those who exclude themselves from that first category because of the religious or moral lives they live.

Application

- Have we set different standards for our lives than for other people? If we think we are better than another group of people, than it is very likely that we might fall into the same trap of thinking that we are good and beyond judgment. We might even think God's judgment of others and His kindness to us means that we are free from God's anger.

- How does doctrine affect my life? Do I merely know it or does it shape how I act and think?
- Detect delusion: Search out people around you that are deluded about some important aspect of life.

B. Everyone Faces a Just Prosecution (Rom 2:5-11)

Everyone is judged according to his works and gets what he deserves.

2:5 But because of your stubbornness and unrepentant heart you are storing up wrath for yourself in the day of wrath and revelation of the righteous judgment of God 6 who will render to every man according to his deeds 7 to those who by perseverance in doing good seek for glory and honor and immortality, eternal life; 8 but to those who are selfishly ambitious and do not obey the truth, but obey unrighteousness, wrath and indignation. 9 There will be tribulation and distress for every soul of man who does evil, of the Jew first and also of the Greek 10 but glory and honor and peace to every man who does good, to the Jew first and also to the Greek. 11 For there is no partiality with God (Rom 2:5-11).

Starting in verse 5, the principle of 'works' is explained. Everyone will be impartially rewarded for what he has stored up. Paul, quoting from the Old Testament (Ps 62:12; Jer 17:10) states, "Who will render to every man according to his deeds" (2:6). They will reap what they have sown. Underlying these verses is the basic concept that man has a will and is therefore accountable for all of his actions. God records a person's actions and thoughts, and will reward people according to whether

> **Self-righteousness distorts doctrine and our perception of wickedness.**

they are good or evil. Do they measure up? Do we? No one but Jesus Christ the Righteous One can because we are all sinners (see chapter 3).

- 2:5 "Stored up wrath" - God is patient! He does not instantly judge every sin. Neither does delay imply our innocence.
- 2:5 "Day of wrath" - The day will come when no one can change what they have stored up. It is the day our accounts are closed and carefully examined. Man is accountable before a righteous God for all their deeds.

Romans 2:1-11 The Prosecution of Mankind

- 2:5 "Righteous judgment of God" - No one needs to be concerned about justice. God as the moral governor will fairly judge all. What we need is grace!
- 2:6 "According to his deeds" - Man will not be judged by what he hoped to do or thought about doing but by what he did. The issue is not what we wanted to do but what we did do.
- 2:6 "Who will render" - God will repay, good for good and bad for bad. He keeps careful accounts of all the things we do with our choices, time, motives and resources.
- 2:7 "Eternal life" - Only given to those who persevere in doing good. (cf. Romans 3:10-12) This is not a simple reward system on how a believer acts.
- 2:8 "Wrath and indignation" - God will release His wrath and indignation upon those who disobey Him and are selfish.
- 2:9-10 "For every soul" - God does not judge differently for those under the covenant and those not under the covenant. He seeks out those who are righteous.
- 2:11 "No partiality" - There is no special group or experience that might exclude anyone from God's scrutinizing eye, Jew or Gentile. This includes both sexes, all ages, all backgrounds, cultures, and religions.

These moralists thought they would be treated differently than the pagans whom they despised, but all men are equally accountable for their moral behavior. Paul states that God will judge the unrepentant on "the day of wrath and revelation of the righteous judgment of God." That day closes the opportunity to repent or do further good works. They all will get their fair portion on that day. Paul's argument will be seen to be true that no one except Christ Jesus has lived out that righteous life. By defining God's standard of righteousness, the apostle (He well understood this problem from his own life) is not afraid that anyone would be able to include themselves in the righteous group that will gain eternal life. He will expand on this as the chapter progresses.

Questions for Reflection
- Is anyone righteous enough to pass God's test?
- What do those who fail to meet up with God's standards do?

Romans 2:6

The general principle of works is given in verse 6, "Who will render to every man according to his deeds." Every man will get according to his deeds. Everything has a consequence, not only here on earth but also in the future. We are not only accountable for the treatment of our neighbor, but we are also liable to God's judgment. We would be fools to believe that what happens on earth is the final point of justice or reward.

Paul presumes people have received certain things for which they are responsible to handle properly. Earlier on, in chapter one, he has mentioned the gift of the knowledge of God, but he also mentioned the 'ordinance of God' in 1:32. God's moral law has been given to us, and therefore we are accountable to adjust our behavior accordingly.

Romans 2:6-8 The Two Paths

Paul mentions two categories within which mankind fall into: those who do good (2:7,10) and those who disobey (2:8-9). Each maintain their own activity and gain their due reward. The concern never needs to be whether God is just or fair. The problem is that when He exercises His justice upon our works, we will be found to be guilty. We need compassion and mercy, which is only found in Jesus.

The Good Path (2:6-7,10)

> 6 Who will render to every man according to his deeds: 7 to those who by perseverance in doing good seek for glory and honor and immortality, eternal life. ... 10 but glory and honor and peace to every man who does good, to the Jew first and also to the Greek.

This 'good' path is one of perseverance in doing good. To say that you are well because of some past good acts is hardly sufficient to claim that you are on the road to eternal life. Paul's chief complaint from the beginning is the way the Jews also "practice the same things" (2:1).

Verse 10 parallels verse 7 by announcing the honor that comes to those who live uprightly. A person's life needs to be confirmed by his or her commitment to doing good. These are the ones who show they are seeking glory, honor, and immortality. "Glory and honor" is a familiar phrase to Jewish ears. Paul strips away any excuse for those who say that, because they 'try to be good' or have such and such religion, they can gain eternal life. Even Nicodemus had to be born again (John 3).

Interpretations of 2:6-7

Verses 2:6-7 are difficult to properly understand because people often forget the context. Here are a few interpretations–though do note that not all are correct: (1) Paul is stating that a person is saved and goes to heaven by good works, (2) Most commentators think it refers not to the unbeliever and salvation but to the rewards a believer gets from the way he lives out his life. (3) I personally believe this is part of Paul's argument, consistent with this section, that he is catching the Jews who think they are immune from their wrongdoings just because of their Jewish connections. Each point will be discussed in detail below.

(1) The first view holds that Paul is teaching that a person gains eternal life by living a good life. Clearly this viewpoint is untenable. The thrust of the whole book of Romans is to declare that the Gospel is not based on a person's good works but on the righteousness of Christ (Rom 4:25). Paul repeatedly elaborates the reasons people are not saved: by trying hard or depending on a religious background. All are sinners (3:9), and therefore fall short of the glory of God (3:21). It is for this reason we all stand condemned, needing a Savior. This suggested interpretation is counter-gospel. D.M. Lloyd Jones summarizes this nicely, "I say that the suggestion that verses 6 and 7 refer to justification by works is shown to be utterly and completely impossible."[17]

(2) Most conservative commentators reject the first interpretation, but then conclude that this passage is encouraging believers to do good; in other words, they believe Paul is speaking about believers here and not about salvation at all (because believers are already saved). Albert Barnes, for example, says that this does not refer to gaining eternal life but obtaining rewards. And so many commentators think this verse describes the Christian, the upright believer.

The believer is always in need of encouragement to obey (Paul will encourage believers in the following section on sanctification); but this is not Paul's argument in this passage. Paul is focused on implicating all of us as sinners who therefore need salvation. Paul sums up this section by showing us that we are all sinners and have turned aside (3:9-10). This chapter has nothing to do with rewards for believers but rather is about exposing how the Law (i.e. the OT quote) exposes our imperfections.

---

[17] D.M. Lloyd-Jones, Romans Chapter 2:1-3:20. Zondervan, 1989, p. 92.

Frankly, I am very disappointed with the majority of commentators who take up this view. It is as if they have a myopic view of the text at hand and exclude the greater context. Each commentator takes a slightly different approach, but in the end, their conclusion comes very close to denying what Paul is asserting, that men are not saved by their good works.

(3) This third view best fits into Paul's argument. Paul speaks this way to catch the moralists who say, "I am good and not like the rest. Everything will be okay." They think of themselves as the righteous ones. Paul clearly is not speaking of rewards because he states 'eternal life' here in verse 7 rather than 'rewards in eternal life'. The issue is about whether a person will gain eternal life, not the amount of rewards he or she has, though Paul does speak about rewards in other places (1 Cor 3:14-16).

Paul is deeply committed to showing the Jewish self-righteous sinner that he has not lived out a godly and acceptable life. There is no such thing as a man that gains eternal life because he is good (because we are Adam's descendants Rom 5:12-21). Paul has categorized the Jews as being disobedient to the truth, and so they should see themselves in the 'bad' category (2:1,3), but he knows they will not think of themselves this way and will attach themselves to this 'good' group.

The apostle has given much thought to this, especially when one considers the fact that he had righteous men killed (e.g. Steven) and yet thought he was serving God. After these Jews award themselves the stamp of righteousness, Paul powerfully demonstrate that there are no righteous people. No one seeks God of his own free will. Lloyd-Jones not only asserts that works cannot save a man, "but he is equally anxious to show that works can condemn a man."[18]

The Gospel tells us that before a person can claim Christ's righteousness, he must first admit (confess) to his lack of a righteous life. This acknowledges his need for Christ's righteousness, because otherwise he would not be able to obtain it. Paul will amplify this thought in the verses to come. It is important for us to realize that Paul is not addressing the issue of finding eternal life (he does this later), but who is going to heaven (no one, because they fall short–second part of chapter 2 and first part of chapter 3).

---

[18] Ibid. p. 94.

Our works do not commend us for eternal life but condemn us!

The Bad Path (2:8-9)

> 8 But to those who are selfishly ambitious and do not obey the truth, but obey unrighteousness, wrath and indignation. 9 There will be tribulation and distress for every soul of man who does evil, of the Jew first and also of the Greek (Rom 2:8-9).

This second group has shown that they belong to the 'bad' category by their choices of disobedience. The Law has revealed their sin. They are going contrary to God's way. They are known for their self-ambitious plans rather than life in God's truth. Man's ways are typified by the word 'unrighteousness.'

Those who have disobeyed the Lord will surely find wrath and indignation as a reward. God is being patient now, but that time will end. Judgment will come and man will find himself facing God's fierce wrath, which is born from His sense of justice. They will be judged by God's standard of truth rather than man's own standard of judgment.

Paul is attacking the false security of the men and women who are supposedly saved by their righteous deeds or their Jewish connections. Paul confronts them where they feel the strongest, but it is their deception that makes them so blind. Again, one cannot presume to be saved on the basis of being a Jew, an elder, a faithful church goer, or having gone through a ceremony like circumcision or baptism. Paul challenges everyone to look at their own behavior rather than at their background, otherwise they will be in for a great shock on Judgment Day. Once they are able to evaluate themselves according to their deeds, they cannot again excuse themselves by their religious connections. Paul pushed them to lean only on their lifestyle choices and then used the Old Testament to show that all are under common condemnation.

Neither Jew nor Greek will be excluded from the general examination of their behavior. The Jew prides himself on the covenant; the Greek prides himself on his wisdom and education. Both will be judged according to their deeds. The phrase "the Jew first" can have two meanings. It might refer to the Jewish people being first in time. They heard the gospel first, as is explained in Acts 1:8. The "first" might also refer to the greatest degree of responsibility.

They knew more about God. Perhaps both are true, but clearly God will hold the Jews at least as responsible as the Gentiles, if not more.

Romans 2:11

"For there is no partiality with God" (2:11). God is fair, as He is just. He does not only apply appropriate punishment to the disobedient but also rewards good behavior with glory, honor, and peace (2:10). Notice again how Paul uses the two extremes of good and bad, righteous and unrighteous, just as John did. There is no middle ground. Put clearly and succinctly, there is no partiality with God. God will examine everyone's moral life and the person will stand or fall. Our works illuminate which road we are walking on and where that path leads.

Application

These verses provide a good check on whether we are guilty of hypocrisy, that is, whether we believe our spiritual state is better than it really is. Paul provides a simple test.

> Step one requires us to analyze those things that we deem to be wrong done by others (e.g. gossip, murder, not being sufficiently sensitive to another's needs).

> Step two asks us to see whether we are actually doing those very same things that we accuse others of.

> Step three has us evaluate our lives to see whether we are consistently good according to this standard or not. If we are not completely good, then we fail the test.

Insight into Theology

Before God's scrutinizing light, all men have sinned (read further into Romans 3). None of us have sought God's way. We all are found to be unrighteous.

But what if there was a righteous man? He would be considered one who earned or at least did not lose eternal life. Paul approaches our lives in this way to uncover any hidden sins. The Apostle Paul has deep insight into this area because of his past. He is pushing everyone into the situation where they need to evaluate their lives according to their moral behavior. In the end, mankind will be shown to have failed miserably, but Jesus Christ, the second Adam, will have been shown to have secured eternal life through his righteous life. We need Him as our Savior.

Reflection on evangelism

The assumption that everyone is contaminated by their own evil deeds is a basic theologic proposition that greatly affects our evangelical message. For example, we do not need to worry that people are able to live righteous lives. No one is righteous. Paul will explore this concept more in the next verses.

So what are we to do with those people who say they try to be good? We can affirm their statement that the righteous one will gain eternal life but then you can try to explore this with concrete questions about their behavior. "You mean you have never deceived anyone?" The issue is that they really have not reached that point. Even if a person is righteous from this point onward, they still have a past that proves that their lot is placed with those who will be utterly judged. All have missed the mark.

Romans 2:12-29
Three Lousy Excuses

Paul addresses three false confidences of the self-righteous Jew (though the moralistic Gentile is always kept in distant view). Confidence can be a good thing, but in the case of the Jews, it was used to justify themselves before God, just as many religious Christians do today. These religious activities were never meant to excuse the Jew from simple obedience.

> Excuse # 1 Rom 2:12-16
> Not Knowledge of the Law
> but Keeping of the Law
> Excuse # 2 Rom 2:17-24
> Not Heritage - the name,
> but Hearing the Law
> Excuse # 3 Rom 2:25-29
> Not Circumcision
> but Completion of Law

Unfortunately, the Christian church is filled with those who similarly think that their relationship with God is fine because they meet certain requirements like owning or reading the Bible, regularly attending church, baptized, belong to the church, tithes, etc. Paul knocks the three false confidences of the Jews down, one by one: the possession of the Law, their heritage as Jews, and their rite of circumcision.

The Jews are being condemned not because they have certain covenantal privileges, but because they do "the same things" as the Gentiles (non-Christians) do, and so deserve a similar judgment. Paul denies "covenantal nomism" where everyone in the covenant is saved and adopts "covenantal pistism," which states that it is faith within the covenant that deems them saved.[19]

---

[19] Wycliffe Exegetical Commentary. Moo, p. 126. Covenantal pistism is from the Greek word for faith. In other words, they are saved by the faith that enables them to be part of the covenant.

A. Excuse #1: "I have the Law!" (Rom 2:12-16)

Not Knowledge of the Law but Keeping of the Law

Not what you know but what you do.

> 12 For all who have sinned without the Law will also perish without the Law; and all who have sinned under the Law will be judged by the Law; 13 for not the hearers of the Law are just before God, but the doers of the Law will be justified. 14 For when Gentiles who do not have the Law do instinctively the things of the Law, these, not having the Law, are a law to themselves, 15 in that they show the work of the Law written in their hearts, their conscience bearing witness, and their thoughts alternately accusing or else defending them, 16 on the day when, according to my gospel, God will judge the secrets of men through Christ Jesus (Rom 2:12-16).

Paul reinforces his former statement: Anyone who has fallen short of a righteous life will perish.

> This paragraph defends the equality of all people before God's judgment seat against the charge that the Jews' possession of the law gives them a decisive advantage. This is not the case. Paul argues, because (1) it is doing, not hearing or possessing, the law that matters (v. 13); and (2) even the Gentiles, who do not have God's law in written form, have it in a different sense (vv. 14-15).[20]

From the Possession or Knowledge of the Law (Rom 2:12-16)

Here Paul focuses on the two general backgrounds: the Jew and the Gentile. The Gentiles are those who have sinned without the Law and will perish without the Law. They do not need the Old Testament Law to condemn them because their societal norm will condemn them. They will be incriminated by the standard they hold.

Those, however, who hold the Law of God will be judged by it. God's specially delivered set of standards given on Mount Sinai is more demanding. The Jew will be judged on completion of the Law and not whether they are part of the covenant. This is different from the New Covenant where the Law is perfectly fulfilled and implemented within the believers' hearts.

---

[20] Moo, p. 142.

An Inclusive Judgment

Paul is thorough in his arguments so that no one can exclude themselves for their disobedience. The 'for' of verse 12 indicates a coming explanation and connects this section with the previous one. Judgment will be fair because it will be based on the same standard whether anyone thinks he has sinned or not. They will not be excused by what they know, but judged by what they have done.

Paul speaks of two categories in verses 12 and 14. The word "without the Law" (*anomos* – ανομος) does not refer to law-breakers but to the Gentiles, which, as a group, never received God's covenant (the Law). Those having the Law are the Jews.[21]

Differing Witness

Those under the Law will be judged by the Law. Although the Law points to God's blessed standards, it also stands as an accuser when not kept, quite the opposite of being the basis of their salvation and hope.

The Gentiles, not being under the Law, will not be judged by it. They did not commit to this covenant as the Jews did (Jos 24:21-22). They do not need the OT Law to condemn them because their societal norm signifies the presence of a "Law written in their hearts" (v. 24), and it is here where their consciences will condemn them.

> The Law, whether it be the Jewish Law or the "work of the Law" written in the heart can never save. Man's striving to get to heaven by his attempt to fulfill God's standard is ridiculous. This is completely different from the New Covenant where the Law is perfectly fulfilled through faith in Christ's work and genuinely implemented within the believers' hearts by the Holy Spirit.

Insight into Theology

The ramifications of this argument is significant. "God will judge the secrets of men through Christ Jesus" (2:16). God is extremely just so that each of our sins will be condemned by the slamming of the gavel. Though many believe

---

[21] "From earliest times, three basic alternatives have been proposed: Gentiles who fulfill the law and are saved apart from explicit faith in Christ; Gentiles who do some parts of the law but who are not saved; and Gentile Christians." Supporters of view 1 include Pelagius, Chrysostom. 2nd view: Moo, Calvin, Hodge, Murray, Kasemann. 3rd view: Cranfield, Augustine. -Moo, pp. 144-145.

God is unfair to send a person to hell (especially loved ones) it is precisely this judgment that God must deliver in order to exact a fair sentence. There is one judgment of everlasting fire, but according to this teaching, we are forced to conclude that judgment will differ in that place. All will be guilty but judgment is based on what a person knows and how he responds.

Reflection on Evangelism
These truths about accountable knowledge are critical to properly sharing the gospel. People are different. They will be judged differently. Paul spoke to those at Athens using a different approach (Acts 17:17-31) because their situation differed from the Jews who had the law. We need to be sensitive to these various approaches.

Everyone, however, has a body of truth to which they are accountable, whether it is through instruction, a traditional religion, or embedded in their conscience (cf. Jn 1:19). Those we speak with have some knowledge of truth. We should discover the level of truth to which they are aware and step into their lives at that point. Even those without religion and law have their conscience to bear witness to their sin, that is, there are things they know they should and should not do, and yet fail to follow that knowledge. Although this standard is imperfect (doesn't fully reflect God's righteousness), it leaves each sincere person able to perceive their lack of obtaining that righteous life as he or she should. These and the following arguments develop the basis for followup discussions on sin and guilt in succeeding chapters.

B. Excuse #2: "I am a Jew!" (Rom 2:17-24)
Not Heritage - the name, but genuinely hearing the Law

Not who you are (in name) but what you do.
---

[17] But if you bear the name "Jew," and rely upon the Law, and boast in God, [18] and know His will, and approve the things that are essential, being instructed out of the Law, [19] and are confident that you yourself are a guide to the blind, a light to those who are in darkness, [20] a corrector of the foolish, a teacher of the immature, having in the Law the embodiment of knowledge and of the truth, [21] you, therefore, who teach another, do you not teach yourself? You who preach that one should not steal, do you steal? [22] You who say that one should not commit adultery, do you commit adultery? You who abhor idols, do you rob temples? [23] You who boast in the Law, through your breaking

the Law, do you dishonor God? ²⁴ For "THE NAME OF GOD IS BLASPHEMED AMONG THE GENTILES BECAUSE OF YOU," just as it is written (Rom 2:17-24).

From their Jewish Heritage (2:17-24)

First, let us look closely at this passage and see the number of things they trusted in that led to their false confidence: cultural status of Jew, possession of the Law, pride in their God, guide to the blind, a light to those in darkness, corrector of foolish, teacher of immature, and embodiment of knowledge of truth. What a list!

Paul in 2:17-20 describes how many Jews thought about their Jewishness. They bore the name Jew. They tended to look at the outward aspect of their people as a race rather than by the characteristics of the inner person. As a Jew, they claim to know all about God, and have been taught by God's Word. Notice the contrast between Romans 1:17 and Jeremiah 9:23-24 (c.f. 1 Cor 1:31).

> For in it (the gospel) the righteousness of God is revealed from faith to faith; as it is written, "BUT THE RIGHTEOUS man SHALL LIVE BY FAITH" (Rom 1:17).
>
> ²³ Thus says the LORD, "Let not a wise man boast of his wisdom, and let not the mighty man boast of his might, let not a rich man boast of his riches; ²⁴ but let him who boasts boast of this, that he understands and knows Me, that I am the LORD who exercises lovingkindness, justice, and righteousness on earth; for I delight in these things," declares the LORD (Jer 9:23-24).
>
> Just as it is written, "LET HIM WHO BOASTS, BOAST IN THE LORD" (1 Cor 1:31).

They have confidence of their relationship with God through their Jewish heritage and their association with the Law rather than in the revelation of God. Unfortunately, they do not back up their profession with a clear obedience of the Law (it is impossible to keep the Law). They lack precisely what should differentiate them from the Gentiles: a righteous life.

Translations for 2:18

"Approve the things that are essential" has three alternative translations:

1) "You distinguish the things that differ [from God's will]" ("know right from wrong" NEB); Hodge);

2) "You distinguish the things that really matter" (Kasemann; Cranfield; Dunn) or

3) "You approve of those things that are excellent [that are worth the most]"(Murray, Moo).

Missions found in 2:19

"And are confident that you yourself are a guide to the blind, a light to those who are in darkness" (Rom 2:19). "A light to those who are in darkness" refers to the strong mission message in the Old Testament.[22] The Jews were supposed to be examples to the whole world but Paul later challenged them on account of discrediting God's name (2:24).

Are we talking about how the Jews are as Gentiles or that the Gentiles can be like good Jews?

They lack precisely what should differentiate them from the Gentiles–a righteous life. So Paul continues his argument by crystallizing certain issues that they claim to have answers for.

Generally, the principal can be summarized as in verse 21, "You, therefore who teach another, do you not teach yourself?" If they teach others not to steal, are they also not accusing themselves because they steal. Paul enumerates such sins as adultery, robbing temples, and general disobedience of the Law. There are some things the Jews would probably never do–such as deny the covenant, but they do other things they ought to refrain from.

They defend their guilt by reasoning, maybe renaming it (e.g. gambling to gaming) or justifying it with some good motive (e.g. give 10% profit of gambling to non-profits). Paul is very acquainted with the Jews' weaknesses as he has probably used these same methods (e.g. justifying the murder of Christians). He has seen their sin and is not apologetic for his generalization. He even quotes the Old Testament prophets, "The name of God is blasphemed among the Gentiles because of you" (Rom 2:24). Their inconsistency has even been noticed among the heathen!

We have a problem understanding how the three sins Paul pointed out might incriminate all Jews. There is no evidence that these sins among the Jews grew to a high proportion. Paul, however, proved his point through them. The Jews possessed no special relationship with God that would, theoretically, excuse them from judgment. The argument can be handled two ways:

---

[22] Moo, p. 158.

- The first would incriminate all Jews, but Paul's usage of idolatry doesn't seem to be a sin of all the Jews; or
- Paul clearly incriminates some Jews. He might be arguing that when we look at these Jews, it is obvious that they are sinners. So if some Jews, because of disobedience disclaim their inheritance, then is it not true that anyone who breaks the Law will not be able to use their inheritance to avoid judgment? If these Jews cannot get by with special privileges with God, then neither can others.

In other words, as Paul concludes in 2:28-29, it is not being part of the outward Jewish community that makes the difference but a life that lives in light of God's moral law. They focused their trust on the name and knowledge of God rather than on God Himself. They are boasting in what they know rather than in who they know. Faith in Christ remains crucial for salvation (the reason for this will be given in a later section).

From Romans 2:1-2 we discover that the faults most self-righteous people point out in others is the same sin that they themselves are committing. They clearly recognize the sin in their own lives. Perhaps it is because of this principle that Paul picks out certain sins in verse 22, such as idolatry, adultery, and stealing, and charges them with doing the same. If we have not experienced grace in a certain area of our lives, we become hypersensitive to it and therefore are quick to see the same sin in others.

Furthermore, if the Jews have in some areas fallen under the guilt of the Law, does not their disobedience bar them from their inheritance? If this is the case, then no Jew can claim exemption from their disobedience by their Jewish name. These Jews simply have no such special privileges with God.

Application
Do you see any parallels between these religious Jews and religious people today (including Christians)? Remember, these Jews thought they were good religious people. How do you think they did these evil acts in good conscience? Do you ever "know what to do and do not do it"?

C. Excuse #3: "I am circumcised!" (Rom 2:25-29)
Not Circumcision but Completion of the Law

Not what you have followed, but what you do with your lives.

> ²⁵ For indeed circumcision is of value, if you practice the Law; but if you are a transgressor of the Law, your circumcision has become uncircumcision. ²⁶ If therefore the uncircumcised man keeps the requirements of the Law, will not his uncircumcision be regarded as circumcision? ²⁷ And will not he who is physically uncircumcised, if he keeps the Law, will he not judge you who though having the letter of the Law and circumcision are a transgressor of the Law? ²⁸ For he is not a Jew who is one outwardly; neither is circumcision that which is outward in the flesh. ²⁹ But he is a Jew who is one inwardly; and circumcision is that which is of the heart, by the Spirit, not by the letter; and his praise is not from men, but from God (Rom 2:25-29).

From their Religious Rite of Circumcision (Rom 2:25-29)

In verses 25-29 he continues his argument. Since they are Jews, they have no special favor with God excluding them from God's judgment. In verses 12-24 Paul has shown that the possession of the law and their Jewish heritage will not protect them from an exacting judgment. And now in these verses (25-29), he affirms that circumcision is not able to protect them from God's judgment of their sin. No one cannot escape a fair judgment.

> To become uncircumcised means to become like a Gentile and to forfeit any defense that one's membership in the people of God might provide on the day of judgment... For in contrast to Jewish teachers, who held that only a radical decision to renounce the covenant invalidated one's circumcision. Paul argues that simple transgressions of the law can have the same effect.²³

Theological Insight

Paul makes a two-pronged argument to compel Jews to accept the Gentiles as equals in their Christian faith (cf. 3:1, 9).

- First, all peoples will be equally judged, the Jew along with the non-Jew.
- Second, he shows how those not being circumcised can become one with God's people (2:29). This circumcision of the heart refers to the process of being 'born from above' where the 'flesh is cast off' (Col 2:11). This topic is based on Deuteronomy 30:6.

Application

Religious people call themselves Christians because they were baptized and go to church, and yet live like the world. From the last two verses, how should we think and approach these religious people?

---

²³ Moo, p. 165.

Summary

Paul concludes this argument in 2:28-29. It is not being part of the possession of the Law, or by belonging to the covenant, or even an attachment to the Jewish community, which gives life but those who live in light of God's moral law. But they, like all us, have not lived out a righteous life. Paul will now press this argument in chapter 3 and draw some powerful conclusions: we all need God's sent Savior, Jesus Christ.

Romans 3:1-20

Total Depravity

The term 'total depravity' might be used often in some circles, but it generally is not well understood. As we look into the later part of this chapter, we will see that Paul's argument contributes much to our understanding of the malign effect of sin upon our lives and thus clarifies this teaching of total depravity.

Continuing from the end of chapter 1, Paul systematically eliminates any excuses a person, either Jew or Gentile, might depend upon to excuse themselves from their sinful behavior, whether it be through their own works or heritage. Paul utilizes five questions in Romans 3:1-20 to destroy the false ideas that keep people from finding the Savior Jesus Christ. He briefly addresses four of these excuses in 3:1-8 before continuing on with the last question in Romans 3:9-20, where he reveals the depravity of all men.

A. The Grand Excuses (Rom 3:1-8)

Paul gets at the heart of these false understandings by asking four questions. Two of them (3:4,6) are marked by Paul's common "May it never be!" phrase. The question and the "May it never be" combination is used ten times throughout Romans, the first being here in 3:4. These questions might seem a bit extreme, but when we understand that they are based on other misunderstandings, we can better see how people's judgment easily becomes warped and can develop such conclusions.

Question #1 (Rom 3:1-2)

"Then what advantage has the Jew? Or what is the benefit of circumcision?"

> ¹ Then what advantage has the Jew? Or what is the benefit of circumcision? ² Great in every respect. First of all, that they were entrusted with the oracles of God (Rom 3:1-2).

Paul first addresses the probable reactions from his former conclusion in chapter 2 by his Jewish readers. They might, perhaps, think that Paul's conclusions are faulty because he is blinded to the great benefits of the Law. Paul, however, anticipating their response, dismissed their wrong conclusion by stating that there is much advantage to being a Jew and having the holy Word of God: "Great in every respect."

The apostle highlights the honor of being entrusted with the oracles of God, the Word of God. God spoke to them (rather than to others). They heard the mighty Creator's voice and could reach out to Him through those words. It is interesting how becoming a believer in Christ incorporates these same benefits.

Paul clearly does not want to get off track, however. He states 'first of all' in verse 2 but neglects to state a second or third point until later, in 9:3-5.

Question #2 (Rom 3:3-4)

"What then? If some did not believe, their unbelief will not nullify the faithfulness of God, will it?"

> ³ What then? If some did not believe, their unbelief will not nullify the faithfulness of God, will it? ⁴ May it never be! Rather, let God be found true, though every man be found a liar, as it is written, "That Thou mightest be justified in Thy words, and mightest prevail when Thou art judged" (Rom 3:3-4).

Others will contend with Paul that if unbelief is found among the Jews then this will make God unfaithful. The apostle is unwilling to accept this line of reasoning for it is totally impossible for any of our interpretations or conclusions, no matter how reasonable they sound to us, to prove God's unfaithfulness. God defines faithfulness! It would be better for every man to be a liar than to accuse God of being unfaithful to His words. (Notice the underlying absolute trust in the accuracy of God's Word as that which is recorded in the Old Testament. We would do well to put such trust in the Word of God.)

He quotes from a well-accepted Old Testament passage where David is confessing his sin before God in Psalm 51:4. David declares that God is righteous in all His judgments. Therefore there must be another way to resolve the unbelief of the Jews with God's promises.

Question #3 (Rom 3:5-6)

"But if our unrighteousness demonstrates the righteousness of God, what shall we say? The God who inflicts wrath is not unrighteous, is He?"

> 5 But if our unrighteousness demonstrates the righteousness of God, what shall we say? The God who inflicts wrath is not unrighteous, is He? (I am speaking in human terms.) 6 May it never be! For otherwise how will God judge the world? But if through my lie the truth of God abounded to His glory, why am I also still being judged as a sinner? (Rom 3:5-6)

Others, however, will approach this issue in a different way and conclude that because God gets what He wants and displays His righteous glory through judgment, then man is not accountable for his own sin. Paul retorts with a quick, "The God who inflicts wrath is not unrighteous, is He?" Paul concludes that just because God's glory and righteousness is apparent through the judgment of sinners, this does not mean that man is not accountable.

If human beings are unaccountable, then God would not judge us. But the Lord does judge us, and this means that no matter what understanding we might have of God gaining glory through man's unbelief, we must not conclude that man is not accountable. God is righteous and mankind will suffer judgment because of our unrighteousness.

Question #4 (Rom 3:7-8)

"And why not say (as we are slanderously reported and as some affirm that we say), 'Let us do evil that good may come'"?

> 7 But if through my lie the truth of God abounded to His glory, why am I also still being judged as a sinner? 8 And why not say (as we are slanderously reported and as some affirm that we say), "Let us do evil that good may come"? Their condemnation is just (Rom 3:7-8).

This wrong conclusion, built upon the prior one, brings further contortion. Some individuals were going around in the church slandering Paul by alleging that he says, "Let us do evil that good may come." Paul flatly denies the charge, though he does it indirectly. Ludicrous charges are not fit to be answered.

Summary

Several of these distorted responses question the character of God. Paul strongly defended these attacks by declaring the character of God as written in God's Word. God is holy and righteous. If any argument concludes that God is not righteous, holy, just, or faithful, then the argument is of no substance. They need to look for other explanations.

B. The Fair Assessment (Rom 3:9-20)

> [9] What then? Are we Jews any better off? No, not at all. For we have already charged that all, both Jews and Greeks, are under sin, [10] as it is written: "None is righteous, no, not one; [11] no one understands; no one seeks for God. [12] All have turned aside; together they have become worthless; no one does good, not even one. [13] Their throat is an open grave; they use their tongues to deceive. The venom of asps is under their lips. [14] Their mouth is full of curses and bitterness. [15] Their feet are swift to shed blood; [16] in their paths are ruin and misery, [17] and the way of peace they have not known. [18] There is no fear of God before their eyes." [19] Now we know that whatever the law says it speaks to those who are under the law, so that every mouth may be stopped, and the whole world may be held accountable to God. [20] For by works of the law no human being will be justified in his sight, since through the law comes knowledge of sin. (ESV)

Romans 3:9 also begins with a question, but in contrast to the previous ones, Paul spends a lot of time expanding his point largely through a conglomeration of Old Testament quotes (noted by capitals in some Bible versions such as this NASB). He first clearly summarizes his previous point, "Both Jews and Greeks (non-Jews) are all under sin." Most likely he was referring to Romans 2:11-12.

> [11] For there is no partiality with God. For all who have sinned without the Law will also perish without the Law; [12] and all who have sinned under the Law will be judged by the Law (Rom 2:11-12).

The first section of quotes derives from Psalm 53:1-3. It is interesting that he does not start with the first words of Psalm 53:1, which state, "The fool has said in his heart..." He truncates the quote to fit his argument, and perhaps not to be too offensive. Other verses quoted are Psalm 59, 10:7, Is 59:7-8, Psalm 36:1. They together paint one clear picture of man's sin.

Man's sin is comprehensive.

"Both Jews and Greeks are all under sin." Man's sin is multicultural (both Jews and Gentiles); it does not exclude anyone because of their race or national background. No person is excluded from the accusation of being a sinner, though the witness condemning each might differ (see Romans 5:12-21 for further arguments).

Man's sin is condemning.

"There is none righteous." Man has missed the mark of righteousness. He does not only have a life of sinful behavior that condemns him but lacks the righteous behavior to rightly present him before his Judge. There is no innocent man. Any notion of the innocence of isolated tribes, untouched by sinful human civilization, is an embellished story.[24]

Man's sin is conclusive.

"All have turned aside." Man's will is bent and is so overwhelmingly infected by sinful impulses that every last person on this planet has made wrong decisions, leading him or her, in part, down the wrong path. (Jesus, however, has not only walked the right way but is The Way! John 14:6.)

Man's sin is confounding.

"None who understands." Paul shared at the end of Romans 1 that man has some knowledge of God, but has rejected it. Their knowledge becomes confounded, causing them to draw wrong conclusions (1:21). They became ignorant.

Man's sin is corrupting.

"There is none who seeks for God." Man's heart, or set of affections, is morally polluted as evidenced in the way he desires wrong things (further described later in these verses). He does not want to find God, but instead avoids God's light (Jn 3:20-21). Man's evil inclination leads him into more evil, both in his thoughts and activities as well as in the propensity to encourage others to participate in such activities (1:32). The person who divorces is likely to encourage another to divorce, thus subtly legitimizing one's immoral action in his or her conscience, rather than objectively seeking what God wants.

---

[24] One Indian pastor on a recent evangelistic trip to an unreached people group did not find them to be innocent but instead, because of their sins, needing to hear the gospel of Jesus Christ! Every culture is similarly in need of Jesus Christ.

Total depravity

Total depravity does not mean that man is as evil as he could be. The word 'total' here means that each part of his person is to some degree affected by sin, including his knowledge, conscience, desires (heart), and will. These verses aptly describe the demise of all mankind. Because all mankind is infected by a sinful heart, mind, will, and conscience, he cannot produce what God demands–a life of righteousness. Jesus understood this, but few preachers or parents seem to understand the importance of identifying the huge role sinfulness plays in people's lives.

> But Jesus, on His part, was not entrusting Himself to them, for He knew all men, and because He did not need anyone to bear witness concerning man for He Himself knew what was in man (Jn 2:24-25).

Those who preach the gospel well must properly understand the depth of man's sin.

The Verdict (Rom 3:19-20)

> [19] Now we know that whatever the Law says, it speaks to those who are under the Law, that every mouth may be closed, and all the world may become accountable to God; [20] because by the works of the Law no flesh will be justified in His sight; for through the Law comes the knowledge of sin (Rom 3:19-20).

Verses 3:19-20 conclusively pass a verdict on man's accountability for their sinful behavior which, due to their failure to keep their law, establish their guilt. The Jews, those "under the Law," are guilty as well as the Gentile world. The Gentiles–"all the world"–includes the Jewish people as all are equally guilty. Paul's powerful conclusion, "because by the works of the Law no flesh will be justified in His sight" (3:20) reminds us that God's sight and man's judgment is often quite contrary. Since God is Judge, man's sight does not matter except, as Paul importantly and painstakingly proves to us, that knowledge of our sin can lead to repentance and salvation.

Summary

The evil one uses confusion about these matters of good works and rituals by causing people to overestimate their good works and ignore their sin. An undermining of one's guilt leads to wrong conclusions about one's need for salvation. Paul makes his all-conclusive verdict in the following verses, starting in 3:21, as well as shows the means by which man can be justified (declared righteous).

Application

Christendom has in itself become, in many cases, a religion where many are confident about their good works as the means to be saved, rather than faith in Christ's good works on their behalf. Many Christians assume membership in the organized church makes their sin irrelevant. What about your church? The church near where you live? Do they believe in the inherent nature of sin in everyone?

Romans 3:21-31

Salvation by Faith

The cross gives evidence of God's standard of righteousness and God's satisfaction of righteousness for those who believe in Christ Jesus.

A. The Fact of Justification Declared (Rom 3:21-26)

The essential points of the 'good news' (i.e. the gospel) that are announced in 1:17 are packed into 3:21-26, a passage that Luther called "the chief point, and the very central place of the Epistle, and of the whole Bible."[25] This section can be unpacked into four statements:

- The revelation of God's righteousness is reiterated and related to the Old Testament (3:21).
- All human beings, equal in sin, also have equal access to God's righteousness through faith in Jesus Christ (3:22-23).
- The source of God's righteousness is found in the gracious provision of Christ as an atoning sacrifice (24-25a).
- The atonement not only provides justification of sinners but also demonstrates God's justice. (Moo, p. 218-9) (Rom 3:25b-26)

God's justice and righteousness is innovative, fair, demanding and just.

---

1) The Atonement Provides God's Righteousness (3:21)

But now apart from the Law the righteousness of God has been manifested, being witnessed by the Law and the Prophets (Rom 3:21).

---

[25] http://www.bunyanministries.org/expositions/romans/05_rom_righteousness_of_god.pdf

The old era: Law reigns

The righteousness of God was displayed in the Law by making a statement about God's holy standard. However, when the Law portrayed God's righteousness, man was revealed to be a sinner and demonstrated as wholly unfit to obtain that righteousness. A person was or is not made righteous by circumcision or possession of God's scriptures. Participation in the Old Covenant instead further demonstrated the depth of their sin, having the truth but disobeying it, thus needing sacrifices to ward off God's wrath.

God's revelation to the Jews in the Law could not save man but foreshadowed a more complete way in Christ, "apart from the Law". Everyone who participates in the New Covenant believes in Jesus Christ and in the eternal life He brings. Where formerly God's revelation in the Law revealed the need for righteousness, this present manifestation of God's righteousness in His Son actually enables us to possess God's righteousness in Christ.

The new era: Grace reigns

Reformed theology rightfully teaches that Jesus Christ became our righteousness, but perhaps more is implied by "apart from the Law the righteousness of God has been manifested" than the perfect functioning under the Old Covenant. I am not implying that Jesus did not perfect the Old Covenant but that this perspective, perhaps, limits our understanding of Christ's righteousness. After all, the Old Covenant was made for sinners, not for the righteous. The ceremonies, the tabernacle, and commands all point to a means by which imperfect man could communicate and beg pardon before a holy God. Jesus Christ, as the second Adam, went far beyond the Law by living a righteous life before God.

All men everywhere stand condemned and in need of salvation.

His righteousness was not just a fulfillment of the Old Covenant, for in that case we would only maintain a shallow relationship—one with priests, curtains, etc. Jesus Christ conformed to the Law to be righteous, He fulfilled it, but the righteousness transferred to us far outshines the shadows of the Old Covenant and completely grasps hold of God's glory and holiness. Fulfillment of the Old Covenant might help those under that covenant, but it would be totally insufficient for those outside the covenant. This truth is affirmed by how Jesus stated that He was the Lord of the Sabbath (Mk 2:28).

"But now" does not testify to a new way to obtain God's righteousness, but a new way God's righteousness has been made manifest. Some focus on the past manifestation in the Law in contrast to the present way through Jesus Christ. Others rather focus on the time aspect, what was then available (see 1:18-3:20) and what is now available. "As the 'wrath of God' dominated the old era, so the 'righteousness of God' dominates the new. ... Lloyd-Jones exclaims, "There are no more wonderful words in the whole of Scripture than just these two words "But now."[26]

> "... For all have sinned and fall short of the glory of God, being justified as a gift by His grace through the redemption which is in Christ Jesus" (Rom 3:23-24).

At this point it is good enough for Paul to show that the Law and the Prophets (then the most popular way of defining the scriptures) had pointed to this means of being justified. In other words, this was God's intention all along. God's past truth is still truth, but it foreshadowed a greater revelation of the truth. Many Old Testament prophecies address how the righteousness of God was to be manifested through the Christ, both His demand for righteousness seen through the sacrifice of the Messiah but also how the righteousness was obtained (Gen 15:1-6 by faith; Is 53 by suffering).

2) Atonement Enables All to Gain God's Righteousness (3:22-23)

> 22 Even the righteousness of God through faith in Jesus Christ for all those who believe; 23 for there is no distinction; for all have sinned and fall short of the glory of God (3:22-23).

a. Through Faith (3:22)

"Through faith" reveals the means by which sinful people can gain God's righteousness in Jesus Christ (22). Faith is the only means through which God's justifying work of Christ becomes applicable to man (a detailed explanation is in chapter 4). The word 'through' speaks of the whole phrase 'faith in Jesus Christ' rather than just faith (as some would wrongly construe faith in anything).

---

[26] Moo, p. 221.

This righteousness of God is limited to those who believe–it is only "for all those who believe." Salvation, then, is offered to all (23) but only those who believe will gain salvation. The gap between the teachings of biblical theology and universalism is as wide as the distance between heaven and hell.

b. From Sin (3:23)

The opportunity to find salvation is made available to all because there is a universal need for it. Paul beautifully summarizes the section 1:18-3:20 in these few words, "For all (have) sinned and fallen short of the glory of God." Our sinfulness established our need of the Gospel, and therefore, we must exercise our opportunities to preach this Gospel, offering hope and salvation in Christ (1:16-17). Preaching social uplift or physical healing does not save man from his deepest needs, nor does saying, "I'm sorry" bring pardon.

Mankind's recurring problem is the regurgitation of the same false belief that one's guilt is ignored when man's standards are met. Our pride in our good works is like the foolish man who mistook the ceiling for the sky. The key is not making ourselves better, though we strive to be better, but realizing we all have sadly fallen short of meeting God's standard of holiness, or as this verse exultantly states "His glory".

Paul in this verse is not only summarizing the fact that we all have sinned, Jews and Gentiles alike, but he is also following through with his first point by stating that the Jews' nationality or 'Jewishness' has not made them a bit better. Jew and Gentile alike have sinned. Notice that the Greek word for sin here–"fallen short," is in the present tense and so describes our present condition. The Greek word has the sense of missing the target.[27] Moo says, "So the absence of glory involves a declension from the image of God in which man was first made....The future glory may be regarded as the restoration of the lost, original glory."[28]

God's wrath is to be found wherever the sinning Gentile or Jew is found. They have fallen short of God's glory while the evidence of their sin is seen in the departure from God's ways. The Old Covenant told of man's unrighteousness, but the New Covenant provides the means by which man can obtain this righteousness.

---

[27] Girdlestone's, *Synonyms of the Old Testament*, has remarkable studies on significant words in the scriptures such as sin (chapter 6).

[28] Moo, pp. 226-227.

3) Atonement Satisfies God's Demand for Righteousness (24-25a)

> ²⁴ Being justified as a gift by His grace through the redemption which is in Christ Jesus; ²⁵ whom God displayed publicly as a propitiation in His blood through faith (Rom 3:24-25).

The connection of this verse with verse 23 is not well understood or agreed upon. Some even say verses 24-26 are a quote from an unknown outside source, but we see no reason not to link it up tightly with verse 23. Where in verse 23 all kinds of people have sinned, so here, all kinds of people are saved. The "all" "indicates not universality (i.e. everybody) but lack of particularity (i.e. anybody–a major theme to be expanded later on).²⁹ All who believe receive this justification by grace–none deserve it. A further study of the following words verifies this interpretation.

Grace

We were meant to benefit from the gift God has given us in Christ Jesus. The contrast between receiving as a gift–not earned, and gaining through one's labor or work–earned, is very evident. The source of righteousness comes through another; not from ourselves since we all have sinned. Contrary to the popular saying, "Look to your heart," we are told to look to God who supplied the grace we need in His Son, the Messiah (Christ).

The emphasis on the passive tense, being justified by His grace, where the action is received, is in contrast to the previous verse where we all sinned (active tense) and therefore are accountable for our wayward behavior. Those who believe are justified (present passive) as a gift of His grace. His grace came as a gift. The agent by which it came was through the redemption of Jesus Christ, enabling us to be declared as righteous. It's a shame that we cannot see the connection between the root words of righteousness {δικαιοσυνη -21, 22, 25, 26) & and justified (δικαιοω -24, 26) in the English language. The adjectival form (δικαιος) was used once in 26.

Redemption

The word ransom (same as redemption) literally means "to buy back", a word embedded in the Hebrew culture through the scriptures (it is thought of somewhat differently in the Greek culture). Although it often refers to the purchase of a slave, the Old Testament provides a deeper understanding.

---

²⁹ Moo, pp. 227-228.

Historically, we find the angel of death passing over the firstborn on the Passover. God required an equivalent payment for those individuals that the Angel of Death passed over as a ransom. The Levites became that equivalent payment except a small number with which they were paid for by cash (Num 3:40-51). The Israelites belonged to the angel of death as the others, but Yahweh redeemed them to himself. They became His people. This redemptive act became known as salvation and beautifully pictures New Testament salvation.[30]

We were taken from Satan's possession and brought under the ownership of God. The price was Christ's death by which he submitted himself to Satan's tyranny (even for a short time) (Heb 2:14-15). Once paid by Christ's sacrifice, Satan's claim on those individuals is annulled. Redemption here describes the means by which justification comes about.

Propitiation

God's righteousness is seen in that He does not overlook our sin, but rather fully met the law's demand of our death. Christ suffered the penalty of our sin, essentially becoming before God the sacrifice or propitiation for our sin. Though the word atonement (Hebrew) is similar to propitiation (Greek), atonement is much richer due to the elaborate way the Old Testament scriptures describe how the blood was offered to God in the Holy of Holies.

Propitiation can have either the meaning of mercy seat itself or of appeasing sacrifice, the later being more appropriate. Propitiation is a better translation than expiation because the word 'propitiation' includes both senses to "wipe away" the guilt of sin and to "satisfy the wrath" of God. God's wrath is perfectly satisfied through Christ's sacrifice. The word 'propitiation,' then, speaks of the cost and legal restrictions of this transaction.

4) Atonement Demonstrates God's Righteousness (25b-26)

> [25] ...This was to demonstrate His righteousness, because in the forbearance of God He passed over the sins previously committed; [26] for the demonstration, I say, of His righteousness at the present time, that He might be just and the justifier of the one who has faith in Jesus" (Rom 3:25-26).

---

[30] My book, _Redemption Through the Scriptures_, goes into a full chronological and biblical theological treatment of the theme of redemption. http://www.foundationsforfreedom.net/Help/Store/Intros/Redemption-RTS.html

The word 'demonstration' is given two times in 25b-26. He wants to strengthen our confidence in this spiritual reality. Demonstration, evidence and proof of, relies on the historicity of the Messiah dying on the cross. His death assures us that our sins are fully paid for through Christ's work on the cross. Even if we do not fully understand the legal transactions being made, God does and fully satisfies them through the cross.[31]

a. God is Just (3:26)

Guilty people, or those seeking divine favors from other gods, generally believe that the particularly offended god will overlook the offense in the presentation of a bribe, sacrifice, or attention. People around the world still try to placate the spirits with all sorts of sacrifices and prayers. All such sacrifices to these gods have no true effect on the guilt they have before the Living God.

The true God has publicly declared that this debt incurred by the "one who has faith in Jesus" is fully paid. In the past, God 'passed over' sin, that is, waited until the time came to fully deal with it; He never overlooked it. God does not tolerate sin but effectively deals with the guilt through a just price. Without Christ's sacrifice, man must suffer God's full wrath. No mercy will be seen. Mercy is only found in God's gift of His Son, and therefore, there is only one way to be saved.

b. God is Justifier (3:26)

God at the same time is the Judge who condemns and the Mercy-giver. God, in His great mercy (Eph 2:4-6), satisfies His own wrath by sacrificing His only Son for the unrighteous ones. God made the sacrifice for man. Herein is God's great devotion and zeal to obtain a people who belong to Him. It is amazing and wonderful that we who believe can be the people God has secured at such a high cost to Himself. The Father sent His only Son, Christ Jesus, to die for His people's sins, and thus justifies them once and for all in His sight.

---

[31] Thankfully God knows what needed to be done to save us. Few are the ones being saved who fully understand the technical requirements that had to be satisfied for salvation. Even the Jews who had the scriptures did not understand this.

B. The Results of Justification Presented (Rom 3:27-31)

In 3:27-31 Paul highlights the exclusivity of the means of salvation provided by God–faith in Christ. By faith, God excludes boasting (3:27), provides a means for the Gentiles to be included (29-30) and shows how the gospel complements the law (31). These points will be expanded upon in chapter 4 through the discussion of certain Old Testament passages. The very fact that Paul raises these issues of faith shows that people in the early church tended to question or distort the fact of justification through faith in Christ, just as many do today.

1. Effectiveness of Confidence in Faith (3:27-28)

> 27 Where then is boasting? It is excluded. By what kind of law? Of works? No, but by a law of faith. 28 For we maintain that a man is justified by faith apart from works of the Law (Rom 3:27-28).

Christ's substitutional work on the cross brings powerful evidence that we cannot contribute to our salvation, otherwise He would not die. In any case, we have nothing to offer (see earlier part of Romans 3). There is nothing we can boast about. Our sin was so incurable that God's Son, had to die in our place if we any of us would be saved. Instead of pride, we should be humbled that our sins demanded such a horrible death from the Righteous One.

"Law of faith" refers to the inflexible way of obtaining God's righteousness. There is no other way. Man is justified by faith in Christ, not by works of the Law.

2. Means of Salvation is the Same (3:29-30)

> 29 Or is God the God of Jews only? Is He not the God of Gentiles also? Yes, of Gentiles also, 30 since indeed God who will justify the circumcised by faith and the uncircumcised through faith is one (Rom 3:29-30).

The Jews embraced the concept of God as Creator of all but severely limited His revelation only to the Jews. Paul, however, partly reasoning from God's position as Creator (Rom 1:20-21), states that God is equally concerned for the Gentiles, those from other nations. The Gentiles might not be (nor we) interested in God, but God is! Special privileges of the past will not make a difference when it comes to dealing with sin. Everyone has sin and needs faith in Jesus Christ to obtain righteousness.

3. Still Respect the OT Law (31)

> Do we then nullify the Law through faith? May it never be! On the contrary, we establish the Law (Rom 3:31).

Paul did not want to distract the Jews from his main points regarding their sin and God's means of salvation, but he also did not want them to discard the truths that he had so carefully laid out, so he briefly addresses those that might question whether this teaching despised God's Law.

Paul, however, repudiates this accusation and affirms how God's provision of Christ actually established and fulfilled the Law. Christ was the One who perfectly fulfilled the Law; no one else could or did. Jesus also took care of the guilt according to the condemnation of the Law by dying for our sins. God's Law is fulfilled only through Christ. Apart from Christ, we only see its condemnation through our death.

Summary

Christ's work in His life and death perfectly filled the Law for those under the Law, if they would but believe. Christ did not despise the Law but kept it to please his Father. He is the Righteous One that we can trust to fully represent us before God when our sins are judged.

Romans 4:1-25
The Nature of Saving Faith

Romans 4 is a beautiful chapter that uses Old Testament illustrations to strengthen and clarify the powerful teaching on justification by faith. Paul has used many Old Testament passages to establish the doctrine of man's depravity and need for righteousness (3:10-18), but at this point, he has not solidly established the teaching of salvation by faith. This he does in chapter 4, and so quiets any claims that 'faith in Christ' dismisses the importance of the Law (3:31).

Salvation through faith is a new idea to many, even in our own generation. A new reformation is needed. Upon hearing that they only need faith to be saved, two responses often arise: (1) Some respond by stating, "That's too easy," and dismiss faith's crucial part of the salvation process. They deny their essential need for salvation by thinking highly of their good works. (2) Others state that they believe, but what they mean by 'believe' is quite different from the trust exemplified here. For them belief is a gut feeling or inclination, a willingness to sometimes be influenced by such ideas rather than something that convinces their soul to adopt a new lifestyle.

Paul not only refutes the false ideas of belief and "easy-believism," but buttresses his arguments on the teaching of salvation by faith with the Old Testament to further convince the Jews that the Lord plans to similarly save Gentiles. Throughout chapter 4, Paul demonstrates his points by using two familiar and indisputable historical illustrations from the Old Testament scriptures: Abraham and David.

A. A Look at Abraham's Life (Rom 4:1-5)

⁴:¹ What then shall we say that Abraham, our forefather according to the flesh, has found? ² For if Abraham was justified by works, he has something to boast about; but not before God. ³ For what does the Scripture say? "AND ABRAHAM BELIEVED GOD, AND IT WAS RECKONED TO HIM AS RIGHTEOUSNESS." ⁴ Now to the one who works, his wage is not reckoned as a favor, but as what is due. ⁵ But to the one who does not work, but believes in Him who justifies the ungodly, his faith is reckoned as righteousness (Rom 4:1-5).

Paul first uses the life of Abraham to clarify how a person is saved. Abraham (~2000 BC) predated the Law and Moses by about 500 years (~1500 BC), which makes God's promises to Abraham more significant. Abraham did not gain acceptance before God because he was good (look what he did to Sarah in Genesis 16), because he kept the Law (it did not exist at that time), or through circumcision, which only came when Abraham was 99 years-old (Gen 17:1-10). Abraham was not "justified by works." He had nothing to boast about. He was, however, "reckoned as righteous" because he believed God's promise.

1. Abraham: His Life and Faith (4:1-3)

Verses 1-3 demonstrate the critical part faith plays in our relationships with God. Faith discerns what is true and real, and therefore discloses what is most important, calling us to properly respond in obedience.

"According to the flesh" (1) refers to patriarch Abraham's own life experience as recorded in Genesis 12-25. The chronology of God's interaction with Abram (and its clear documentation) illustrates and defines the teaching of justification by faith. Note how the Old Testament, that which is accepted by the Jews, is used to verify the truth of the gospel, that which is unfamiliar.

"Justified by works" (2) is clearly ineffective in gaining righteousness before God. The use of this phrase infers its common acceptance in the world. Religion and human moralism largely depend on their virtuous works that consist of moral and financial contributions, mixed with certain rites and ceremonies, in order to make individuals more presentable before God. These works do not bring cleansing, but are performed in hopes to cover up, when present, a plaguing sense of guilt instigated by our moral deficits. This is the whole spirit of works, which must be outright rejected.

How sad it is to see how legalism has crept into so many places of Christendom, even though the scriptures, Old and New, expose the futility of depending upon works to gain salvation. There is a constant propensity for churches to move from conservative to liberal, where man again insists on his worth. Despite this, God makes it impossible for us to earn our salvation with a life well-lived; the Lord wants us to boast in His grace (Eph 2:9). We are saved in order that we might magnify His glorious wisdom, mercy, and grace. Abraham, along with the rest of us, clearly lacked the works needed to make up for a moral deficit (see 4-5).

"What does the Scripture say?" (3) Abraham was declared righteous (Genesis 15) before he was instructed to be circumcised (a Jewish religious initiation ceremony first given in Genesis 17:10 as a seal belonging to the Old Covenant). We, therefore, should not conclude that acceptance before God was dependent upon his efforts. The scriptures (the Old Testament scriptures are in view here) are clearly held authoritative for our doctrine and life (2 Tim 3:16-17).

"Reckoned to him as righteousness" (3,5). Though lacking righteousness, God reckoned (credited, imputed, calculated) righteousness to Abraham's account due to his faith. 'Reckoned' is an accountant term referring to our debts and credits before God who weighs all our thoughts, words and deeds. This phrase is quoted from Genesis 15:6 where God pledges to award Abraham righteousness considering his faith in God's promise.

> If salvation is dependent on our belief, then the obtaining and preserving of this belief stands to be the most important object of our life, without which, we will most certainly perish.

Note that faith is not considered a work. The idea that our faith is what we contribute to our salvation has recently become popular, though it be unbiblical. Faith is not something we do, like a work; we would boast in our faith-work rather than in the cross, which is God's gracious work for us. Faith is, in actuality, our response to God's work in our lives and occurs as God imparts spiritual insight to us through these truths. Faith surely is needed but is theologically seen as a gift (Eph 2:8), not as a work.

Looking back, we should be amazed at how well these verses fit into the overall gospel plan. God planned it all along that way, revealing the true nature of faith and how He would, through the Messiah, save His people. He would save people through faith, not by works. Again he states in 4:5, "His faith is reckoned as righteousness" because there is no inherent righteousness in the person; righteousness must be imputed.

2. Abraham: His Need of Righteousness (4:4-5)

God awarded righteousness to Abraham due to his faith (4:3), not his works. The scriptures are clear that Abraham was not a righteous man and needed to gain righteousness through another means. Paul says the Lord "justifies the ungodly" (5) with reference to Abraham and us all. Abraham selfishly lied about Sarah not being his wife (Gen 12:10-20; 20) and in doubt listened to his wife and took Hagar as his concubine to produce a descendant (Ishmael– Gen 16). If Abraham was righteous, associated blessings would have followed. However, he was blessed because of his faith in God's gracious promise and the justification that God declared.

The stress we put on faith cannot be underrated. Belief in Christ, the object of our faith, becomes central to our relationship with God. Similarly, those who believe in Christ today gain faith through God's promise to forgive us through Jesus Christ, not through our good works.

Legalism's Danger

Underneath the massive confusion over legalism lies misunderstandings of the Law. Part of the confusion is the various ways the term is used. Interestingly, the term 'legalism' is not used in scripture and therefore does not have a scripture passage to serve as an anchor to clarify its definition or regulate its usage. Legalism, however, does project concern for an erroneous idea that is commonly pointed out in the scriptures, largely rooted around the notion of salvation by works. For example, Paul says, "Who has saved us, ... not according to our works, but according to..." (2 Timothy 1:9).

Paul refers to this issue early in Romans 4 three times. "For if Abraham was justified by works..." (Rom 4:2). "Now to the one who works, his wage is not reckoned as a favor, but as what is due" (Rom 4:4). "Just as David also speaks of the blessing upon the man to whom God reckons righteousness apart from works" (Rom 4:6). The source of legalism stems from man's reliance on works to gain approval before God. This, in turn becomes the source of the two other references to legalism.

(1) The Apostle Paul frequently refers to those who have, or are, contemplating a return to their old faith, usually Judaism, and departure from the gospel as seen in Galatians (Gal 1:6-7) or the Book of Hebrews. Due to pressure from Jews, many converted Jews rejected their faith in Christ and

resumed a life of the Law. The term legalism needs to get its primary definition from here, where a person lives in hope of gaining his acceptance before God by conforming to the Law. Legalism is the opposite, then, to the faith in the gospel or justification by faith. Legalism is the attempt to be justified by works. The Seventh Day Adventists traditionally face this problem of staring into the Law, which keeps them from the gospel (though it ought to be noted that one group has affirmed the gospel).

(2) The term 'legalism' is also used in the area of sanctification for the believer. The confusion arises over the increasing uncertainty of the basis of salvation, by emphasizing the place of works in gaining acceptance before God. Instead of resting in one's faith, the believer focuses on his works, which will invariably have a detrimental affect on his basic understanding of Christian growth. They identify various rules or standards to be critical in acceptance by God, and then begin to see others and themselves in light of these adopted standards. Traditionalists have their own variation of this, but often the standards are more general, perhaps relegating the 'law' or essential things to carry out as some rite, going to church on Christmas or even as general as giving to the poor.

Believers always need to be careful not to move back under the influence of believing acceptance before God is by works. A new unfounded believer can be easily confused. Standards are good and required, but they will never deliver the righteousness that is demanded by God. By focusing on God's gift of grace in Christ, we can humbly admit our inability to please God, and we can meditate our minds on the fact that our faith is based on Christ's work on the cross.

Legalism for the believer directs attention from Christ's work and onto their performance of some self-defined standards, some required by the scriptures, some not (e.g. abstinence from alcohol). Either way, when we focus on our acceptance of keeping these 'laws', we take our eyes off the Lord's grace found in the cross and focus on the rules we think are important. Christian growth is virtually impossible in such situations until we break through this false mentality.

B. A Look at David's Life (Rom 4:6-8)

⁶ Just as David also speaks of the blessing upon the man to whom God reckons righteousness apart from works: ⁷ BLESSED ARE THOSE WHOSE LAWLESS DEEDS HAVE BEEN FORGIVEN,

AND WHOSE SINS HAVE BEEN COVERED. 8 BLESSED IS THE MAN WHOSE SIN THE LORD WILL NOT TAKE INTO ACCOUNT (Rom 4:6-8).

King David is the second person exemplified in Romans 4 to verify the theology of imputed righteousness. David was promised a royal heir who would become the righteous and glorious Messiah everyone would come to long for, "When your days are complete and you lie down with your fathers, I will raise up your descendant after you, who will come forth from you, and I will establish his kingdom. He shall build a house for My name, and I will establish the throne of his kingdom forever" (2 Sam 7:12-13). David's example derives its power not from the timing, as in Abraham's case (also see 4:9-12), but from his situation.

David spoke of a "righteousness apart from works" (4:6). He was not a righteous man, but a sinner. Instead of speaking about His righteousness, David boasts about forgiveness, wherein he clearly admits his sin. David's acceptance before God was not due to his righteousness, but despite his sin. Verses 7-8 are taken from Psalm 32 where David confesses his sin. Nobody can read the Old Testament historical books without reading of David's two major sins that cost the lives of many. The whole of Psalm 32, and particularly these quoted verses, remind us how unrighteous a king David was. He admitted that the blessed man is the forgiven one, the one who is no longer guilty for his sins. His good works or merits did not contribute toward his righteousness, but instead, having experiencing mercy, he acknowledges his imperfection and need for forgiveness.

Summary

The ways God blessed Abraham and David testify to God's amazing grace and love. Covering sin (7) speaks of a forgiving mercy (i.e. atonement) where sin is covered by blood (i.e. Christ's blood and death). This covering of sin greatly differs from covering up sin, which mocks God's justice and elevates man's works before God. Romans 3 is a clear statement of man's depravity shutting out anyone's claim to righteousness. Any approach to God, other than through the forgiveness in Christ, counters the truth of God's grace, effectively discarding God's mercy by man's sinful boasting.

"Blessed" (7,8) speaks of the grace given to the sinner on top of forgiveness. The Christian life is based on mercy and grace (1 Tim 1:2). Mercy speaks of forgiveness, the withholding of God's just judgment, while grace describes the blessings given despite one's sin (Romans 5 explains this).

C. A Look at Old Testament Truths (Rom 4:9-12)

Paul did not stop with articulating the case for imputed righteousness through faith by Abraham and David's lives, but continued by showing that the Gentiles, like the Jews, are saved by faith, just like their forefathers.

1. The timing of circumcision (9-10)

> 9 Is this blessing then upon the circumcised, or upon the uncircumcised also? For we say, "FAITH WAS RECKONED TO ABRAHAM AS RIGHTEOUSNESS." 10 How then was it reckoned? While he was circumcised, or uncircumcised? Not while circumcised, but while uncircumcised (Rom 4:9-10).

Paul's argument in 4:9-12 was subtly laid in the former verses. The Jews relied on circumcision as the mark of their heritage as the people of God. Paul turns back to the argument of timing. The scriptures teach that Abraham received the promise of righteousness at a time when he was not circumcised (Gen 15:6). Circumcision came later (Gen 17:9-14).

Paul's goal was to establish the argument that righteousness was gained by Abraham apart from circumcision's ceremony, thus making circumcision irrelevant to those gaining righteousness. The quote from Genesis 15:6, "Then he believed in the LORD; and He reckoned it to him as righteousness" proves that Abraham received this righteousness before he was circumcised, opening the door for the uncircumcised to gain righteousness through faith. In other words, the Gentiles could gain access through faith too, without circumcision.

2. The ceremony of circumcision (11-12)

> 11 And he received the sign of circumcision, a seal of the righteousness of the faith which he had while uncircumcised, that he might be the father of all who believe without being circumcised, that righteousness might be reckoned to them, 12 and the father of circumcision to those who not only are of the circumcision, but who also follow in the steps of the faith of our father Abraham which he had while uncircumcised (Rom 4:11-12).

The Jews did not easily embrace Paul's conclusion, so he repeatedly refers to the historical timing: Abraham was accepted by God as righteous before he was circumcised. Paul concludes his point by establishing Abraham as father of all those who believe, whether circumcised or not (avoids discussion of what kind of faith so as not to distract from his point of accepting the Gentiles by faith).

- Circumcision as a sign (11a) or wonder points to something greater, in this case his gained righteousness and favor with God.
- Circumcision as a seal (11b) settles the authority of what has been done and makes it irrevocable.

So Abraham became the father (Abraham literally meant 'father of many nations') of all those who would receive righteousness through faith, whether circumcised or not (i.e. Jew or Gentile). More important than the ceremony of circumcision was the presence of a faith like Abraham's. Circumcision was only the *seal* of the faith, not the faith itself. Circumcision is, therefore, unconnected to obtaining righteousness. Faith's importance is reemphasized, however, by proving our shared faith with Abraham, "Follow in the steps of faith." Circumcision is of no real value, at least in the case of becoming a true child of Abraham. Being a Jew or Gentile does not matter, but having a genuine faith like Abraham's, which brought both forgiveness and blessing, does matter.

Before the cross, a non-Jew needed to first become a Jew in order to become one of God's chosen people. This greatly limited God's redemptive message to the non-Jews. However, once faith's door opened with the gospel, salvation for the Gentiles was not dependent upon rituals and sacrifices in Jerusalem, and they could become a part of God's people in any region. This teaching on the open door of salvation to the Gentiles is presented throughout the book of Romans. Paul suffered greatly for the proclamation of this one truth as he went from city to city preaching the Gospel.

Paul does not refer to baptism here (though he does later), but for clarity, let us state that Christian baptism, like circumcision, is a sign and seal of our faith, not the means by which a believer is saved. The scriptures do not allow for baptismal regeneration, the saving of the soul by baptizing a person, but instead instruct us on believer's baptism, which seeks faith before the confirming sign of baptism.

This understanding is confused by an early church tradition of baptizing believers very soon after their faith conversion. As a result, baptism was very closely associated with one's conversion. Peter said, "Repent, and let each of you be baptized" (Acts 2:38). The two should be closely linked but remember, baptism is only a sign, not the essence of salvation. Another church tradition that confuses the order, faith before baptism, is infant baptism. In their understanding, salvation is not dependent on the person's faith but the parents' faith. Again, much confusion arises since the sign of faith, baptism, is given to those who do not themselves believe.

Summary

Paul stated in Romans 1:16 that the gospel "is the power of God for salvation to everyone who believes, to the Jew first and also to the Greek." What God did through the small nation of Israel has great implications for the whole world and therefore our lives. Salvation can be gained by all of us, no matter our nationality. Our sin, though great and awful, should not keep us from possessing that faith, from believing in the promise of God for forgiveness of sins.

Self-confidence is the anti-gospel because it despises God's clear pronouncement of our sin and provision through His Son (Ps 2). Instead of boasting in our works, let us humbly receive God's mercy, being renewed by God's desire to impute righteousness to us through the costly gift of His Son on the cross.

D. The Nature of Saving Faith (4:13-25)

Paul might have persuaded the Jews that the Gentiles and Jews in Rome were similarly in need of salvation, but they needed further persuasion if they were going to be convinced that salvation was also for the Gentiles. There is one way to be saved; there is no difference for the Jew and Gentile. There are not two churches, but one (Eph 4:4-6).

1. The Treachery of the Law (Rom 4:13-15)

> 4:13 For the promise to Abraham or to his descendants that he would be heir of the world was not through the Law, but through the righteousness of faith. 14 For if those who are of the Law are heirs, faith is made void and the promise is nullified; 15 for the Law brings about wrath, but where there is no law, neither is there violation.

The promise spoken of (in verse 13) clearly refers to Genesis 15:5,

> And He took him outside and said, "Now look toward the heavens, and count the stars, if you are able to count them." And He said to him, "So shall your descendants be."

Even though the prospect of having many descendants looked dismal at his old age, Abraham believed God. God "reckoned it to him as righteousness" (Gen 15:6). The promise of righteousness did not come from the law but from his belief in God's promises.

If one, however, insists on heirship (i.e. belonging to God and inheriting His blessings) through the Law, then he must accept the responsibility of gaining righteousness through one's good deeds (which one cannot do - Rom 3:19-23). The Law, due to our sinfulness, can only bring about the horrible curse of death, delivering its observers into the wrath of God. Faith, however, delivers promises of hope and life. The wrath of God stems from His powerful, righteous nature that exercises His just condemnation against all forms of defiance against His upright and sovereign rule.

The opportunity to become a descendant of Abraham is not dependent on whether one observes the Law. It is dependent upon whether one believes as Abraham did, and like Abraham, be reckoned as righteous.

One can only be heir to one entity. If one claims the heirship of the Law, then he does not gain the promises of God and thus excludes himself from the promises of Abraham. However, even the Jew who has been brought up under the Law, can, like the Gentile or like Abraham (as this passage has been stressing), focus on the heirship of Abraham's promise, which is not based on the Law. The Law, then, is not a means to salvation but condemnation. The focus is on the great advantage of faith in the promises of God over trust in one's virtue.

2. The Character of Faith (Rom 4:16-22)

> 16 For this reason it is by faith, that it might be in accordance with grace, in order that the promise may be certain to all the descendants, not only to those who are of the Law, but also to those who are of the faith of Abraham, who is the father of us all, 17 (as it is written, "A FATHER OF MANY NATIONS HAVE I MADE YOU") in the sight of Him whom he believed, even God, who gives life to the dead and calls into being that which does not exist. 18 In hope against hope he believed, in order that he might become a father of many nations, according to that which had been spoken, "SO SHALL YOUR DESCENDANTS BE." 19 And without becoming weak in faith he contemplated his own body, now as good as dead since he was about a hundred years old, and the deadness of Sarah's womb; 20 yet, with respect to the promise of God, he did not waver in unbelief, but grew strong in faith, giving glory to God, 21 and being fully assured that what He had promised, He was able also to

perform. 22 Therefore also IT WAS RECKONED TO HIM AS RIGHTEOUSNESS.

In 4:16, Paul affirms that God's purpose for His timing and method of revelation to Abraham was to incorporate the Gentiles into the faith. God incorporates His divine purposes into His plan. Because God cannot be seen, our relationship with Him is built on faith. Without faith, there is no relationship. Our faith, therefore, reveals the status of our relationship with God.

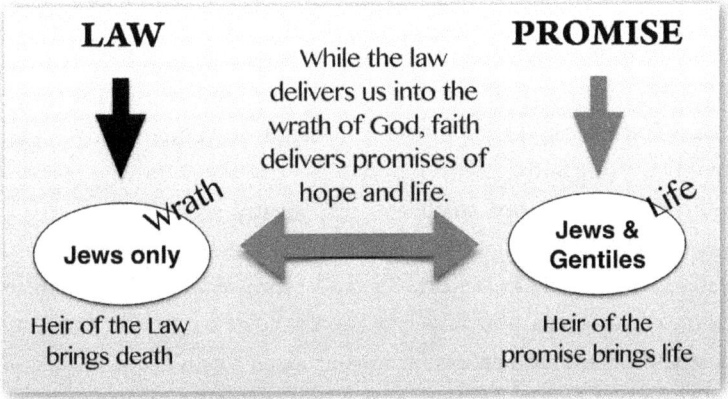

A purposeful faith (16-17a)

Paul continues in 4:16–"for this reason"–by identifying God's purpose of bringing the Gentiles into this faith. When it was by faith, those from all the nations could believe and belong to Abraham's children. This is evidenced by the stress on Abraham's faith and the meaning of his name, "father of many nations" (17a). (The '*ham*' literally means peoples or nations or Gentiles.)

> 4 As for Me, behold, My covenant is with you, and you shall be the father of a multitude of nations. 5 No longer shall your name be called Abram, but your name shall be Abraham; for I will make you the father of a multitude of nations (Ge 17:4-5).

If one insists on being Abraham's heir, then he must accept faith as the means to gain salvation. The opportunity to become a descendant of Abraham is not dependent on having, or not having, the Law, but dependent upon whether one believes as Abraham did, and like Abraham be credited as righteous.

Abram **Abraham**

A powerful faith (17b-20)

Abraham was at one point asked to offer up his only son, upon whom all the promises that God made to Abraham were built. Abraham manifested his faith by more faith! "...In the sight of Him whom he believed, even God, who gives life to the dead and calls into being that which does not exist" (Rom 4:17). The phrase "So shall your descendants be" found in 4:18, clinches the argument. God openly declared that Abraham's descendants would, like him, have an unwavering faith.

Abraham's faith, not small or easy, greatly pleased God. His faith is elaborated on because it is the source from which he would gain a great inheritance. The timing is important: God promised and Abraham believed. The promise was given first and was then followed by faith. Later and in a similar way, our own faith would be a response to God's promise that whoever believes on Jesus Christ would not perish but have everlasting life.

> **God's promise (Gen 15:4-5) => Abraham believed (15:6a) => God reckoned it as righteousness (15:6b)**

The difficulty for Abraham to maintain his faith is clearly brought out through several phrases: "Without becoming weak in faith" (19); "his own body, now as good as dead" (19); "deadness of Sarah's womb" (19); "did not waver in unbelief" (20); "but grew strong in faith" (20).

It was not the promise that brought our righteousness, but our faith in the promise, and so it is with a believer's faith. Faith is what positively connects God to our lives. Our salvation does not come to us because God is good or generous, though that is true, but because of our faith in God who forgives us through the propitiatory death of Christ on the cross. But certainly, Abram responded to God's revelation, and the Lord therefore worked with him.[32] Paul further clarifies this faith in the following summary.

---

[32] Whether God had revealed Himself and beckoned others to follow Him before Abram is pure conjecture. In any case, if so, they did not believe (Rom 1:20-21). Abraham did and went to the Promised Land (Gen 12:1-3).

The Place of Faith (20-22)

Abraham believed that the Giver of the Promise was faithful, and thus believed the promise. The promise, without the Promise Giver, had no substance.

"And being fully assured that what He had promised, He was able also to perform" (4:21).

Our faith in the invisible God will be tested to affirm our relationship with Him. We are tested not by whether we state that we have faith, but whether we act on what God has revealed to us (Hebrews 11:1). Some people believe that faith itself does not gain faith in God! "It doesn't matter what you believe, just so you believe." The Lord trained Abraham in this issue of faith through many years of trial, waiting on God to have a son. He resigned himself that though he might not be able to see the promises fulfilled, he could still believe them! Abraham had an enduring faith.

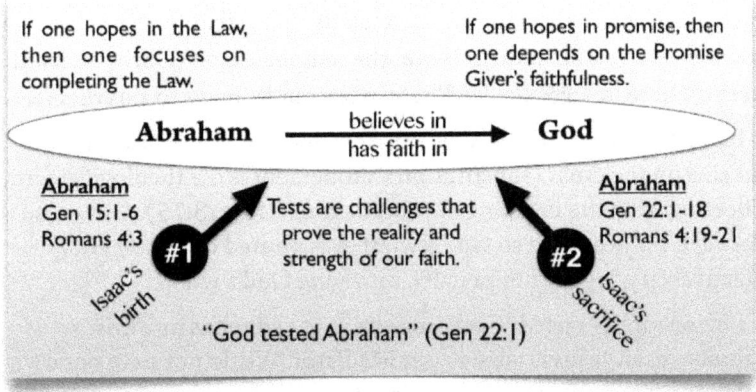

E. The Promise of Faith (Rom 4:23-25)

Paul closes his arguments by restating the doctrine of justification by faith along with a new supporting reference to an Old Testament passage.

> 23 Now not for his sake only was it written, that it was reckoned to him, 24 but for our sake also, to whom it will be reckoned, as those who believe in Him who raised Jesus our Lord from the dead, 25 He

who was delivered up because of our transgressions, and was raised because of our justification (Rom 4:23-25).

1. Salvation's Application (23-24)

To emphasize the application of this point to our lives, Paul states that the phrase, "It was reckoned to Him" (23) was written back then, not for Abraham, but for us, the readers, even those "who believe in Him who raised Jesus our Lord from the dead" (24), those in Paul's time as well as ours.

2. Salvation's Effect (4:25)

Verse 4:25 was taken from Isaiah 53:11, the end of the most popular prophesy of Christ's work on the cross.

> As a result of the anguish of His soul, He will see it and be satisfied; By His knowledge the Righteous One, My Servant, will justify the many, as He will bear their iniquities (Is 53:11).

This thought forms a powerful closing proof for (1) the Gospel's uniformity with Old Testament teaching, as well as (2) the fact that God wants to save the Gentile as well as the Jew. This verse also summarizes chapters 1-3 (because of our transgressions) and chapters 4-5 (was raised because of our justification). Note the emphasis on Christ's death and resurrection here in 4:25. Paul will return later in Romans to this theme.

> Life taken away - death: Our sins are wiped away because Christ bore our sins on the cross (substitutional atonement is the theological term reflecting from the meaning of propitiation in Rom 3:25). Our curse was placed upon Jesus and so God's wrath was poured out upon Him, effectively paying for our penalty, satisfying God's wrath.

> Life restored - raised: God presents us as righteous in Christ's righteousness. Jesus is alive as our Mediator. We do not have our own righteousness but hide ourselves in Christ's righteousness (e.g. in Christ, in Him) and therefore His ongoing life. As such, we belong to Him. We are part of the body of Christ, the church.

Summary

Paul showed the Romans how a person can, through faith, become Abraham's child. This faith is a saving faith because it does two things: brings forgiveness of past wrongs and presents us as righteous in Christ!

> **"Who was delivered up for our trespasses,
> and raised for our justification" (Rom 4:25 ESV).**

Romans 5:1-11
A Faith Worth Believing

In the preceding chapters, Paul has adequately introduced the need for man's reconciliation with God and the means by which reconciliation is obtained. Abraham believed God's promises and was reckoned as righteous. The apostle builds upon these assumptions in chapter 5 and from there begins to enumerate the results of this amazing 'justification by faith.'

The apostle presents three things in which we should put our confidence or faith. A different response (faith rather than doubt; trust instead of rejection) projects a whole new sphere of living. Peace substitutes rebellion. Love replaces rejection. Hope overcomes helplessness.[33]

Since God blessed Abraham, we should be able to see these blessings in Abraham's seed (descendants). While focusing on our confidence, we will also observe six blessings that follow justification.

What does justification mean to me? What affect does Christ's work on the cross have on my own life?

A. Confidence in God's Acceptance (Rom 5:1-2)
Established in the Past

5:1 Therefore having been justified by faith, we have peace with God through our Lord Jesus Christ, 2 through whom also we have obtained our introduction by faith into this grace in which we stand; and we exult in hope of the glory of God (Rom 5:1-2).

1. Our Security Through Jesus Christ (5:1)

The beginning verses of chapter 5 ("Having been justified by faith"... compare 5:9) summarize the first four chapters (aorist tense). It is on this

---

[33] Perhaps Psalm 28:7 influenced Paul's thinking here.

basis of declared righteousness that the blessings to be announced are introduced into our lives.

2. Our Privileges in Christ (5:1b-2b)

We must think of this peace as the official peace treaty implemented through the sacrifice of Christ, which resulted in a subjective peace, blessing our personal lives and experiences.

Privilege #1: Peace with God

Peace is the first fruit flowing from justification. This implies a time of conflict or war before God's work of reconciliation, the context of which is supported in the first three chapters of Romans. We were not right before God, living reprehensible lives and violating God's rule. In the description of Romans 3:9-21, men's mouths are full of cursing. They do not seek God and in fact have turned aside. They have transgressed.

> ## War (1-3:20) -> Propitiation (3:21-4) -> Peace (5)

This peace, resulting from God's work, is more than an emotional plateau or unwarlike life (cf. 3:17). The wrath of God is against natural man (Rom 1:18 to 5:19), but through Christ, the wrath of God has been propitiated and man's sin and guilt expiated so as to make a true peace between the two parties. This was no mere compromise as seen through the great pain and suffering of Jesus Christ's death (Rom 4:24-25). There was no other way to make peace.

Privilege #2: Access before God into His grace

"Obtained our introduction": Through Christ and our humble confession of His Name, Christ becomes the doorway that leads us into God's presence–it is our introduction. Christ is said to have led us, the justified, into this grace as one would lead a person before a king. Satan might blast doubt in the mind of the guilty sinner's worth of being presented before the Holy God, but our confidence is not in our abilities but in Christ our representative.

3. Our Response (5:2c)

Privilege #3: Exulting in the hope of God's splendor!

The ability to exult in the hope of the glory of God is the third blessing listed. The word 'hope' emphasizes the future, even though it is based on present glory or splendor. The greatest part of His glory is to be shared with His saints, for we are co-heirs with Jesus. God's glory is our glory because of our justification through Christ. God's plan is greater than simply our salvation from the penalty of our sins; it leads us onto a path where we can experience the greatest blessings the world can ever know.

B. Confidence in God's Purpose for Hardship (Rom 5:3-5)

Coming through the Present

> 3 And not only this, but we also exult in our tribulations, knowing that tribulation brings about perseverance; 4 and perseverance, proven character; and proven character, hope; 5 and hope does not disappoint, because the love of God has been poured out within our hearts through the Holy Spirit who was given to us (Rom 5:3-5).

1. Our Test (5:3a)

Privilege #4: Glory in Tribulation

Paul and his friends also exult in tribulation. This fourth blessing is introduced by a strong 'but' (*alla*), which brings out the ensuing positive attitude toward tribulations. It's one thing to exult in hope, but quite another to exult in one's tribulations. Many 'saints' have removed themselves from tribulations just so they could 'rightly exult in God'. Paul found his troubles to be a blessing in disguise.

Reflection Questions

Do we exult in hardship, pressure, and suffering?

What is our attitude toward these trials?

2. Our Life's Design (5:3b-4)

Hardship leads to patience which leads to proven character which in turn leads to hope.

Christian maturity is tested on whether we can accept a long term perspective of our present trials and testings.

Paul looks beyond the trials and observes their long term outcomes in his life. He has learned that trials bring about perseverance, and perseverance proven character, and proven character, hope. Proven character produces hope for our future total glorification.

3. Our Assurance (5:5)

Hope can disappoint us if the object hoped in fails to come about. Divine hope, however, does not disappoint us because it continues to shine even through times of tribulations.

God's great and genuine love has taken root within our hearts. This love is said to have been poured out, and yet continues to refresh our hearts (perfect passive tense). This is done through the Holy Spirit who at one time had been given to us (vs. 5).

There is no doubt that the Holy Spirit illumines us to the fact of Christ's love, but there is more to it. He entwines the facts of Christ's work so closely with our lives so that we can be deeply moved. The Holy Spirit has a key role (aorist passive participle) in revealing God's love for us. The context emphasizes the fact of God's love for us rather than our love for God.

C. Confidence in God's Risen Son (Rom 5:6-11)
No fear of the future

1. In Ourselves Hopeless (6-8)

> 6 For while we were still helpless, at the right time Christ died for the ungodly. 7 For one will hardly die for a righteous man; though perhaps for the good man someone would dare even to die. 8 But God demonstrates His own love toward us, in that while we were yet sinners, Christ died for us (Rom 5:6-8).

These verses point out the extremity of God's grace by using three powerful descriptions of his work in our lives. Notice how Paul uses the pronoun 'we' to include himself in this list.

a. **Helpless** (6a) literally means sick and weak. We were unable to help ourselves. We needed a Savior.

b. **Ungodly** (6b) reminds us how unlike God's intention we were. Even with all our good works, we were best described as ungodly. Note that our lives, including Paul's, is not thought of in a positive light. If we believe that we are worth saving, then we cannot fully understand God's great anger toward us, nor His wonderful grace for us in Christ Jesus.

c. **Sinner** (8), the last of the negative descriptions of our lives apart from Christ, means we are transgressors. We have crossed over the boundary of the law that was revealed to us. Christ's death proves our unrighteousness (6b-7a). If we were not sinners, He would not have died.

Christ's life is equally important, but his death is emphasized here. Not until verse 10 is there mention of His life. Paul is still preoccupied with the deep significance of Christ's death on the cross.

2. In Jesus Christ Hopeful (5:9-11)

> 9 Much more then, having now been justified by His blood, we shall be saved from the wrath of God through Him. 10 For if while we were enemies, we were reconciled to God through the death of His Son, much more, having been reconciled, we shall be saved by His life. 11 And not only this, but we also exult in God through our Lord Jesus Christ, through whom we have now received the reconciliation (Rom 5:9-11).

Christ's death for His enemies brings salvation to them (9-10a)

Privilege #5: Saved From the wrath of God

Christ's deliverance from God's wrath becomes our fifth blessing. This stresses the opposite point of view of the resulting peace of God. Interestingly, Paul speaks of the future. It is here Jesus' life (resurrection) is mentioned. Paul has adequately established the fact of God's wrath against mankind in the beginning of his epistle (1:18, 2:3-5:4; 15). This is hope for the future.

His life for the reconciled confirms our real hope (10b)

The phrase "reconciled to God" is based upon our justification, but the word 'reconciliation' moves beyond gaining a righteous standing. Man is the one being reconciled, not God. Literally, reconcile means to make one with. In the NT we do not find God making friends with man; man is reconciled to God. The basis of reconciliation is the work of Christ at the cross. Through the cross we have been initiated into a new, healthy relationship with God.

His death and life give us reason to exult in our God (11)

Privilege #6: Glorying in God

This exultation in God is the sixth blessing of justification. Present joy stems from justification and reconciliation. God loved us while were ungodly. Through Jesus, our reconciliation to God presents a whole new perspective of Him. This justification restores the fellowship once held between God and man.

Summary

A different response to troubles (faith rather than doubt; trust instead of rejection) enables us to live on a whole new level of life. Peace substitutes rebellion. Love replaces rejection. Hope overcomes helplessness.

- **Peace substitutes rebellion**

Man's relationship has been restored with God (Ro. 5:1-2). Peace
Obedience instead of rebellion. We don't need to seek power, pride and money to demonstrate our importance for we can simply come before God. He knows who we are. We were created to have a relationship with God and that relationship is possible through what Christ did on the cross long ago. This relationship comes through faith in Christ.

- **Love replaces rejection**

Man's environment is controlled by God (Ro. 5:3-5).
When handling crises, we might use words to describe our frustration over some life experience; "It was a disaster" or "I can't handle it." But now, we know God works through the most difficult situations to bring about the best in our lives. Our lives do not consist in living comfortably as the materialist says, but by nurturing our spiritual lives and being more like our holy Father in heaven.

- **Hope overcomes helplessness**

Man's future is ensured by Christ's resurrection (Ro. 5:6-11).
Our secular society teaches us that our lives consist of the here and now. They say man consists in only what he can see. But if we really understand man, with his hopes and fears, there is another part of us that continues beyond the here and now–our soul, the immaterial part of us. God's wrath is real and will be unleashed upon the human race. Christ's resurrection and His ever-present intercession on our behalf is the basis for our hope.

Justification from our sins through Christ's blood is real so as to profoundly affect our lives today. Salvation comes to us as a package of blessings, a part of Abraham's blessings resulting from his faith.

Romans 5:12-21
Further Proof of Justification by Faith

Romans 5:12-21 clinches the argument for the need of justification by faith. It is apparent that Paul is still providing proof for why human beings cannot be justified by their works. His thoroughness leaves no wiggle room for his opponents. Chapter 4 showed that justification by faith is a teaching that originated before the Law as evidenced by Abraham, and yet God blessed Abraham. In Romans 5:1-11 Paul proves that Abraham's blessings regarding faith are released upon God's people–not because they were good, but because of Jesus Christ. Lastly, here in 5:12-21 Paul destroys any relative or comparative arguments on the virtue of a man's good works by demonstrating how everyone is a sinner and therefore guilty of death.

> *"For I am not ashamed of the gospel, for it is the power of God for salvation to everyone who believes, to the Jew first and also to the Greek."*
> Romans 1:16

One person's decisions can affect another, especially in the cases of Adam and the Second Adam, Jesus Christ. Due to his sin, Adam passed his sin and guilt to his descendants, while Jesus, due to his obedience, passed his righteousness and its ensuing life onto those representative of him.

Those from Western countries can face a problem following Paul's logic. They cannot comprehend how one person can so drastically affect the lives of so many. It should be obvious. Stalin or Hitler are negative examples, President Lincoln of a positive example.

The concept of representation is present in our society but is hardly made notice of. For example, if my property as a father incurred a lien, then even if I was to die, the lien would be attached to those who inherited the property. The head's decisions affects those under him. In this case, the sinful choice of one man (Adam) brought condemnation on us all. It is easier for many to accept what Christ has singularly done for us by dying and rising, than it is to embrace the way we became guilty through belonging to the human race (as descendants of Adam). This headship, however, allows Christ to represent those who put their trust in Him.

One may ask, "Why do we need further proof of justification of faith?" The Jews, simply speaking, needed further convincing that people like you and I (the Gentiles) are part of this salvation plan. Let's first review how this passage of Romans 5:21-31 fits into the major outline before discussing its content.

Review of previous chapters

After presenting the gospel in Romans 1:1-17, Paul quickly jumps into a logical argument of how all men, Jews and Gentiles are equally sinners and receive just condemnation of the Lord in 1:18-3:20. Paul deliberately makes the case against all mankind but, at the end of the section, also shows how Christ became an effective sacrifice (propitiation) for all those who believe, whether Jew or Gentile.

Starting in 3:21, we see him strategically turn his argument toward the means by which we gain needed righteousness. If all mankind lacked the righteousness needed and the law was no help, then they would need another means to gain that righteousness. The work of the righteous one, Jesus Christ, on the cross is presented to us in the rest of this section. Romans 3:21-5:21 shows how one acquires righteousness by faith (trust) from the Old Testament. 5:1-11 is best understood when stripped from any trust in one's good works for salvation.

1:18-3:20 Need of Righteousness

All are sinners and guilty before God

All can be saved through work on the cross

3:21-5:21 Means of Righteousness

The gospel Provision by faith

The gospel Promise by faith
- Abraham by faith (4:1-5)
- David by faith (4:6-8)
- OT truth (4:9-12)
- Abraham's blessing (4:13-5:11)
- One died for all (Rom 5:12-21)

Reflective Questions to Our Lives

Here are some reoccurring questions made throughout the centuries. Perhaps you have heard of some:

- How come I am suffering from another person's sin?

- What about those people who didn't know the Law. Are they going to suffer judgment?
- How can Christ's death and resurrection really help people from across culture and time?

An Outline of Romans 5:12-21

The last half of Romans 5 can prove to be difficult to understand because of the many comparisons and anti-comparisons presented. Fortunately, the comparisons are only between two individuals, Adam and Jesus Christ. An outline will help clarify Paul's argument.

A. Worldwide Stain of Sin and Death (5:12-14)
1. Effects of Sin (12)
2. Sin before the law (13)
3. Grip of sin (14)

B. Adam and Christ Contrasted (5:15-17)
1. Object and result of their work (15)
2. The various operations of their work (16-17)

C. Adam and Christ Compared (5:18-19)
1. Regarding their work and its effect (18)
2. Regarding their obedience (19)

D. The Purpose of God (5:20-21)
1. In respect to the law (20)
2. In respect to grace (21)

Let's now briefly look at each section.

A. Worldwide Stain of Sin and Death (Rom 5:12-14)

> 12 Therefore, just as sin came into the world through one man, and death through sin, and so death spread to all men because all sinned — 13 for sin indeed was in the world before the law was given, but sin is not counted where there is no law. 14 Yet death reigned from Adam to Moses, even over those whose sinning was not like the transgression of Adam, who was a type of the one who was to come (Rom 5:12-14 ESV).

1. Effects of Sin (12)

The "therefore" connector in verse 5:12 means 'on account of' or, more simply, 'because.' The link with the previous verses (5:1-11) is essential. Paul was not moving on to a completely different topic. Many, however, believe Paul got off track and did not finish verse 12. We will later discuss how his completed thought is found in verse 17. Each cycle includes the presentation of a type and fulfillment. This type is better described as a counter type (anti-type) for the fulfillment finds itself in the opposite way.

2. Sin before the Law (13)

"Sin entered into the world by one man..." Much can be implied from this verse. At the very least, one should be able to conclude that before Adam the world had no sin. Adam was the door through which evil entered the human race. God commanded Adam that on the day you eat of the fruit of the tree in the middle of the garden, that day shall you die. Perhaps it can be likened to a cancer that is passed on to all of his descendants (all of mankind).

Death here began as an 'unnatural' part of man's life. Sin and death were not inherent in the nature of man, rather they stand as a mark of judgment. This teaching has a great impact on our concept of man, especially in today's modern circle where the "natural man" is to be sought after as the most liberated man (i.e. free from culture), when in fact he has a curse on him from which he cannot be free.

> **"... For all have sinned and fall short of the glory of God, being justified as a gift by His grace through the redemption which is in Christ Jesus" (Rom 3:23-24).**

How is it that some people were guilty of sin before there was a law? The apostle's point is that there is another principle at work, which is only explainable by our association with Adam.

3. Grip of Sin (14)

We know for fact that Adam's sin affected everyone by how everyone, even those without the Mosaic Law, died, as God promised Adam ("You shall surely die" Gen 2:17). Death is the sign of sin, but if the law was not transgressed among non-Jews, then another principle was at work in order for there to be any death.

We need to remember that some people, even now, are living without the laws of scripture. These laws have not been revealed to them. But this does not make them innocent. Each man was represented by Adam, and they will be judged in Adam. Our sin and judgment proves Adam is our representative.

B. Adam and Christ Contrasted (Rom 5:15-17)

> 15 But the free gift is not like the trespass. For if many died through one man's trespass, much more have the grace of God and the free gift by the grace of that one man Jesus Christ abounded for many. 16 And the free gift is not like the result of that one man's sin. For the judgment following one trespass brought condemnation, but the free gift following many trespasses brought justification. 17 For if, because of one man's trespass, death reigned through that one man, much more will those who receive the abundance of grace and the free gift of righteousness reign in life through the one man Jesus Christ (Rom 5:15-17 ESV).

One For All

Verses 13-17 are virtually a parenthesis; and verses 20-21, contain two remarks that are merely incidental to the discussion. Verses 12, 18, 19, must therefore contain the main idea of the passage.

> The purpose of 15-17 is to drive home the vast dissimilarity between Christ and Adam, before the formal comparison between them is made in verse 18f, and so to preclude possible misunderstanding of the comparison.[34]

The phrase, "For if many died through one man's trespass" (v.15) could allude to one of two explanations: (1) verse 12 where the inherited evil nature brings each man to sin and therefore die or (2) their death was due to their position in Adam, so when Adam fell, all fell. Both are true.

---

[34] <u>Romans: A Shorter Commentary</u> by Charles Cranfield (Wm. B Eerdmans), p. 117.

Verse 16 distinguishes the two various operations by which Adam and Christ's work were accomplished. Regarding Adam, one transgression brought judgment (a verdict), which in turn brought condemnation. Regarding Christ, many transgressions brought forth a free gift and this brought about justification.

Verse 17 explains 5:16 by emphasizing differing outcomes. Death is the ruler in one, while the people who have been favored will reign in the next. There is every difference between the two (see diagram below).

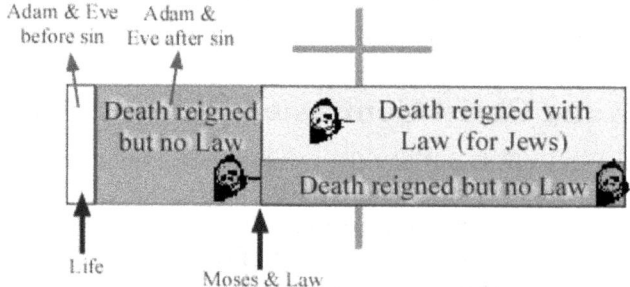

Those who will reign have an abundance of grace and have received the gift of righteousness. The sphere of their reign will be in life and all of this comes from abounding grace in Jesus Christ. These verses reflect the sense of 5:1-11 and specially the second point, "We have obtained our introduction by faith into this grace." The words grace (*charis*) and gift (*dorea*) emphasize our unworthy, undeserving, and helpless state and nature.

Let's look at the 3 contrasts:		
Condemned in Adam	**(yet) Justified in Christ**	**15a But the free gift is not like the transgression.**
15) One sinful person (i.e. Adam) brought condemnation to many.	One gracious person (Jesus) brought righteousness (= gift) to	15b For if by the transgression of the one the many died, much more did the grace of God and the gift by the grace of the one Man, Jesus Christ, abound to the many.

16) Condemnation (to all) came from the one sin of Adam.	The benefits of justification grew having seen the great number of sins forgiven–more mercy and grace.	16 And the gift is not like that which came through the one who sinned; for on the one hand the judgment arose from one transgression resulting in condemnation, but on the other hand the free gift arose from many transgressions resulting in justification.
17) Death reigns over over all mankind because of one man.	Life reigns over all those in Christ Jesus because of the One, Jesus Christ.	17 For if by the transgression of the one, death reigned through the one, much more those who receive the abundance of grace and of the gift of righteousness will reign in life through the One, Jesus Christ."

> **It is not only that our curse was taken away, but that we have gained every imaginal good through Christ's righteousness and life. We eternally reign in Christ's abounding grace!**

C. Adam and Christ Compared (Rom 5:18-19)

¹⁸ So then as through one transgression there resulted condemnation to all men, even so through one act of righteousness there resulted justification of life to all men. ¹⁹ For as through the one man's disobedience the many were made sinners, even so through the obedience of the One the many will be made righteous (Rom 5:18-19).

1. Regarding Their Work and its Effect (5:18)

It appears that Paul continues his interrupted statement from verse 12, "so death spread to all men because all sinned..." Verse 5:18-19 represents the previous words by pointing out several similarities between Adam and Christ. Adam was a type of the one to come. Generally, Adam was a type, but in the form of an anti-type.

Adam lead the human race into condemnation, whereas Jesus Christ led her into justification. Adam broke the fellowship between God and man, but

Christ brought them together. Positively, they were both very influential people. Their lives, acts, and submissiveness to God determined the future course of mankind. Paul does stress the negative side, though, not to discredit Adam but to properly embellish Christ's work and God's grace.

> The design of this section is the illustration of the doctrine of the justification of sinners on the ground of the righteousness of Christ, by a reference to the condemnation of men for the sin of Adam. ... The ground of the sinner's acceptance with God is not in himself, but the merit of Christ. ... As this idea of men's being regarded and treated, not according to their own merit, but the merit of another, is contrary to the common mode of thinking among men, and especially contrary to their self–righteous efforts to obtain the divine favour, the apostle illustrates and enforces it by an appeal to the great analogous fact in the history of the world.[35]

1. Regarding Their Obedience (5:19)

The anti-comparison is displayed in the diagram below:

The parallels are seen in the opposites:

Condemnation	Righteousness
Death-oriented	Life-giving
Disobedience	Obedience

Grace Abounds!

D. The Purpose of God (5:20-21)

> [20] And the Law came in that the transgression might increase; but where sin increased, grace abounded all the more, [21] that, as sin reigned in death, even so grace might reign through righteousness to eternal life through Jesus Christ our Lord (Rom 5:20-21).

1. In Respect to the Law (20)

The apostle discussed the Law earlier (3:27-31) but not its purpose or timing. Paul uses the Law as a highlighter to display of the magnificent grace of God. The Law came so that transgression might increase. As the Law came, man failed all the more. He could not come near the target God had set for him. But because sin increased, God's grace increased. God had planned for

---

[35] Charles Hodge, A Commentary on the Epistle to the Romans, pp. 142.

Christ's work (Eph. 1:4-5). This work of grace has now created a wonderful new course of life for man.

2. In Respect to Grace (21)

The Law came so that abundant grace might come. The consequences of death come from sin. Death is natural though only due to its commonality, yet it remains unnatural and properly hated. Whatever way we may describe this deadly grip upon mankind, let us remember that grace is now a greater ruler. Greater because it promotes righteousness and eternal life, because God is seen in His great love in the work of Jesus Christ, and because no merciless principle dictates our lives. Only the love of God can do that.

> If men are thus justified by the obedience of Christ, for what purpose is the law? 'It entered that sin might abound,' i.e. that men might see how much it abounded; since by the law is the knowledge of sin.
>
> The law has its use, although men are not justified by their own obedience to it, verse 20. As the law discloses, and even aggravates the dreadful triumphs of sin reigning, in union with death, over the human family, the gospel displays the far more effectual and extensive triumphs of grace through Jesus Christ our Lord, verse 21.[36]

Adam sinned
    the result of Adam's sin
    passed on to man along with its evil tendencies
        so it penetrated into their lives
        and became their own sin
            sin & death

Jesus obeyed
    the result of Jesus' righteousness
    passed on to man along with its righteousness & justification
        so it came into their lives
        and became their own righteousness
            righteousness & life

Summary

In the case of any remaining pride residing in his heart, Paul releases the major disputation, unleashing an absolutely crushing argument against man's ability

---

[36] Hodge, p. 144.

to be confident about himself before God. All people are committed to sin and death from Adam onwards. In Adam, all died–revealing our failures to obey God. But fortunately, the same principle of federal representation works on a positive side too. If we doubt that Christ's death can be effective for many, then we only need to look at the former evidence, which is abundantly clear: because of Adam all are sinners and all die. This work of God, then, ought to set off an eternal spark of joy and grace in Christ, freeing man from the horribleness of sin and death in Adam, and releasing them to experience life and peace in Christ.

Romans 6-7
Eliminate Misunderstandings

The purpose of Romans 6-7 is to identify the misunderstandings that sometimes stem from erroneous understandings of justification by faith so that believers can avoid being ensnared by them, so that they can grow properly. Paul's thought seems to be that sanctification naturally grows out of our justification by faith. We do not need to do special things to grow as believers. We do, however, need to be careful of false teaching that has the ability to cripple our spiritual health. Not until Romans 8 does Paul more positively present a full picture of a believer's life (essentially carrying on from 5:11).

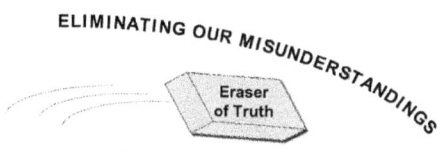

Romans 1-5 Summary

Romans chapters 1 to 3 poignantly declares the sin and condemnation of all mankind. Chapters 4 to 5 definitively pronounces that people are totally forgiven for all their sin, not on the basis of any good they do, but upon their faith in Christ's work alone. Paul then uses these two chapters of arguments (6-7) to avoid abuse and misunderstanding before going on in Romans 8 where he positively presents a Christian's relationship with God through Jesus Christ.

#	The Pattern
1	Starts with general introductory question
2	A followup question indicates the misunderstanding
3	Paul's strong answer, "May it never be!"
4	Strong refutation follows contrary conjunction

Romans 6-7 Overview

Certain individuals were trying to make excuses for their sin and as a result mislead many sincere Christians. This still happens today. Behind each argument is a certain attitude that can be easily passed on to others.

Chapters 6 and 7 carefully eliminate the most dangerous misunderstandings that arise because of a misunderstanding of the biblical teaching of justification by faith. Paul decided that it was necessary to clear up any potential confusion before further developing the impact that justification of faith has on our Christian lives and perspectives. These misunderstandings are perpetrated by those who are trying to make excuses for their sin, thus misleading the average sincere believer. Each argument is closely connected to a certain attitude or approach that can detrimentally influence others.

Each of these four misunderstandings are easily marked out in chapters 6 and 7 by Paul's "may it never be!" phrases (6:1-2, 6:15, 7:7, 7:13). The repetitiveness of this phrase shapes the format of this section. The traditional and uninspired paragraph divisions will only confuse Paul's points. Paul tries to minimize the influence of each false interpretation before it has a chance to carry out its harmful influence. When carefully scrutinized, there seem to be three sections rather than four. The fourth introductory clause is different from the first three but is a modified form of the third, though varies in its focus. We treat it separately, though the argument is more refined and outwardly similar to the third. Let's look at the structure of the phrases.

A. The Romans 6 and 7 Pattern

The introductory phrase of the four sections (6:1-14; 6:15-7:6; 7:7-12; 7:13-25) differs only slightly. The greatest difference is in the fourth section. All four sections use a question to frame the attack against the section's misinterpretation. The later two sections utilize the word 'but' along with strong argumentation. They all accomplish the same purpose of stating a strong rebuttal and clarification. Here is a description of how the arguments progress.

- An introductory question phrase
- A question raised indicating a misunderstanding

    (6:1) What shall we say then?

    (6:15) What then?

    (7:7) What shall we say then?

(7:13) Therefore did that which is good become a cause of death for me?

- The resounding answer, "May it never be!" (μη γενοιτο)
- A strong refutation through either a question of refutation or a strong contrary conjunction (but – αλλα) followed by argumentation.

Wrong conclusions are dangerous! They become the breeding ground for all sorts of temptations that can twist our logic and allow us to continue in our sin. A proper understanding can dislodge these lies, discard incorrect conclusions and enable us to live uprightly before the Lord. What you believe matters! Right doctrine develops right thinking and believing.

B. Misunderstanding #1

Romans 6:1-14 – Baptized into Christ

6:1 What shall we say then? Are we to continue in sin that grace might increase? May it never be! How shall we who died to sin still live in it? 2 May it never be! How shall we who died to sin still live in it?

Wrong conclusions

Oh, we can do whatever we want now. We are free from sin under grace. If we are living under grace, then we are free to sin. God even gives more grace if I do sin. We can sin with the full confidence that God in His glorious wisdom can turn our sin into acts of His grace bringing further glory to His name.

Danger of poor teaching

It is dangerous to presume upon God's forgiveness for deliberate sin and folly and conclude that freedom from sin's curse enables one to act free from a lifestyle requiring obedience. Instead of identifying with Christ as our head, we follow a sinful path justifying our sin.

Truth

Although God has graciously freed us from sin and the curse of the law, we need to fully recognize that being released from our sin does not put us into a neutral position but positively unites us with Christ's life. We find the necessary theology for this argument in Romans 5:12-21. A believer escapes from his old nature, under the head of Adam, and is ruled by another nature, under the headship of Christ. He is totally reoriented around Christ's empowering life and leadership.

Discussion on Romans 6:1-14

> ³ Or do you not know that all of us who have been baptized into Christ Jesus have been baptized into His death? ⁴ Therefore we have been buried with Him through baptism into death, in order that as Christ was raised from the dead through the glory of the Father, so we too might walk in newness of life. ⁵ For if we have become united with Him in the likeness of His death, certainly we shall be also in the likeness of His resurrection, ⁶ knowing this, that our old self was crucified with Him, that our body of sin might be done away with, that we should no longer be slaves to sin; ⁷ for he who has died is freed from sin. ⁸ Now if we have died with Christ, we believe that we shall also live with Him, ⁹ knowing that Christ, having been raised from the dead, is never to die again; death no longer is master over Him. ¹⁰ For the death that He died, He died to sin, once for all; but the life that He lives, He lives to God. ¹¹ Even so consider yourselves to be dead to sin, but alive to God in Christ Jesus. ¹² Therefore do not let sin reign in your mortal body that you should obey its lusts, ¹³ and do not go on presenting the members of your body to sin as instruments of unrighteousness; but present yourselves to God as those alive from the dead, and your members as instruments of righteousness to God. ¹⁴ For sin shall not be master over you, for you are not under law, but under grace (Rom 6:3-14).

Verses 6:3-4 Romans 6 often confuses Christians because it mentions baptism, but doesn't mention water. The baptism discussed here is not talking about the form or ceremony of baptism, but the meaning of baptism itself. It is not something that we do as a church but something that is done to us. Indeed there is only one baptism where we were baptized into Christ's death and thus died to the power of sin (note 'Law' is not used here). Christ's death fully satisfies the penalty assessed to sin: death. But because we were baptized into Christ's death, we were also raised by Christ's power. This then binds our new heart to live like Christ.

Verse 6:5 Paul clearly states that those who are united with Christ in His death are also necessarily those who are united with Him in Life. In other words, one cannot make an exception that he was merely baptized with Christ and not raised with Him. This is senseless–this would leave him still dead! The word "certainly" puts doubt out of the question. If we claim the effectiveness of Christ's death and propitiation, then we must also lay hold of His power in His resurrection and life. To deny one is to deny the other; and conversely, to accept one is to accept the other. There are no stages or advanced levels of acceptance.

Verses 6-11 Paul amplifies the meaning of baptism starting with verse 6 right up to verse 11. Though the word baptism symbolizes both death and resurrection, the word was no longer used after verse 4, avoiding any confusion with the ceremony of baptism. He is discussing the meaning of the ceremony as stated in verse 3.

Paul coins this new term "old self" (only Rom 6:6, Eph 4:22, Col 3:9). It originated in its contrast with the new life or self. The 'old self' died. The phrase "crucified with Him" emphasizes the certainty of our death even as Christ's death was real.

The purpose of the crucifixion of our old self is simply so that our body of sin might be done away with and that we would no longer be held under its sway. "For he who has died is freed from sin" (7). He died and no longer lives. He is not looking for excuses to sin, but recognizes that his true self is identified with the new self rather than the old. Paul in part is explaining the means we have escaped the reign of death and sin in Adam. Christ suffered in our stead. But to be sure, our old self has also died. The old self's ugly head was crushed. How remarkable and wonderful that we could escape sin's grasp. This is the wonderful power of the gospel.

As verse 8 states, if we have so died with Christ, we also believe we shall live with Him. "In Christ" is frequently used, but here (and Phil. 1:23 and Col 2:20) the preposition 'with' (*sun*) is used instead of a general pronoun. Paul further confirms our participation in the event.

This joint identification with Christ is profound in its simplicity. We have confidence we shall live with Christ mostly through Christ's powerful resurrection. He shall not ever die again. If Christ has overcome death, He has also overcome it for us because we are united in Him. There is no reason, even theologically, that requires Him to die again. So we dare not think this truth implies that we sin and so He dies; we sin again, and He dies again. No. This is not what has happened. He died. We sinned. We died in Him. We became alive with Him and will live with Him forever. This is life eternal, life without end. This is probably one of the clearest explanations of eternal life in the scriptures.

Verses 12-14 So Paul, with one of his signature linking words "therefore" (used 24 times in Romans), concludes this theological discussion. Practically, since we are alive with Christ, we should prohibit sin to reign in our mortal bodies. When sin rules, we will always obey its lusts. We do not give ourselves over to these sins. Instead, positively, we are to deliver ourselves over to God so that His righteousness can be exercised through us. Being under the Law would mean that we were still part of Adam. Those under the Old Covenant lived under Adam. Today we live under the power of God's grace; we live out God's righteousness. We are not only objectively declared righteous, but are righteous people. Sin is not reigning, but Christ is.

If someone says that he cannot help it, then we must believe either he has not died with Christ and come alive with Him, or that he does not sufficiently understand this truth. Just because someone falls into sin and stays there does not mean Christ will again die for his sin. Christ died once and so we indeed are really free from the power of sin.

Summary

Scripture warns us not to presume upon God's grace but instead to favorably respond to His goodness. We are not to continue in sin so that grace might increase. Though one can find God graciously dealing with His stubborn people as one looks through the annals of history (e.g. Jacob), but we can equally find places where He did not deal in grace but judgment. Paul intended to amplify the means by which we escaped from Adam's group and leaped upwards into Christ's group (cf. 5:12-21).

C. Misunderstanding #2

Romans 6:15-7:6 – Servant of Only One Master

> 15 What then? Shall we sin because we are not under law but under grace? May it never be! 16 Do you not know that when you present yourselves to someone as slaves for obedience, you are slaves of the one whom you obey, either of sin resulting in death, or of obedience resulting in righteousness?

Wrong conclusions

> Ah, you mention we are not under the Law. Does this not infer that we can live any lifestyle we choose? After all, this is an age of grace, is it not? We are free to do what we wish. I don't have to live by the law anymore. I'm free. I can do whatever I feel like doing.

Danger of poor teaching

Freedom from the law is erroneously interpreted to mean that one is free from living a lifestyle bound to God's righteousness.

Truth

Yes, the sin's condemning power over us is gone, but we have gained a new Master. Living under grace means that we have transferred Masters. Before, we served sin, but now we serve righteousness under Christ. Remember how when under the Law, your sin was roused? "Don't..." But now you are free from this old authority by your faith in Christ where you have died to yourself, thus freeing you to serve in newness of the Spirit.

Discussion on Romans 6:15-23

> 17 But thanks be to God that though you were slaves of sin, you became obedient from the heart to that form of teaching to which you were committed, 18 and having been freed from sin, you became slaves of righteousness. 19 I am speaking in human terms because of the weakness of your flesh. For just as you presented your members as slaves to impurity and to lawlessness, resulting in further lawlessness, so now present your members as slaves to righteousness, resulting in sanctification. 20 For when you were slaves of sin, you were free in regard to righteousness. 21 Therefore what benefit were you then deriving from the things of which you are now ashamed? For the outcome of those things is death. 22 But now having been freed from sin and enslaved to God, you derive your benefit, resulting in sanctification, and the outcome, eternal life. 23 For the wages of sin is death, but the free gift of God is eternal life in Christ Jesus our Lord (Rom 6:15-23).

Verses 6:17-18 The phrase, "You were... you became" (17) highlights the change that comes with being in Christ. We are either without Christ or with Him. We cannot be neutral, amoral creatures because we were created in God's image and followed in Adam's path. As fallen creatures we have 'joined' the rebellious forces against our loving Maker. Freedom is illusory among God's moral creatures and should only be proclaimed when we boast in our opportunities to serve Christ! Later Paul says, "Now having been freed from sin and enslaved to God" (22).

Verses 6:19-23 We should note that even though the unregenerate person is ensnared by his flesh, we must accept that he is still the one presenting his members (body parts) as slaves and therefore is accountable for his sin. We choose whom we serve. Our nature, affected by our desires, shapes our decisions, but is still counted as our decision. In our sensual world, for example, we must include how men and women use their body parts in illicit sexual encounters, some in real life, while many more in virtual porn scenes.

Slavery is used six times in 17-23. The notion of slavery is protested everywhere, and yet, because it powerfully carries the imagery of a binding obligation to someone outside ourselves, it remains a most accurate and useful description. "Free in regard to righteousness" (21) does not mean that the wicked have no accountability before God for living a holy life, for this is something he has clearly articulated, but he instead refers to the notion that their immediate master is their sin nature and that is what they live for. Being so preoccupied with their own lives, they are blind to God's expectations.

Even the Christian relationship to God is described here as "enslaved to God," but instead of attaching it to shameful or burdensome behaviors and desires, Paul uses it to positively shape our opportunity to properly serve God. This is freedom, or as Paul officially calls it, 'sanctification' (22), which is used 8 times, two of which are here in Romans 6 (19,22). Our freedom to live as Christ's slave is actually our path to holy living, bringing all sorts of benefits, which, in turn, lead to eternal life (22).

Having been freed from Master Sin, we are now obligated to serve Lord Christ, who is known for righteousness. Freedom from one brings captivity to another. This section addresses the need for Christ-filled living under one's new status under grace. Paul uses the 'master illustration' at the end of chapter 6:16-23 to communicate this idea.

Discussion on Romans 7:1-6

> 7:1 Or do you not know, brethren (for I am speaking to those who know the law), that the law has jurisdiction over a person as long as he lives? 2 For the married woman is bound by law to her husband while he is living; but if her husband dies, she is released from the law concerning the husband. 3 So then if, while her husband is living, she is joined to another man, she shall be called an adulteress; but if her husband dies, she is free from the law, so that she is not an adulteress, though she is joined to another man. 4 Therefore, my brethren, you also were made to die to the Law through the body of Christ, that you might be joined to another, to Him who was raised from the dead, that we might bear fruit for God. 5 For while we were in the flesh, the sinful passions, which were aroused by the Law, were at work in the members of our body to bear fruit for death. 6 But now we have been released from the Law, having died to that by which we were bound, so that we serve in newness of the Spirit and not in oldness of the letter (Rom 7:1-6).

In chapter 7 Paul turns from the illustration of baptism to the illustration of marriage to highlight what happens when a person in Christ dies to his sin and becomes bound by a new relationship with Christ. To properly understand this argument, we need to rightly understand the Old Testament law. The law, as a covenant, has obligation over a person as long as he lives. One cannot leave its jurisdiction except through death. The typical wedding vow states the same, "Until death do us part." The legalization of divorce and proliferation of remarriage has created different understandings of marriage that confuse the biblical understanding.

The married woman is bound by law to her husband while he is living; but if her husband dies, she is released from the law concerning the husband. But if she joins up with a man while her husband is living, she is an adulteress. But if her husband dies, she is free from the law, so that she would not be an adulteress, though she is joined to another man (7:1-3).

We are legally bound to obey the covenant or agreements that we are under until death. Before the woman was married, there was no obligation. But once the 'knot' is tied, there is a serious obligation that nothing but death will destroy. The only way to escape our enslavement to sin is to die to it, and this is secured only through the cross. "But now we have been released from the Law" (7:6) reveals that our death with Christ has released us.

We cannot join with Christ in His death unless we join ourselves to Him in belief. Apart from belief in Christ, we have no lawful case to join another, but are bound to our sinful passions (v. 5). It is theologically impossible to get out of the legal obligations of the first until we have joined with Christ through dying with Him.

Paul returns to his main point in verse 6 that we cannot properly assert that believers are not bound to serve Christ, having been set free by Him. "We serve in newness of the Spirit and not in oldness of the letter" (v. 6). The word 'serve' again shows that we are bound to do as Jesus leads through the power of the Holy Spirit. God helps us with satisfying our guilt, giving us our new nature and blessing us with the Holy Spirit to obey Him. This is in stark contrast to the Old Testament Law, which although is God's Word, did not empower us to serve Him.

A comment on marriage and divorce

Although divorce, and its implied freedom to remarry, has become legalized in many places, we should note Paul's clear affirmation (and Jesus' clear statement Mk 10:1-12) that marriage does not allow divorce.[37] Divorce differs from death and does not nullify the marriage covenant. This is the reason remarriage is considered adultery for the divorcee but remarriage is fine when one's spouse has died.

D. Misunderstanding #3

Romans 7:7-12 – Sin Comes from Me Not from the Law

> 7 What shall we say then? Is the Law sin? May it never be! On the contrary, I would not have come to know sin except through the Law; for I would not have known about coveting if the Law had not said, "YOU SHALL NOT COVET."

A Wrong Conclusion

Sin isn't my fault, but the Law's. The Law brings about my sin.

Danger of Poor Teaching

When people associate the Law with sin, they erroneously pass responsibility of their sin onto the Law. Once the Law is associated with sin, its moral compass is dismissed. Guilty people tend to blame others to redirect the focus from themselves and onto others. In this case, as they pin their guilty consciences onto the Law, they are then free to continue unrepentant in their sin, and perhaps, justify more sin, convinced that their fault is the Law's responsibility.

The doubt about the goodness of the law, then, becomes the root of antinomianism, which seeks the opportunity to choose a lifestyle of one's own choice because one has been freed by grace. This mentality has become quite prevalent by the modern world, which sees the law as a hinderance to the development of human beings rather than an aid in their development. Hedonism is one offshoot of antinomianism that assumes the law is the impediment to the quest for pleasure, interpreted as the indulgence of one's senses and desires:

> Those who reject the Law become hardened, self-righteous individuals rather than humble and repentant.
>
> Instead of the Law inspiring them to live holy lives, people hold negative and suspicious attitudes toward it.

---

[37] Jesus stated His perspective in Mark without any qualifications. The exception clause from Mat 19 was given to the Jews who knew the Law which dealt with that specific situation.

Rejection of the Law removes God's cautions that keep us from falling further into evil (Rom 1:26-28).

Truth

The Law does not make us sin; it only exposes it when we break it. The Law warns us of our coming peril if we remain unchanged (7). The Law is holy, righteous and good, just as the author of the Law is holy. Without the Law, we would miss the opportunity to know the truth about our sin, the truth that would lead to salvation ("result in life" 10).

The real problem is our sin nature (8). We disobey the law and fall under its curse. When we become more conscious of the Law, our sin tends to get worse, but this is only due to our sinful tendencies, or "Sin, taking opportunity" (8). When we rightly appraise the Law and humble our hearts, we can then seek and find God's grace.

Discussion on Romans 7:7-12

> 8 But sin, taking opportunity through the commandment, produced in me coveting of every kind; for apart from the Law sin is dead. 9 And I was once alive apart from the Law; but when the commandment came, sin became alive, and I died; 10 and this commandment, which was to result in life, proved to result in death for me; 11 for sin, taking opportunity through the commandment, deceived me, and through it killed me. 12 So then, the Law is holy, and the commandment is holy and righteous and good (Rom 7:8-12).

Rules and laws are commonly looked down upon as the obstacle of proper personal development. "The rules are no good. If it weren't for the rules, I wouldn't be so rebellious." Antinomianism has extended its hold in the world, making immoral thoughts and actions legal and proper by suppressing the laws that restrain immorality by associated guilt. And so, modernity removes law, guilt, truth, and rules from public awareness, allowing people to further stray from God's design, suppressing their real (old) self. Without the Law, lust and selfish impulses overtake the real person.

Coveting, immorality, etc. cannot exist without the Law. "When the commandment came, sin became alive." The Law names the sin and instantly implicates the sinners. This is the reason modernity aggressively seeks to obliterate any Laws.

The Blame Response

People are persistently looking for a means to suppress the guilt that comes from knowledge of the Law. The more religious or traditional a society is, the more pronounced the norms are. Unregenerate hearts must somehow repress their surging guilt so that they can seek opportunity to fill their lusts. This third misunderstanding, where the Law is criticized as being the source of the problem, explains why many are suspicious toward the Law's inherent goodness. Instead of concluding, like Paul, that "the Law is holy, and the commandment is holy and righteous and good" and that they are protected by it, they subjugate it as being an evil–or at least an incompetent set of rules– and having done so, they can easily dispose of them. By shifting blame, they are 'free' to pursue their lusts.

Summary

There can be two very different responses to the Law: (1) they blame the Law for their sin, dismissing its holiness, and continue in their sinful behavior and greed, or (2) they allow God to make them sensitive to His holy standards through the Law and, as necessary, repent, find Christ's forgiveness in the cross, and seek to live pleasing to God by helping others.

---

dormant sin > commandment > active sin > death

E. Misunderstanding #4

Romans 7:13-25 – Death Comes from My Sin Not from the Law

^{7:13} Therefore did that which is good become a cause of death for me? May it never be! Rather it was sin, in order that it might be shown to be sin by effecting my death through that which is good, that through the commandment sin might become utterly sinful.

A Wrong Conclusions

What a dirty trick! Here, I've been thinking God's law was helping me, but instead it's convicted me. I wish God would never have dealt with us at all. Without the Law, I would have been okay. It's really God's fault; He shouldn't have given us the Law.

Danger in this Poor Teaching

- They accuse God, the Lawgiver, of being responsible for their personal sin.

- Criticism and pride cause a person to avoid confession, which leads to a humble heart, the cross, and freedom.
- Instead, they erroneously associate sin and death with God's will rather than seeing the law as a wonderful expression of His care.
- They develop a helpless and fatalistic attitude: "I can't help it." "God made me do it."

Truth

Upon close examination, this fourth 'misunderstanding' seems to be a fuller development of section three, which speaks directly about the Law but rather focuses on the Lawgiver, being "a cause for death for me" (13). Paul is primarily addressing the religious Jews, who refuse to directly mention God as the source of the problem. Not many people directly blame God, but their insinuation is that, as the Lawgiver, the Lord is not genuinely concerned for them. They believe, however, that life would be a whole lot better without the Law and so hold suspicion of God's treatment of them, doubting God's love for them.

The passage of 7:14-25 is not a new topic but is part of the misunderstandings. The word "for" connects verses 14-25 with verse 13. For further confirmation of this view, after each "May it never be", a strong rebuttal occurs (at the end of verse 13) along with an intensive explanation for that rebuttal. Verses 7:14, 15, 18, 19, 22 all use the word 'for' to emphasize Paul's ongoing explanation. This approach is further supported by the way the passage persistently explains the correct view one should have toward the Law and our flesh, a theme Paul has been defending in chapters 6 and 7 (and elsewhere such as Gal 6).

Discussion on Romans 7:13-25

> [14] For we know that the Law is spiritual; but I am of flesh, sold into bondage to sin. [15] For that which I am doing, I do not understand; for I am not practicing what I would like to do, but I am doing the very thing I hate. [16] But if I do the very thing I do not wish to do, I agree with the Law, confessing that it is good. [17] So now, no longer am I the one doing it, but sin which indwells me. [18] For I know that nothing good dwells in me, that is, in my flesh; for the wishing is present in me, but the doing of the good is not. [19] For the good that I wish, I do not do; but I practice the very evil that I do not wish.
>
> [20] But if I am doing the very thing I do not wish, I am no longer the one doing it, but sin which dwells in me. [21] I find then the principle

that evil is present in me, the one who wishes to do good. ²² For I joyfully concur with the law of God in the inner man, ²³ but I see a different law in the members of my body, waging war against the law of my mind, and making me a prisoner of the law of sin which is in my members. ²⁴ Wretched man that I am! Who will set me free from the body of this death? ²⁵ Thanks be to God through Jesus Christ our Lord! So then, on the one hand I myself with my mind am serving the law of God, but on the other, with my flesh the law of sin (Rom 7:14-25).

Disrespect for authority, who are those who give and enforce the law, has become rampant in our corrupt modern society. Young people are not the only ones who despise authority figures, but they are the ones who have never matured. This is commonly seen in the rage people hold against their parents, "My parents only care about themselves. If they didn't give me these rules, then I wouldn't be so bitter toward them." While Misunderstanding #3 focuses on the inherent problems of the Law, Misunderstanding #4 questions the motives of God who gave us the Law.

1. The Law is Spiritual (7:14-16)

¹⁴ For we know that the Law is spiritual; but I am of flesh, sold into bondage to sin. ¹⁵ For that which I am doing, I do not understand; for I am not practicing what I would like to do, but I am doing the very thing I hate. ¹⁶ But if I do the very thing I do not wish to do, I agree with the Law, confessing that it is good (Rom 7:14-16).

The Law is a spiritual expression of God's righteous rule (14). He asserts, "I am not practicing what I would like to do" (15) and in the next verses astutely observes, "I agree with the Law, confessing that it is good" (16). The scriptures do not allow a dualism to arise between Law and Spirit, or as some imply, between the God of the Old Testament who uses the Law to control and the God of the New Testament who uses love to inspire. The Law is spiritual! The Law is the means by which the Spirit prods us into obedience.

From the outset, Paul embraces the honor of the Law and the destructive influence of the flesh, our sinful nature. By identifying with people's experiences instead of head knowledge, Paul is able to convince a greater number of those that erroneously conclude that the Law has inherent weaknesses and should be dismissed. Those open to examine their spiritual lives will find the source of their problem in their flesh not in the law. People need to understand how devious our flesh is–our lives apart from the rule of the Spirit. The statement, "sold into bondage to sin" offends some but it is in agreement with Paul's description of the sin nature we inherited from Adam (Rom 5:12-21), and is further proven by the common curse of death that plagues humanity.

7:15-16 Not many law-conscious Jews would quickly accept Paul's summary in verse 14 because they consider themselves righteous. But Paul, as a former Pharisee, understands the inconsistency we all face–the great divide between the knowledge of good and the lack of will to carry it out. He uses his present inner struggle–there is no hint of it being merely in the past–to prove there are two sides: one side of him that does what he does not want to do, and the other side that does not do what he wants to do. In acknowledging this battle, which most conscious Jews could identify with, he acknowledges a high and good standard that he and all humans admire. In verse 16 he concludes that this tension is proof that the Law is not causing the problem–for it is good and stands outside of the problem. When we can observe the struggle between the good and right, we are at once admitting to the perfect Law of God as well as our failure to keep it.

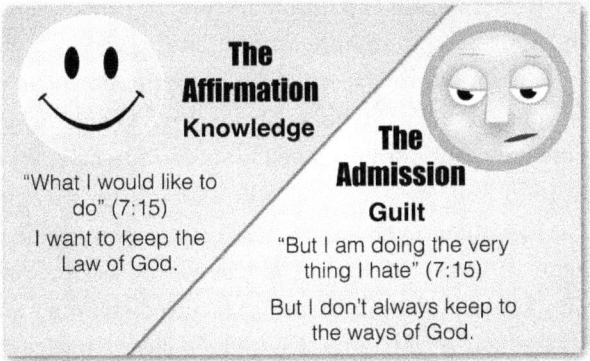

Paul, it seems, is not merely restating former arguments from chapters 1-3 but purposely makes further inroads through yet another means of exposing man's corruption and need for Christ.

2. The Flesh is Evil (7:17-19)

> ¹⁷ So now, no longer am I the one doing it, but sin which indwells me. ¹⁸ For I know that nothing good dwells in me, that is, in my flesh; for the wishing is present in me, but the doing of the good is not. ¹⁹ For the good that I wish, I do not do; but I practice the very evil that I do not wish. (Rom 7:17-19).

7:17 Paul's conclusion here agrees with what verse 13 has to say. The Law is not liable for our sin; we are guilty because of our sin. Paul, however, takes it a step further by portraying the sinner. Notice his words, "no longer am I the one doing it, but sin which indwells me." This is not his attempt to excuse himself from the responsibility of sin; he admitted his guilt in verse 15. Instead, he is linking his sin to his sin nature, which possesses a sick passion to do wrong. Due to a thought or inclination to do good, he shows that he is not abandoned to the flesh, even though it might appear that way on the outward at times (14).

Blame should not be placed on God's Law, but upon the law of our flesh. "So now, no longer am I the one doing it, but sin which indwells me" (17). Believers, like Paul, find contrary thoughts and decisions going through their minds. The thought that we choose to believe and act upon will result in either God's work or our flesh's work being done. There are two operatives or principles at work in our lives: "For the good that I wish, I do not do; but I practice the very evil that I do not wish" (19).

7:18-19 The flesh is 100% corrupted; "Nothing good dwells in me, that is, in my flesh." Our person, represented by "me", is aligned with the flesh, though not totally. A person seems to be caught between two worlds–ensnared by one and yet conscious of another. Our actions betray our alignment to the flesh, but our minds still identify and sense responsibility for that which is good and perfect. Paul is developing another principle, that which he first spoke about in chapter 1; that man is, to some degree, exposed to the revelation of God's truth. This is true for both Christians and non-Christians, but of course, the Christian has received so much more of God's revelation. For the Jew, they had the Law, which clearly revealed more of the good and right. The liability of the person increases as he or she receives a greater amount of God's revelation (see diagram).

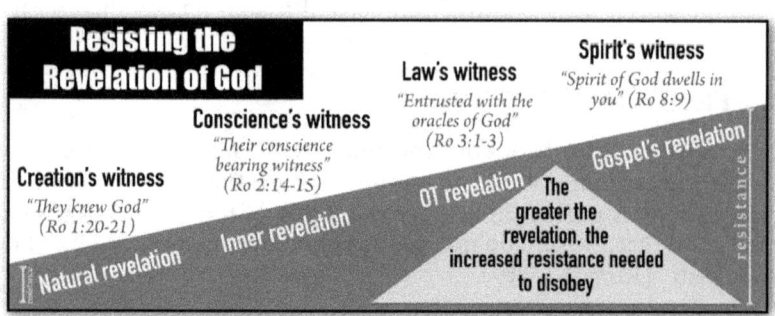

3. The Tension Found (7:20-23)

> [20] But if I am doing the very thing I do not wish, I am no longer the one doing it, but sin which dwells in me. [21] I find then the principle that evil is present in me, the one who wishes to do good. [22] For I joyfully concur with the law of God in the inner man, [23] but I see a different law in the members of my body, waging war against the law of my mind, and making me a prisoner of the law of sin which is in my members. (Rom 7:20-23).

7:20-21 Verse 20 further develops the argument. He reveals that he is not totally committed or identified with the flesh. In 19 he speaks of "the good that I wish" while in 21 he says, "the one who wishes to do good." There is more to him (speaking of all of us) than just our flesh. The tension reveals God's varying levels of revelation, wrestling with our desires trying to convince us into conformity. The evil presence, "sin which dwells in me", however, presents itself to be a formidable inner foe. It rules him apart from Christ (stated in 25) and yet does not totally erase his sense of reasoning. His sin becomes obvious in that he chooses to do wrong while knowing what ought to be done.

Paul allows for a conflict of our identity but does not exclude responsibility. Sin acts as its own person when allowed, "sin which dwells in me" (21). But Paul doesn't avoid accountability, as he still admits, "I am doing" (20). We, likewise, should affirm that God's law is good and that our evil is part of our old nature. Even when in the thick of the battle where our feelings and lust arise, we can, like Joseph (Gen 39:12), flee from sin and make good decisions.

7:22-23 The term 'inner man' is used three times in scripture and only by Paul (also: 2 Cor 4:16; Eph 3:16). It identifies the soul, the invisible part of man, that has been awakened by God's Spirit so that, being enlightened, can rejoice in what is good as defined by the law of God. Our bodies, however, have a degenerate force at work that induces us to live apart from the insight of the inner man. And so, the battle ensues and the body struggles with the mind. The 'me' is made a prisoner of the law of sin, which in the end dominates one's decisions and corrupts one's actions. The 'me' force, in many cases, wins over the law of God. (For references to the renewed mind see Rom 12:2; Ep 4:23, 3:16; 2 Co 4:16.)

4. God's Solution (7:24-25)

> ²⁴ Wretched man that I am! Who will set me free from the body of this death? ²⁵ Thanks be to God through Jesus Christ our Lord! So then, on the one hand I myself with my mind am serving the law of God, but on the other, with my flesh the law of sin (Rom 7:24-25).

7:24 Paul makes his powerful conclusions, all of which fit the rebuttal in verse 13, and yet give the appropriate clues to evaluate his former words in light of what God has done for us through the Gospel of Christ. It is the body or flesh, the 'wretched man', which brings death. The evil principle or rule, amplified through our compliance, convincingly rules our bodies and exposes the utter sinfulness of our nature, making it fit only for death. The law is not the cause of death (13), and Paul is quick to point out that if we can recognize the pure effect of the law, then we will admit to the evil in our own lives, which in turn begs the need for life and a Savior. The Lord Jesus Christ does not only free us from this dominating force of evil, but brings a new burst of light and life into our lives that helps us obey the Lord. The flesh has so overpowered the mind that, without God's grace, man cannot understand and grasp the truth of God.

> Thanks be to God through Jesus Christ our Lord! So then, on the one hand I myself with my mind am serving the law of God, but on the other, with my flesh the law of sin (Rom 7:25).

7:25 Paul's conclusion highlights an answer to his question from the former verse and gives testimony of what Christ has done for himself and all who believe on Him. The power of the flesh is at work in unbelievers and believers, and it always results in the work of sin. For Paul, and all genuine believers, they see and serve the law of God–which is not contrary to the Spirit of God, but in harmony with it. The battle between our flesh and mind depicts the battles Christian face daily in their spiritual lives.

We must not trust our old nature to bring any good thing. If, as a believer, I serve the Spirit with my mind, then I will as a Christian walk in the Spirit. If I don't focus on those holy things with my mind, I will go astray and sin. Can a Christian sin? Yes, but it remains our duty and obligation to live according to God's higher principles as seen in the Law that reflects God-given values.

Paul highlights the goodness of the Law of God. The unbeliever toys with obedience: first against general revelation, then the conscience, then the Law itself. These 'small lights' all point to God Himself. Infraction to the instruction of these smaller lights reveals our antagonism against God. If we want to find spiritual guidance, start with identifying the voice of truth, no matter how small it might be (during temptation that voice may seem almost incomprehensible at times). Recognize that God wants to fully enlighten and empower you through His Holy Spirit whom He has poured out to us when we believe in Christ (Rom 5:5). Unequivocally embrace God's way in your life through Christ. (In chapter 8 Paul expands on this topic.)

Summary

Those who understand the truths stated here can escape many spiritual setbacks and be able to help keep many other believers from stumbling. The Christian life is a fight between our two natures. Yes, we are victors through Christ and can win, but if we are not careful, we can, through temptation, give control over to our sinful nature where our lusts will again lead us astray.

The spiritual nature that God gave us is such that it doesn't give rise to sin. The Law is a spiritual expression of God's good and righteous rule. It is only the flesh that we inherited from Adam that causes sin and brings death (Rom 5:12-21). Though sin and death are common, the Christian has discovered by faith in Christ the principle that brings eternal life.

The evil one does everything he can to hold back our spiritual growth. What better way is there than to have us adopt some false teachings in regard to salvation. In this manner we tend to forget our true salvation and focus on other matters that end up compromising our faith. Unless we dismiss these misunderstandings, we will not be able to move forward in our Christian lives. Instead of considering God as the instigator of sin, we need to consider God as the Savior who in love sent His Son Jesus the Messiah. Fortunately, within the Law was a sacrificial system foreshadowing God's full redemptive program and grace in Christ Jesus (7:25).

F. Two General Views of 7:13-25

There are two approaches to this passage that can shape one's interpretation and application, but it is the greater context seen above that directs us toward the proper interpretation.

(1) Pre-Christian view

Paul uses his past life to describe what life is like for those under the flesh. His use of the present tense is a tool to catch the reader's attention. Romans 7:25, especially the last part, "So then, on the one hand I myself with my mind am serving the law of God, but on the other, with my flesh the law of sin," clearly expresses Paul's tensions early on before he was a believer.

(2) Christian view

Paul shares from his inner struggles as a Christian believer in order to engage his readers in his argument to remove any blame on the Law for their sin and pins the whole problem of sin on their own nature and choices. This passage, therefore, can be used to describe the inner struggle of the believer. Those who object to this interpretation identify 7:14, "sold into bondage to sin" as the "negative and uncompromising language of Christians"[38] and therefore adopt the pre-Christian view.

(3) My view

Paul was not working out the Christian doctrine of sanctification in chapters 6 and 7, but was focusing on eliminating false understandings about our faith. This section of 7:13-25 is no different. The key verse is verse 13, which provides a strong rebuttal to the false supposition that the law could be the cause of our death. Paul, almost desperate to communicate the truths of the gospel message, divulges his inner spiritual struggles. By exposing his own struggles, past and present, he reveals the ugliness of the flesh, and its ongoing and desperate attempt to counter God's ways in all of us.

Like the parables, the description of man's relationship with evil and truth will possess some strong similarities. The unbeliever, however, is often oblivious to the spiritual battle. The Christian, though, now has a living inner man due to another power, Christ's resurrected power, which allows him to serve God and others from a heart of thankfulness. His old flesh still hangs about, but it no longer holds him under its dark powers. Like a disguised hook, it remains nearby hoping to snag him into temptations.

As Christian believers, we must get beyond this battle with our flesh and onto living and walking by the power of the Spirit, not focusing on our selfish desires but on God's glorious purposes, will, and love, all themes that will be more carefully presented in chapter 8.

---

[38] Ziesler, p. 194.

Romans 8:1-17

The New Man

In Romans 5:1-11 Paul shared about the personal inner joy and peace that can be derived from faith in Christ Jesus. But the changes don't stop there! In 8:1-11 he continues to teach what happens on the inside that makes such an outward difference. Christ freed us from the arena of selfishness, which results in death, and brought us into the Spirit's love, power, and life. Romans 8 positively presents the new nature and position of the Christian believer.

A. Freed by the Spirit (8:1-11)

There is no condemnation! Compare 5:1, which speaks of being justified by faith, with 8:1, which declares the believer as free from condemnation.

1. Declared Free! (Rom 8: 1)

There is therefore now no condemnation for those who are in Christ Jesus (8:1).

This verse powerfully summarizes all the chapters that have preceded it. Notice the logical development through the first seven chapters of Romans leading to this point, where Paul makes this declaration: Sinful => condemned => needs salvation => man's unable to save => Jesus as Savior => Belief in Jesus => Free from sin => Belong to Christ => Can sin but doesn't have to sin, because of Christ (7:25).

Paul, here and elsewhere (4 "who do not walk..."), carefully defines the group that can put their full confidence in escaping condemnation for their sins. The whole message of salvation, its urgency and potency, would be swallowed up if there was no a clear distinction kept between those who are saved and those who are not. Freedom from condemnation is only offered to those "who are in Christ Jesus" (also verse 4), which makes the spreading of the gospel an urgent matter.

The gracious freedom from condemnation that we have received lays the foundation for a gracious and forgiving life as Paul later delineates. For example, we are not to take revenge (12:19) but instead ought to be extra kind to those weak in faith (14:1 ff.) and avoid judging others (14:10).

2. Set free (8:2-8) from Law of Sin and of Death

> 2 For the law of the Spirit of life in Christ Jesus has set you free from the law of sin and of death. 3 For what the Law could not do, weak as it was through the flesh, God did: sending His own Son in the likeness of sinful flesh and as an offering for sin, He condemned sin in the flesh, 4 in order that the requirement of the Law might be fulfilled in us, who do not walk according to the flesh, but according to the Spirit. 5 For those who are according to the flesh set their minds on the things of the flesh, but those who are according to the Spirit, the things of the Spirit. 6 For the mind set on the flesh is death, but the mind set on the Spirit is life and peace, 7 because the mind set on the flesh is hostile toward God; for it does not subject itself to the law of God, for it is not even able to do so; 8 and those who are in the flesh cannot please God.

It is critical that we have a real picture of the horror of being condemned and eternally separated from Christ lest we make an erroneous conclusion like the Israelites when they became convinced that slavery in Egypt was better than the freedom of going to Canaan (Num 11:5-6).

"The Law of the Spirit of life in Christ Jesus" (8:2) is an enhancement from the Old Testament Law. The Old Testament Ten Commandments were recorded on stone while these are engraved on our heart through the Spirit of God (Heb 10:16-18). The believer now has a desire to obey God. The OT law motivates from the outside, using guilt to enforce its laws, while the NT is energized by the Holy Spirit from the inside out. By using the term "Law" he reinforces the good aspect of God's teaching, both the OT and the NT teachings, that which complements God's holy being.

The Manner We are Set Free

The OT law is wholly inadequate compared to Christ's saving work: "For what the Law could not do" (3). The Law pointed to the way of righteousness, but our sinful flesh could not satisfy its demands. God became man and became "an offering for sin" –a sacrifice (3:5). "Condemned sin in the flesh" is a good depiction of how bad sin is; bad enough to require Christ to come to earth and carry our sentence of death upon Himself. A righteous human had to die for a human to satisfy the Law's sentence.

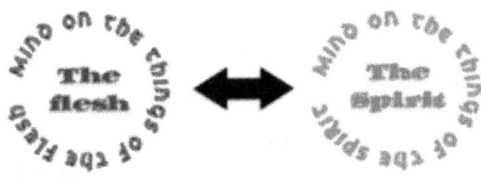

The Reasons We are Set Free
> ... in order that the requirement of the Law might be fulfilled in us, who do not walk according to the flesh, but according to the Spirit (Rom 8:4).

Christ satisfied the law's claim on our lives, and so the law, the principle or rule of the Spirit of life, takes control of our lives. We run by a different operating system or law now (cf. baptism 6:1-11; marriage 7:1-6). The phrase "In order that the requirement of the Law might be fulfilled in us" (4) includes the condemnation required by the penalty of death as well as the life of righteousness given in the life of Christ.

For us to commune with God, we need to walk uprightly. This cannot be done on our own as was demonstrated through Romans 1-3. God the Father required that Christ be born and die for us so that the curse of the law would fall upon Christ instead of us. This, in effect, brought us into the righteousness of Christ. We then walk in the fullness of the Spirit of God and are rescued us from our dominating flesh that was leading us to death.

The Great Escape
Notice the description of the flesh from Romans 8 upon us before physical death takes place–these are things we are now freed from:
- "The mind set on the flesh is death" (Rom 8:6).
- "The mind set on the flesh is hostile toward God" (Rom 8:7).
- "It does not subject itself to the law of God" (Rom 8:7).
- "It is not even able to subject itself to the law of God" (Rom 8:7).
- "Those who are in the flesh cannot please God" (Rom 8:8).

Death infiltrates each part of our lives. Paul is no longer stating that death just impacts all of our lives (and thus shows we are all sinners - Romans 3), but that it completely destroys any hope of gaining holiness and communion with God. Sin's power is in death. If a person sins, he will die, "... as sin reigned in death" (Rom 5:21).

Note the conditional aspect: "Who do not walk according to the flesh, but according to the Spirit" (Romans 8:4). Paul in this first phrase is not reflecting on those who might sin, but on the unregenerate who are given to sin. The second half of verse 4, "but according to the Spirit" (4), is similar to verse 1 "for those who are in Christ Jesus", depicting the specific atoning work of God in Christ for those who believe.

Not under obligation to the flesh!

These verses reveal the horrible state of our old nature and give us an idea as to why trying to live a good holy life on our own just does not work! Unless we gain new life in Christ and the Holy Spirit, we will not have what it takes to live a holy life.

By again establishing the just condemnation upon us, he accentuates the powerful and tyrannical nature of our flesh and why we all need to know Jesus Christ. What a great summary of what Paul means by spiritual deadness (Eph 2:1-3)!

Verses 4-6 describe the difference between those who receive the new spiritual nature and set their minds on the things "according to the Spirit" (4-5). Christ freed us from the arena of selfishness that results in death, and brings us into the hands of the Spirit's love, power, and life. "The mind set on the Spirit is life and peace" (6) reflects the new standard of love by which a person lives in contrast to the self-serving tendency that leads to death. While life is set in contrast to death, peace triumphs over the desperate fretful pursuit of our wants and needs.[39] The principle or rule of the Spirit of life takes over control of our lives. We run by a different operating system or law (in Christ, 5:12-21); alive in baptism (6:1-11); marriage (7:1-6)–death and subsequent life with new spouse.

Summary

---

[39] This peace differs from 5:1 where it speaks of our peace with God, having formerly been at enmity. This peace of heart results from the former, though both are true (5:3-4).

The condemnation of the flesh is obviously deserved when it's closely examined with the ways of God. The old nature's inherent hatred of the things of God is set in stark contrast to the new nature's beautiful love for the things of God. The old man does not fulfill the Law of God, not only because he is unable, but because he doesn't want to! This old nature will never change–even when we become a Christian.

Check yourself: Do you have a desire to please God? What is your life motive?

3. Freed for the Spirit (Rom 8:9-11)

> 9 However, you are not in the flesh but in the Spirit, if indeed the Spirit of God dwells in you. But if anyone does not have the Spirit of Christ, he does not belong to Him. 10 And if Christ is in you, though the body is dead because of sin, yet the spirit is alive because of righteousness. 11 But if the Spirit of Him who raised Jesus from the dead dwells in you, He who raised Christ Jesus from the dead will also give life to your mortal bodies through His Spirit who indwells you (Rom 8:9-11).

Paul does not allow us to focus on what a believer is freed from because dwelling on that will lead the believer into mediocrity. Instead, he leads us to focus on what we are saved from. This is where an appreciation of grace begins, we must understand and hold onto those things we were freed for! What does this "grace might reign through righteousness..." (Rom 5:21) look like?

"In the Spirit" (8:9) Paul first highlights our new position in Christ, "in the Spirit." God's people are connected to God through the Spirit-enabled network.[40] With the proper connection to God through Christ's work (8:1-4), we have access to all of God promises. This is in contrast to "in the flesh" where our self-seeking flesh controls.

The indwelling is referred to several times in this passage starting with "the Spirit of God dwells in you" (9; "given to us" 5:5). The Spirit of God mysteriously resides in believers (9-11). This is repeated in verse 11 and restated in verse 10 as "Christ in you." Though the temple concept is not stated as it is in other places (e.g. 1 Cor 3:16-17; 6:19; Eph 2:22), it certainly is implied and forms an important basic truth to help us understand the

---

[40] First joining an invisible wifi network for internet connection serves as a wonderful example how we can suddenly relate to God on a whole different sphere. The network existed before we believed, but faith in Christ enables us to join through the gospel.

characteristics of our new lives and what our relationship with other Christian believers should look like (later in Romans).

Verse 9 relates ownership to indwelling. It negatively speaks of those of the flesh not belonging, but from clear and anticipated inference, those having the Spirit of Christ do belong to, or are set apart for, Him. Freedom means free to serve the Lord. The old slavery is replaced with a new owner–the Spirit of God, who is not a cruel taskmaster but a liberator who freed us for the purpose of fulfilling God's wonderful plan for our lives.

The Spirit lives through us (10-11)! Both verses speak about how Christ through the Spirit enable us, though still in our earthly bodies (i.e. flesh), to live out the purposes of God. The original Greek does not differentiate 'spirit' from "Spirit" as the English versions do; the proper meaning must be discerned. Verse 10's "spirit is alive" could refer to the Spirit of God being alive and working in us or the "spirit is alive" meaning our spiritual nature is engaged and active. Probably the first is correct due to the clarification in verse 11. In other words, it is correct to think of our spiritual nature not as an impersonal force but as the Spirit of God working His purposes in us. We can communicate with Him.

"He... will also give life to your mortal bodies through His Spirit who indwells you" (11) speaks not only of new life, living in light of God's holy purposes, but also of the ongoing aspect of eternal life that will usher us into eternity. There is a holy repossession of our mortal bodies for God's holy purposes. It would, therefore, be wrong to conclude that we can live a spiritual life without living a holy life through all the daily life decisions that we make.

Christ satisfied the law's claim on our lives and so the law, the principle or rule of the Spirit of life takes control over our lives. We run by a greater program (law): by the Spirit.

Summary

Become convinced! Our evil nature is not just a little bad. Our sinful nature will always betray us. Don't ever trust it. But the Spirit of God? Yes, trust Him always. God is eager to teach us how to live in harmony with Him, just as Jesus lived. Our life is about choosing to live for the Lord and carrying out His principles by the direction and power of the Spirit.

B. Living by the Spirit (8:12-17)

Christ satisfied the law's claim on our lives and so the law, the principle or rule of the Spirit of life takes over control of our lives. Having escaped control of our flesh, we are now led by the Spirit of God as the children of God. We are not free to simply do anything, but are obligated to follow the Spirit of Jesus through the different means taught below.

1. Not Under Obligation (12)

> So then, brethren, we are under obligation, not to the flesh, to live according to the flesh... (8:12).

I don't have to!

What a liberating statement. We don't have to live by the flesh, our old nature. Do you get mean, upset, anxious, jealous, lustful? You don't have to live by those feelings and impulses. You might feel like you need to live by them. This is Satan's goal. He makes you feel as if you need to live by them so that you choose to serve those feelings. The key question is: Who do you choose to serve? Remember, you no longer have to serve the old nature if you are a genuine believer. Christian growth comes from faith that we do not need to live by the flesh. Without this confidence, we will give into our old desires.

Key = Clarifying who you serve

Application

By making a clear commitment and renewing that commitment on a daily basis (such as through meaningfully saying the Lord's prayer) we take a great leap forward in our Christian lives as we clarify who we serve.

2. Putting to Death (13)

> But if by the Spirit you are putting to death the deeds of the body... (8:13).

Out you go!

We should not be naive. We cannot flirt with sin and escape unharmed. The maturity of a believer depends on his spiritual disciplines like fasting, praying, and engaging in regular devotion to God's Word. It also depends on learning to say "no" to your anger, jealousies, and lusts. This is the important spiritual discipline of "putting to death the deeds of the body." Give your body a chance and it will stuff itself with too much food (glutton) or feed your mind with lustful thoughts (fornication/adultery). Spiritual disciplines, however, are those intentionally cultivated habits that help strengthen our focus and dependence on the Spirit of God so that we can more easily dismiss the bait that these old desires attempt to hook us with. We can simply choose not to carry them out. How awful our lives would be if we carried out all the things we thought! Praise God the Holy Spirit helps us.

Key = Active non-participation

Application
What spiritual disciplines do you participate in? Connect each spiritual discipline with how it might help you 'put to death the deeds of the body.'

3. Being led by the Spirit! (14)

> For all who are being led by the Spirit of God, these are sons of God (8:14).

Here I come!
Above, we focused on the spiritual discipline of "putting to death" but we can't stop there. We need to remember that we ought to be led by the Spirit. The Holy Spirit helps us discern evil, notice temptation, remind us what He wants, and brings God's Word to our minds. He is actively taking part in a believer's life. If we are not trained to notice how the Spirit moves and leads us (an important part of discipleship), we will be oblivious to His work.

Consciously talk to the Lord and seek His wisdom, faith, strength, and hope. Walking in the Spirit is one aspect of Christian living that very few believers have actually learned to do (also 6:4). The Spirit's work in us is real and so we need to observe how He works and go alongside Him. Jesus sets a great example for us.

Key = Taking conscious orders from the Spirit

Application
Examine a three day period for the times you consciously prayed or communed with the Spirit about what He wanted for your life, needs in people around you, etc. Make the necessary changes in your life.

4. Affirm Belonging and Purpose (15-17)

¹⁵ For you have not received a spirit of slavery leading to fear again, but you have received a spirit of adoption as sons by which we cry out, "Abba! Father!" ¹⁶ The Spirit Himself bears witness with our spirit that we are children of God, ¹⁷ and if children, heirs also, heirs of God and fellow heirs with Christ, if indeed we suffer with Him in order that we may also be glorified with Him (8:15-17).

I belong!

The evil one tries to persuade the believer that he is too evil to find forgiveness from the Lord. He attempts to undermine our confidence in our status as a child of God. This passage, however, reminds us of our heritage in Christ. We are God's children, and "have received a spirit of adoption as sons" (16). We are His forever!

We only have two options. We will either live in deceit, believing we are under the power of our sin (i.e. "spirit of slavery"), or we live by faith in the promises of God that are part of our heritage in Christ and will live out righteous lives by the Holy Spirit.

- Spirit of slavery > Fear
- Spirit of adoption > "Abba, Father!"

Key = Serve as a child

But Paul does more than remind us of our belonging and need of His Lordship. He plants in our minds the idea of our divine roles as "fellow heirs with Christ." As children, we focus on the fulfillment of our needs; this tendency will never disappear, but learning of our calling as fellow heirs, we are reminded that we are meant to grow up and take our part in the cultivation of the kingdom of God, even if it means suffering. This is all part of the process: suffering leads to glorification as exemplified through Christ's own life. Things are not "wrong" when we suffer, but right! God is with us just as He was with Jesus during His time of suffering. The Lord's promises does not mean avoidance of difficulties but grace to endure them for His glory.

Children > heirs > fellow-heirs with Christ

Believers, then, are to glory in their call to share as fellow-heirs with Christ for this hope leads them to a greater faith fostering a more complete obedience in His presence. This hope for the future creates a stronger faith in the present where God will tenderly and protectively care for them as His children. God will not abandon them but always, even in their desperate times, carefully watch over them and faithfully supply their needs.

Summary

Paul finally fills in what the Christian life should look like: deferring from our ever-present fleshly desires, and affirming the presence and leadership of the Holy Spirit in our lives. Nothing is as grand as the active "no" (to the flesh) and "yes" (to the Spirit), for therein lies our hope of actively serving with Christ so we can, at the proper time, share in His glory. Our service is not a meaningless set of rituals or avoidance of sin, but participation in Christ's holiness, work, and glory.

Romans 8:18-39

Conquerors Through Christ

Paul addresses God's children who live on the edge of two powerful worlds at tension with each other. The world at enmity with God is caught in the web of sin and death; God's redeemed people have by God's grace stepped into life and light (see Rom 5:1). One might think that God, having favored His children, would keep them from the evils of the world along with all of its suffering, but they too must persevere through this world in sin-tainted bodies. However, God does grant His people His Spirit and a special confidence that enables them to grow strong in their faith if the face of difficult times.

Perhaps Paul sensed an impending persecution against believers in Rome. In any case, the Roman Christians and other believers at various times in history including the presence have and do greatly suffer, and need to understand their experience in light of God's rich promises.

Understanding God's Greater Purposes of Suffering

We should not be surprised when God takes what is perfect and subjects it to a humble status so that a greater good might be accomplished. This is what He did with Christ's life. Take hope! The stage of suffering is merely a transitional period when God further refines us to work closer with Him.

Below we will discuss how the believer ought to deal with suffering (18-25), how the Spirit helps in that (26-27), the Lord's beautiful design (28-30), and God's proof of love (31-39). The Lord wants to give us a solid understanding of His care and comfort so that we know, in spite of what happens, that nothing can go perfectly wrong and that everything will work out for His glory in the end.

A. The Christian Faces Suffering (Rom 8:18-25)

> ¹⁸ For I consider that the sufferings of this present time are not worthy to be compared with the glory that is to be revealed to us. ¹⁹ For the anxious longing of the creation waits eagerly for the revealing of the sons of God. ²⁰ For the creation was subjected to futility, not of its own will, but because of Him who subjected it, in hope ²¹ that the creation itself also will be set free from its slavery to corruption into the freedom of the glory of the children of God. ²² For we know that the whole creation groans and suffers the pains of childbirth together until now. ²³ And not only this, but also we ourselves, having the first fruits of the Spirit, even we ourselves groan within ourselves, waiting eagerly for our adoption as sons, the redemption of our body. ²⁴ For in hope we have been saved, but hope that is seen is not hope; for why does one also hope for what he sees? ²⁵ But if we hope for what we do not see, with perseverance we wait eagerly for it (Rom 8:18-25).

In Romans 8:18-25 we learn that the Christian will likely face difficult situations. This pattern is very clearly set in verses 17-18. Romans 8:17 starts by connecting suffering with glorification. "...If indeed we suffer with Him in order that we may also be glorified with Him" (Rom 8:17). Along with the freedom of a new life comes a transitional period into this life. Verse 21 and 23 carefully explain this:

> The creation itself also will be set free from its slavery to corruption into the freedom of the glory of the children of God (8:21).

> But also we ourselves, having the first fruits of the Spirit, even we ourselves groan within ourselves, waiting eagerly for our adoption as sons, the redemption of our body (8:23).

		PARALLEL EXPERIENCES	
Romans 8:19-22	The creation suffers & waits glorification.		God's children suffer & wait glorification.
Romans 8:23-25	Jesus suffered & was glorified.		God's children suffer & will be glorified.

There is a parallel experience going on between the creation and the children of God, and Jesus and our lives, though the later is mentioned in different places (8:17 and 32). Both are pictures of how God will work out splendid things in the lives of the believers. There are many promises that have not yet been seen: the glory of creation (the creation groans), Christ's glorious rule (injustice seems to rule), our resurrected and glorified bodies (our bodies get sick and die). Though we face distress in life, the ultimate plan of freedom is coming. Although we are the Lord's, we are still affected by the sin-stained world. As Christians, we are caught in the frailty of our human bodies and creation. Our bodies have not experienced redemption even though our souls have. Our real potential is hidden behind the weakness of our human bodies.

Theological perspective

Great doctrinal passages such as this one are not 'cold' theological treatments, but deliberate instructions designed to provide relevant truths that enable God's people to powerfully live out peaceful and loving Christian lives in a tumultuous world.

We should remember that man brought sin into the world, not God. Because of God's abundant grace, Jesus suffered alongside God's creation. If man did not sin, then both the creation and Christ would not have suffered at all. Despite man's foolishness, God has chosen, in His amazing grace (He did not have to), to bring forth good out of evil. This brings a great sense of relief and joy to the hearts of His people.

> For He has not despised nor abhorred the affliction of the afflicted; Neither has He hidden His face from him; But when he cried to Him for help, He heard (Ps 22:24).

> The afflicted shall eat and be satisfied; Those who seek Him will praise the LORD. Let your heart live forever! (Ps 22:26)

Bottom Line

Trials are to be expected. Suffering is part of this life. We are to keep our faith and strengthen our trust in Him during these times of trials because we can trust that God will create a greater good out of the many sad events on earth (e.g. beheadings of Christian believers). How great to know that everything will work out for His glory in the end!

Romans 8:28

We will go on and learn more about the place of suffering in the lives of His people and the creation in general through the rest of chapter 8. This path leads us to some of the most powerful redemptive verses in the scriptures.

B. Three Questions on Suffering (Rom 8:26-39)

By understanding how God's truth applies to questions of suffering, we can prepare ourselves for times of suffering, distress, and persecution, whether our own or others. Note below the three ways Satan instigates doubt in our minds and how, if we are off our guard, he can throw us into despair and depression.

- Can I make it through? (Rom 8:26-27)

    Satan's voice: "You can't make it!" "He's left you alone!" "You may as well give up."

- Is God really in control? (Rom 8:28-30)

    Satan's voice: "God is not doing a very good job taking care of things is He? He doesn't involve Himself in such matters."

- Does He really love me? (Rom 8:31-39)

    Satan's voice: "If He really loved you, He wouldn't have you go through these things."

Paul instructs us on three ways the Lord helps us cope with sufferings. By obtaining a firm grasp on the truth, we will be able to counter Satan's lies and embrace God's wonderful promises.

- Strength: The Lord understands us and helps us pray through the Spirit.
- Confidence: The Lord works out everything for our (His people's) good.
- Love: The Lord has assured us nothing can separate us from His love in Christ.

1. The Spirit Helps Us in Our Weakness (Rom 8:26-27)

> ²⁶ And in the same way the Spirit also helps our weakness; for we do not know how to pray as we should, but the Spirit Himself intercedes for us with groanings too deep for words; ²⁷ and He who searches the hearts knows what the mind of the Spirit is, because He intercedes for the saints according to the will of God" (Rom 8:26-27).

In the former section we were first shown that the creation groans (22), then how we, through the Holy Spirit, express deep groans awaiting the promise of the new world, and lastly, how the Spirit helps us during our weaknesses

Romans 8:18-39 Conquerors Through Christ

through prayerful groanings (23). At times, our situations are so oppressive, our minds so confused, that we do not know how to pray for ourselves.

The Spirit of God comes to help us by interceding on our behalf. This is not the words of a tongue-speaking Christian but the groanings or sighs–no words that compose a sentence, that come from our deep inner spirit. People who have experienced crises understand this. These groaning are the cries of the distressed. The Spirit asks God the Father what needs to be asked as He is well-acquainted with our difficult circumstances. Here are some principles we can draw from this.

- God completely understands our distressing situations.
- We are limited even in our prayer life. We need His help.
- The Spirit intercedes for us according to God's will, that which is good and perfect (Rom 12:2).

We must not undermine the way the Spirit helps us pray. He will only pray according to the will of God for He knows what the will of God is. It is during times of distress that we often become very subjective and need this kind of clarification, confidence, and inner strength. For this reason we need to make sure our lives are clear from sin and doubt.

> *Strength through Spirit's understanding and help*

Once, during an extreme testing, I was very worried about having sufficient financial resources for a mission trip. Worry overcame me so that I could not even prepare for the trip. I did, however, persevere in seeking God for help. He heard. The Lord first brought peace and faith to me by bringing to my mind two special scriptures. This enabled me to break out of my anxiety, find His peace, and patiently watch Him provide for the mission trip.

Reflections through Questions
- What does He pray?
- Who does He help pray?
- How does He affect our prayers?

Let us gain the strength the Lord wants to give us during these times through the knowledge of the Spirit's intercession for us.

2. The Lord Designs Things for Our Good (Rom 8:28-30)

> ²⁸ And we know that God causes all things to work together for good to those who love God, to those who are called according to His purpose. ²⁹ For whom He foreknew, He also predestined to become conformed to the image of His Son, that He might be the first-born among many brethren; ³⁰ and whom He predestined, these He also called; and whom He called, these He also justified; and whom He justified, these He also glorified (8:28-30).

Romans 8:28, along with the former verses on adoption and calling, all become our spiritual backbone. The truths in this verses are incredible! God can and will work out all things for a greater good. No matter what sickness, shortness of life, poverty, persecution, difficulty in life, family rejection, or even horrible physical features we might have, we can fully trust God to bring about a greater good. In other words, the trials in His wise providence are designed to accomplish His greater purpose.

God began a great work in each of us before the creation of the world, but He also has continued to work it out until our full glorification.

Before creation	CREATION	Life on earth	CHRIST'S RETURN	Glorification
Plan designed		Plan initiated		Plan realized

- His design for our lives confirms His full involvement (Eph 1:4).
- His plan assures us that He perfectly oversees all that happens in our lives.
- His design reminds us of His great work already done on our behalf.
- His plan reminds us of our goal.

What a comfort, knowing that nothing can go wrong! His ways are personal, powerful, prepared, and purposeful. "And we know that God causes all things to work together for good to those who love God, to those who are called according to His purpose" (28).

Personal ~ Powerful ~ Prepared ~ Purposeful

The Overall Design of Our Salvation (Rom 8:29-30)

The power of these verses is seen in the way that individual events are connected to others in the overall scheme of redemption. The whole eternal redemptive plan is set before us. Everything must fit into this eternal plan. Sure, we might misunderstand or even disagree with the way God says He intervenes in the salvation of man, but we should instead focus on the fact that through His mercy we are saved.

'**Foreknew**' does not mean that God knows your choices ahead of time, including your choice to believe in Christ, and so chooses you. That thinking is based on works and depends on a heart to seek Him, which is quite contrary to the facts. "There is none who seeks for God" (3:11). Foreknew (see Rom 11:2; 1 Pe 1:2) instead is to be understood in light of the use of 'know' as in Gen 18:19; Jer 1:5; and Am 3:2. Ziesler says the 'fore' not only shows that God's choice preceded the knowledge of it by the Christian but also shows that it was done before the world was created (see Eph 1:4, 2; 2 Ti 1:9).[41]

Predestination is quite the opposite to fatalism since God, quite involved in the lives of His people, delights to graciously help many (not a few) escape their sin. Though often maligned, God is most merciful and compassionate. The word 'predestined' is used six times in the scriptures: Ac 4:28; Rom 8:29, 8:30; 1 Co 2:7; Ep 1:5, 1:11.

> Whom He **foreknew**
> He also **predestined**
> These He also **called**
> These he also **justified**
> These He also **glorified**

'**Called**' is the specific way God draws His people to Himself. While many associate calling with direction and God's will, it is largely confined in scripture to the way the Lord saves people and calls them to serve Him. "For many are called, but few are chosen" (Mt 22:14). "And it was for this He called you through our gospel" (2 Th 2:14).

'**Justified**' is the special way God, through our faith in Christ, has declared us righteous and restored us with Him. Chapters 3-4 addressed this topic of justification and gaining righteousness.

---

[41] *Paul's Letter to the Romans* by John Ziesler.

'Glorified' is the special eternal state genuine believers will experience in God's presence carrying out His will. Although not fully realized in our lives while on earth, it is written in the past tense as it is being done.

Events in our lives do not happen by accident. God's thread of grace in Christ weaves through the history of man forming it into a grand redemptive masterpiece. This undeniable design is seen in our salvation, in Christ's sacrifice, and in the daily experiences of the saints. If one of these aspects are true of us, they all are.

Predestination is not associated with a select few, but a great many and presents before us a most merciful, involved, and compassionate God.

---

3. The Lord Proves His Love for us (Rom 8:31-39)

When God sent His Son, He did not choose another person like Job, but volunteered Himself to suffer and die. Since He did not spare His own Son but gave Him up, will He not freely give us all things? We should have every confidence that God is working on our behalf and if this is so, then there is no enemy that is able to threaten us.

> *Security through Christ's sacrificial help*

Three questions and answers found in the passage further develop our understanding of the depth and power of God's love toward His people in Christ.

- Who will bring a charge against us (33)?
  God made us righteous!

- Who will condemn us (34)? Christ was condemned for us!

- Who can separate us from Christ (35)? Nothing, nowhere, never!

Being helped in our weakness is a great comfort, but more needs to be said. God has so designed all things that all things work together for good to those who love God and are called according to His purpose.

a) The Providence of His Son (Rom 8:31-34)

> 31 What then shall we say to these things? If God is for us, who is against us? 32 He who did not spare His own Son, but delivered Him up for us all, how will He not also with Him freely give us all things? 33 Who will bring a charge against God's elect? God is the one who

justifies; ³⁴ who is the one who condemns? Christ Jesus is He who died, yes, rather who was raised, who is at the right hand of God, who also intercedes for us (8:31-34).

The presence of suffering among His people is not because God does not love us, nor is it because He is weak. The fact that His only Son suffered for sinners clearly testifies to God's greater design. He loved us and therefore sent His Son. By His power, Christ and His people are raised.

If suffering brought Him or us completely down, then we could see the rationale behind those who complain about God's toleration of evil in this world. But when God chose to place that tree in the middle of the garden, He demonstrated that He, too, was willing to suffer, if that was what it would take to bring about a people who loved Him and could share His glory. If we stood condemned and Jesus laid still in the grave, then perhaps we would see God's limited power, but we do not see that. Christ is alive and now intercedes for us! Evidence of His love and perfect power resounds in our lives. How special it is that we see Paul echoing the Old Testament prophecy of the Messiah here in these verses:

> ¹¹ As a result of the anguish of His soul, He will see it and be satisfied; By His knowledge the Righteous One, My Servant, will justify the many, As He will bear their iniquities. ¹² Therefore, I will allot Him a portion with the great, And He will divide the booty with the many; Because He poured out Himself to death, And was numbered with the transgressors; Yet He Himself bore the sin of many, And interceded for the transgressors (Is 53:11-12).

He did not spare His own Son (the agony of the Messiah).

He delivered Him up for us all (poured out Himself to death).

God is the One who justifies (will justify the many).

He will freely distribute good things to them (divide the booty, 53:12).

Who also intercedes for us (And interceded for the transgressors).

When we begin to realize that this saving Servant from the Old Testament is the same as God's own Son who came from heaven, we then further discover the great depth of God's love for us.

b) The Testimony of the Saints (Rom 8:35-39)

Paul asks a third question in verse 35 and provides an answer. Paul is so confident of the Lord's overriding love that he boldly parades God's powerful protection before his most threatening enemies. The point is that if God's power and love is sufficient for these, then there is no real threat of separation from the love of Christ. Paul formulates two lists: The first list outlines typical threats made to the lives of God's people while the second list includes intangible threats.

(1) Temporal threats (35-37): tribulation, distress, persecution, famine, nakedness, peril, sword.

(2) Intangible threats (38-39): Nothing can or will separate us from the love of God which is in Christ Jesus!

First List of Enemies (Rom 8:35-37)

> 35 Who shall separate us from the love of Christ? Shall tribulation, or distress, or persecution, or famine, or nakedness, or peril, or sword? 36 Just as it is written, "For Thy sake we are being put to death all day long; we were considered as sheep to be slaughtered." 37 But in all these things we overwhelmingly conquer through Him who loved us (Rom 8:35-37).

The first list outlines typical threats made to the lives of God's people. Paul initiates this list with a general "Who shall separate us from the love of Christ?" and specifically identifies many troubles that believers face across time and space. Satan would want us to conclude that a God who loved us would not allow His people to suffer such things, but the apostle states quite the contrary: God carefully watches over His children through perilous times and good.

- Tribulation: general afflictions against God's people
- Distress: inner emotional troubles (e.g. a raped child)
- Persecution: outward oppression brings many kinds of suffering
- Famine: hunger, lack of food
- Nakedness: lack of proper clothing whether due to poverty or oppression
- Peril: includes many kinds of dangers such as thieves and storms
- Sword: where death is threatened either by individuals or movements

> **"A single word covers oceans of dangers and reveals to us all the evils which people encounter in life."** – **Chrysostom**[42]

---

[42] *Ancient Christian Commentary on Scripture*, Vol VI, (IVP) p. 241.

Who dares face such terrible things? We do. We are victors in Christ. Verse 36 is a quotation from Ps 44:22 and was used in reference to the death of the martyrs for Judaism in II Maccabees 7.[43]

> **"But for Thy sake we are killed all day long; We are considered as sheep to be slaughtered" (Ps 44:22).**

Second List of Enemies (Rom 8:38-39)

> 38 For I am convinced that neither death, nor life, nor angels, nor principalities, nor things present, nor things to come, nor powers, 39 nor height, nor depth, nor any other created thing, shall be able to separate us from the love of God, which is in Christ Jesus our Lord (Rom 8:38-39).

The second list focuses on general threats. Paul establishes that there is absolutely nothing that can separate God's people from His love when he crosses over into the intangible, uncontrollable, and unknowable areas such as: death, the future, the spiritual world, and powers. Note the four sets of opposites: death and life; angels and principalities; things present and things to come; and height and depth (see diagram). Surely each of these things reflect the vulnerabilities of human beings as they cannot even see the enemy, let alone know how to fight apart from Christ.

SECOND LIST OF ENEMIES

DEATH>	<LIFE
ANGELS>	<PRINCIPALITIES
POWERS	
THINGS PRESENT>	<THINGS TO COME
HEIGHT>	<DEPTH
ANY OTHER CREATED THING	

God's love forever clings to us by what He did in Christ Jesus our Lord in His death and resurrection. Each of our lives showcases, in one or more

---

[43] Ibid, p. 230.

ways, how God graciously delivers us from such evil. From this side of life, Christ's resurrection and the experiences of His people through the ages provide abundant historical proof that what these scriptures say is totally trustworthy. The glorious resonance found in these verses comes from Paul's vibrant faith acquired through his deep association with these sufferings (1 Cor 11:23-30). The future, with the brilliance of Christ's full glory and unreserved splendor, will soon settle any remaining dust of doubts.

Summary

God's love is made manifest through His Son's suffering in our place. His power is shown in the way He lifts us up from dire circumstances. God's Word and love should sufficiently shape our perspectives so that we too overwhelmingly conquer in Christ. We need to allow God's truth "in Christ Jesus the Lord" to wholly bind our hearts and minds to Him in His love and peace (cf. 6:23; 7:25; 8:39). Even when suffering knocks on our door, we can fully trust that His love is there too, and in fact is even greater than our suffering. He will keep us to the end to fully witness and share His glory!

Election and Predestination

Understanding and Appreciating Romans 8:29-30

Romans 8:29-30

> ²⁸ And we know that God causes all things to work together for good to those who love God, to those who are called according to His purpose. ²⁹ For whom He foreknew, He also predestined to become conformed to the image of His Son, that He might be the first-born among many brethren; ³⁰ and whom He predestined, these He also called; and whom He called, these He also justified; and whom He justified, these He also glorified (8:28-30).

Many people have problems with the doctrines of election and predestination. The apostle's hope is for this teaching to strengthen rather than confuse our faith.

The reason that many believers have a problem with election and predestination is because of ignorance and misunderstandings rooted in distortion. These distortions are hard to unravel. Let me share how, over these many years, I have come to understand these teachings.

First, we should accept the clear fact that God predestines believers (Rom 8:29-30). Denial of this teaching is not acceptable and excludes God's people from an avenue to better understanding God's glorious and marvelous ways. We can admit we do not know what predestination or election means (though we should learn), and that we do not understand its implications (which admittedly are more difficult), but we should be careful not to twist its meaning so to suggest that God does not predestine His people. That is arrogance.

Second, predestination is associated with blessing to God's people. This is the reason Paul so openly teaches it here to comfort His people. It is not a teaching to argue with unbelievers! The apostle is not ashamed of this teaching; neither should we. Paul positively presents it to strengthen our faith. Arguments that do not build up our faith but tear us from our focus on God's truth should be avoided. An example of this is when believers ask if the teaching of predestination means that the Lord also predestines the lost to perish. This is not what is taught here in Romans 8:29-30. We should allow the scripture to provide its own teaching before carefully extending the logic of what has been clearly taught.

Third, if we feel somewhat repelled by the teaching of predestination, it is because it goes against the pride and self-confidence of man. We are easily taken up with arguments against it rather than in reveling in its truth. God has encouraged and helped me in my own Christian life through meditation on the fact that He chose me and absolutely and unconditionally loves me. While I might doubt whether others love me, whether past or present, it doesn't ultimately matter because God my Creator chose to save and love me. His love is sufficient for whatever I shall face. Shall we let arguments distract us from the glory of this truth? No. Refuse them and focus on what is said. Let the truth of God build up your faith!

Remember that our goals are higher than being competent in the presentation of these truths. We need to so shape our hearts and minds so that these truths powerfully shape our lives. Six words or phrases will be explained and defined here in hopes that clear definition will eliminate argument and accentuate our delight in God's plan for us.

1. God's Grace

We are sinners and do not deserve the grace of God. Grace by definition means we are not entitled to His goodness. We should not assume God should or will be gracious to all–that would deny the essence of grace. We are all sinners and due to our rebellion, we deserve no goodness from God; only judgment ("For as through the one man's disobedience the many were made sinners" Rom 5:19).

The false assumption that God needs to be gracious to all is a foundational misunderstanding based on a poor understanding of God's love (though many claim to understand God's love). Salvation is based on God's love for His people. God's love does not mean that He will save all. His general love is seen through His general patience with sinful creatures while He constantly reveals His eternal and divine power to them (Rom 1:18-20).

2. God is Just

We are not really asking for the right thing when we question whether God is 'fair'. The question is based on the assumption that God is not just. God is absolutely righteous. He cannot be unjust. God judges all 'without partiality' (Rom 2:11: "For there is no partiality with God"). Fair should mean that the Lord will treat us as we should be treated. Since we are sinful and rebellious creatures (Rom 3:9-20), the only fairness we deserve is judgment.

Instead of asking for fairness, we should ask for mercy and grace!

A plea for fairness means that we are demanding that God carry out our guilty sentences right away! Notice how in Romans 10:22 it says that God patiently endures vessels of wrath. Instead of carrying out His wrath immediately, God restrains His wrath and, according to his predetermined (i.e. predestined) plan, put His Son to death on the cross (Acts 2:22-24) to save those that would believe. God did not overlook His people's sin. A full payment was paid through the death of Christ for sin. Was God being unfair to treat His people like this? Definitely not. He was being wonderfully gracious! This is an awesome God that we should excitingly declare to others.

3. Man's Choices

Many believers are convinced that man ought to have a choice. This popular teaching has become a stumbling block to many. If God allowed our choice to determine our future, we would all choose to rebel against God (and this is what we did do in Adam and otherwise). By insisting on our privilege of choice, we would exclude ourselves from God's kind, saving work.

Remember Romans 8:5? "For those who are according to the flesh set their minds on the things of the flesh." If we had our way, our choices would, every time, condemn us to eternal judgment. I much prefer God's gracious intervention in my life than the so-called freedom of 'free choice.' This plan revealed in Romans 8:28-30 is God's intervention plan, also called salvation. Does the man in perilous circumstances tell the rescuers to go away? No. He thanks them for their help. The firemen raise a ladder to a man on a ledge of a burning building. The man on the ledge did not ask for help. He did not bargain with them that he would give them one million dollars if they would come; he could not demand help. They risked their lives to save him. We should be overwhelmed with thankfulness for how God saved us. So, what about free will? We exercised it and sinned and face condemnation.

4. God's Eternal Plan

Our salvation is wrapped up in the eternal plan and purpose of God. It is something that is done even before we are conceived. This is the powerful teaching of the comprehensive redemptive plan set before us in Rom 8:29-30. Before we were born, God foreknew us. The word foreknew could be translated chosen. There is a bit of misunderstanding over this word. The four verses that speak of God foreknowing as a verb (Rom 8:29, 11:2, 1 Pe 1:2, 20) all speak of foreknowing persons, either God's people or Christ. The verses say nothing about foreknowing the good works that we would do or of the foreknowledge of our decision to choose Jesus Christ to save us.

The meaning of the relevant verses (Rom 8:29, 11:2, 1 Pe 1:2) is rooted in prior acquaintance. The word is closely connected to the action 'to chose' or 'to elect'. In the Old Testament the word 'to know' is used to intimately know someone, and includes sexual intimacies. If we would separate 'to know' from 'to choose' perhaps we could say that 'foreknow' describes the depth of commitment and intimacy while 'choose' focuses on the aspect of decision. We use the phrase 'get to know' someone, but God did it before we were born. The timing part is hard to explain. Think of this phrase 'for whom He foreknew' (Rom 8:29) as God's inner commitment to take a person as His own. Does anyone blame a man for putting his affection, care, and wealth upon a certain woman, namely his wife? No. Choice reveals commitment.

If God's choice of us was dependent upon on our good works or our own decision to follow Him, then salvation would be dependent upon man's effort. But as students of the Book of Romans, we already have been convinced that "there is none who does good" (Rom 3:12) and "there is none who seek God" (Rom 3:9). We have no good works nor do we have the desire to choose God. Without God choosing us, we simply would not and could not follow Him. We therefore humbly welcome His gracious choice of us secured in Christ. God the Father chose us, the redeemed through the ages across all continents, to be His Son's bride. Our future, then is bound up in serving our Bridegroom while He oversees our needs, comfort and protection. What a wonderful plan!

5. Our Representative

The apostle has argued that our salvation is bound up in Christ. In Ephesians 1:4, he writes, "just as He chose us in Him before the foundation of the world, that we should be holy and blameless before Him in love." Romans 5:12-21 addresses this in a more comprehensive way: "Much more those who receive the abundance of grace and of the gift of righteousness will reign in life through the One, Jesus Christ" (Rom 5:17).

Jesus Christ is our true representative for salvation. If we are hidden in Christ, then we have hope. If we are apart from Christ, we have no hope. Although we tend to think of being in Christ only for justification (i.e. being set from our condemnation), it is better understood that we are hidden in Christ through the salvation process for eternity just as Romans 8:29-30 teaches. Being in Christ is a constant and needed state for the believer as Christ is our Mediator.

6. Predestination

Predestination is used six times in the scriptures, all in the New Testament (Ac 4:28, Rom 8:29, Rom 8:30, 1 Co 2:7, Eph 1:5, Eph 1:11). The Greek word *'proorizo'* can be translated as decreed, predestined, foreordain, decided beforehand, or destined. Different translations use different English words, but they are all one in the same Greek word. Let us think through what Romans 8:29-30 says.

What did the Lord predestine? The Lord predestined His people with the clear purpose of conforming us to His image and so share in His family (among many brethren). Is this not a good and gracious act? Could we ever reach this position without God's help? Never. Neither should we associate predestination with a negative connotation since it represents one of God's highest purposes for us.

I know we tend to ask other questions about predestination, such as why He does not predestine everyone, or whether predestination also means He predestined others to damnation. These are not the questions Paul is posing here. Again, go back to the truth about God not being obligated to save any. He is only obligated to judge us. Romans 8:29-30 reminds us that salvation is not just what happens at an evangelical service, but is one part of an eternal comprehensive process.

Think again of a man marrying a woman. He decides to marry her. He thinks about her (i.e. foreknew) and sets His heart to marry her (predestine) by making arrangements with her parents. In time He reveals his choice (i.e. called) and shares with her the arrangements (i.e. justifies). He has already discussed the proposal with her parents and arranged it all. When she hears of it, she is overwhelmed.

What woman would refuse being married to such a person? She is greatly moved and responds in her heart with great warmth and anticipation (i.e. 'being born again'). She is so thankful that he has taken care of the dowry (the cost: He died for us) and other marriage issues and awaits for the full realization (i.e. glorification).

We focus on the time she 'hears the offer and responds' (modern evangelicalism). We Westernize the whole notion of choice by insisting on personal decisions as against prearranged marriage. These modern concepts sterilize the gospel.

When we see the breadth of the redemptive process, we are humbled at His selection of us and respond with glee. I have been chosen! I will be His! (If we are not yet saved, then we should seek it with all our heart!) Justification speaks of the hidden price that needs to be paid to secure us (Heb 2:14). We had to be bought with a price (i.e. redemption).

Some will bring up other passages that speak of contrary perspectives. These should be studied, but they must be studied in their context. Don't allow a verse here or there cloud the clarity and force of this extended Romans' passage. Romans 8:29-30 reveals God's comprehensive salvation plan, blending many precious truths together. The use of predestination here is in full context, and we must allow that to shape our thoughts and beliefs. If we find contrary verses, we should be honest enough to say that it appears to be contrary while still trying to find a resolution. It is wholly inappropriate to allow a few scattered verses usurp the perspective so clearly spoken of here in Romans 8. Let me provide one example.

Some will support a contrary opinion from 2 Peter 3:9, "The Lord is not slow about His promise, as some count slowness, but is patient toward you, not wishing for any to perish but for all to come to repentance." They state that God does not wish for any to perish. From this, they extract with a few other previously mentioned assumptions that God wills to save all and so conclude that predestination (where God only chooses to save some) is either a wrong teaching, a teaching of a mean God, or something totally different from what is presented in Romans. They are willing to set aside the clear meaning of Romans 8:29-30 and the teaching of election and predestination of some so that they can believe that a loving God wants to (and perhaps will) save all. They might insist, "Since God is all-powerful, then in His love He will save all." This conclusion is premature. We should cease taking what is unclear to support what we want to be said. How should we accept 2 Peter 3:9 then?

First, we should, as necessary, be willing to say, "I do not know how it fits together with the other passages." As humble students, we should ask the Lord to teach us what it means. Understanding takes time and further study.

Second, we should see that this verse certainly does not mean that God will save all since in the following verses He speaks of judgment. So whatever it does mean, it does not mean that God will be save everyone.

Third, we notice that Peter is speaking of God's general call to all mankind to repent (as opposed to the salvation call in Romans 8:30). Just as the Lord in Romans 1 is daily using creation to witness to His glory and power, so He is patiently putting off judgment.

Man chose to rebel. God is calling man to turn from his rebellious ways through the many verses that speak about God's patience and reluctance to judge.

And should I not have compassion on Nineveh, the great city in which there are more than 120,000 persons who do not know the difference between their right and left hand, as well as many animals (Jonah 4:11)?

Summary

There are other verses used to counter election and predestination, but there are adequate explanations for each one. The real problem is the assumptions that one holds to when using these verses to counter the clear and comprehensive teaching in Romans 8:28-30. Paul wants us to take full joy in the redemptive program of the Lord.

If we are disciples of Christ, then let us have His Word shape us rather than using our erroneous assumptions to shape our interpretations of His Word. There is a glorious hope for His people to look forward to. Christ has already died and come alive. The redemptive salvation plan is in operation with the past works already accomplished and the present being fulfilled right now. The full realization of the glory of God is soon to be revealed so we can endure hardship and be confident that this all is part of God's glorious and wonderful plan. We might not see it clearly now, but we should be sure of it.

Romans 9:1-13

Great Hope for True Israel

Paul makes an abrupt change of topic starting in chapter 9:1 that continues to the end of chapter 11. Paul appears to pick up a loose end from verse 8:1 with those who question God's faithfulness to the Jews (or perhaps 3:3). The fact that those in Christ will escape condemnation is great, but what about those who do not believe in Jesus? What about the Jews who possessed the promises of the Christ? Would they be saved? This question has great application to the Jews but also to the professing believer, or the one who grow up in Christian families. Will those with God's Word be saved? Close association to God's promises and His people, however, do not save. Only faith in Jesus Christ can save. Paul dives into this discussion by affirming God's justice and faithfulness.

A. God is Just (Rom 9:1-5)

> 9:1 I am telling the truth in Christ, I am not lying, my conscience bearing me witness in the Holy Spirit, 2 that I have great sorrow and unceasing grief in my heart. 3 For I could wish that I myself were accursed, separated from Christ for the sake of my brethren, my kinsmen according to the flesh, 4 who are Israelites, to whom belongs the adoption as sons and the glory and the covenants and the giving of the Law and the temple service and the promises, 5 whose are the fathers, and from whom is the Christ according to the flesh, who is over all, God blessed forever. Amen.

God's condemnation appropriately comes upon all who are not in Christ, even if they have the promises of God. Implicit in Paul's description is the general waywardness of Israel–they are, as a whole, condemned. Paul weeps because he knows they are condemned for rejecting God's sent Savior the Christ. This judgment brought tears to Paul, but not because God was unjust in condemning his own people. Paul's willingness to be accursed for them is mentioned only because the Israelites as a whole were accursed. This is where we get acquainted with Paul's heartfelt compassion.

1. Paul's Sorrow (Rom 9:1-2)

Paul has "great sorrow" (2) because Israel did not recognize her Messiah (Christ) and now suffers condemnation. In verse 1 he repeatedly affirms his sincerity. He really did believe the chosen people were condemned! So many promises, prophesies, and symbolisms pointed to Jesus as the Messiah. What a glorious fulfillment it could be! But they rejected Him: "Crucify Him!"

This scene is like a dramatic movie where a long-separated mother and daughter, longing to eventually meet, happen to be at the same port but miss each other. The tragedy of Israel, as a nation, to miss Christ brought "great sorrow and unceasing grief" to Paul (2). This was a national tragedy. Israel missed its calling.

Paul's compassion made him willing to be accursed and separated from Christ for them–if indeed it would help, reminding us of Moses' plea for His people (Ex 32:31-33). The heart of Paul is seen by the way he sought yet another opportunity to present Christ to His people (Acts 22), even though it was prophesied, "The Jews at Jerusalem will bind the man who owns this belt and deliver into the hands of the Gentiles" (Acts 21:11). Paul answered the believers begging him not to go to Jerusalem, "What are you doing, weeping and breaking my heart? For I am ready not only to be bound, but even to die at Jerusalem for the name of the Lord Jesus" (Acts 21:13). The point behind the story here was not just Paul's willingness to die for them but that he was willing to die for his beloved people for just one more opportunity to preach to them, hoping that they might turn to Christ. Almost as a prophecy, the scene in Acts would soon lead to Paul's arrest and his being sent to Rome as a prisoner (Acts 21-27).

> **Moses' Intercession**
>
> 31 Then Moses returned to the LORD, and said, "Alas, this people has committed a great sin, and they have made a god of gold for themselves. 32 But now, if Thou wilt, forgive their sin--and if not, please blot me out from Thy book which Thou hast written!" 33 And the LORD said to Moses, "Whoever has sinned against Me, I will blot him out of My book" (Ex 32:31-33).

God clearly showed His favor to the Israelites. Despite their refusal to obey the Lord, God brought forth the Messiah, even Jesus (9:5). Along with this favored status, however, is responsibility. They were placed under the Old Covenant to be a bright light to the nations, but they rejected God's purposes for them. Paul itemizes many ways God favored Israel (also see 3:1-3).

- Adoption as sons (Probably refers to this redemption event: "Sanctify to Me every first-born… it belongs to Me" –Ex 13:1-2). The scriptural understanding of "sons", however, remains somewhat mysterious as the phrase "His people" could imply sonship but it also could refer to slaves.
- Glory (glory of God's presence and Word)
- Covenants (e.g. Abrahamic, Mosaic)
- Giving of the Law (revealed in the Pentateuch)
- Temple service (the temple was in Jerusalem)
- Promises (e.g. Can pray and find God's help–2 Chr 7:14 "If my people…")
- Fathers (The privilege of having ancestors like Abraham, Jacob, David in their lineage.)
- Christ according to the flesh (Christ is the long-awaited Messiah)

Responsibility accompanies this favored status of grace. They were placed under the Old Covenant to be a bright light to the nations, but they rejected God's purposes for them. Despite the Israelites' refusal to obey the Lord, God brought forth the Messiah, Jesus (9:5), providing even more evidence of God's faithfulness.

2. Two Powerful Theological Statements (Rom 9:5)

Two theological arguments are clarified in one verse, "Christ according to the flesh, who is over all, God blessed forever." This is a clear description of both Jesus Christ's humanhood and divinity.

- "Flesh" – Christ became human counters the incipient Gnostic cult, which denied that a holy God could closely associate with a body, having identified the body or flesh as evil. Hindu and Buddhist have similar misunderstandings, believing that the spiritual is good and holy in contrast to the flesh which is evil.
- "Who is over all, God" – Christ was God, and not just a subordinate of God – countered Arianism and Jehovah Witnesses who stress Jesus is the son of God and not God (denying His divine nature). This

teaching of Christ's deity is largely denied by our modern world, rejecting His governing principles and His love.

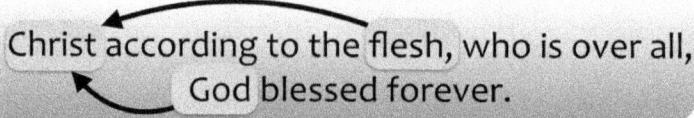

"It is clear from this passage that Christ is the God who is over all. The one who is over all has nothing over him, for Christ does not come after the Father but from the Father."[44] –Origen

B. God is Faithful (Rom 9:6-13)

God is faithful. God's Word did not fail.

⁶ But it is not as though the word of God has failed. For they are not all Israel who are descended from Israel; ⁷ neither are they all children because they are Abraham's descendants, but: "Through Isaac your descendants will be named." ⁸ That is, it is not the children of the flesh who are children of God, but the children of the promise are regarded as descendants. ⁹ For this is a word of promise: "At this time I will come, and Sarah shall have a son."¹⁰ And not only this, but there was Rebekah also, when she had conceived twins by one man, our father Isaac; ¹¹ for though the twins were not yet born, and had not done anything good or bad, in order that God's purpose according to His choice might stand, not because of works, but because of Him who calls, ¹² it was said to her, "The older will serve the younger. ¹³ Just as it is written, "Jacob I loved, but Esau I hated."

1. God is Faithful (Rom 9:6)

God is always faithful, even when His people do not believe. "Their unbelief will not nullify the faithfulness of God, will it?" (Romans 3:3). How can Paul say these wonderful things about God's faithfulness to His people in Romans 8 if God did not prove faithful to His people in the Old Testament? If He was not faithful, it might cast suspicion on God's faithfulness to His people now. God, however, is faithful.

Faithful to God's promises. "But it is not as though the word of God has failed. For they are not all Israel who are descended from Israel" (Rom 9:6). Paul carefully shows through the quotation of scriptures (see diagram) the

---

[44] Ancient Christian Commentary on Scripture, Vol VI, (IVP) p. 246.

way God faithfully carried out His promises to Isaac, Jacob, and his sons (Israel).

"Through Isaac your descendants will be named." God chose to give His blessing to Abraham through Isaac's descendants. Abraham had other children such as Ishmael through Hagar, but Hagar was not a child of promise. He had children later in life too (1 Chr 1:28-33), but it was through Isaac that the promised seed would be born.

"At this time I will come, and Sarah shall have a son." (Gen 18:10). The same time the angels came to destroy Sodom, they announced God's promise to Abram and Sarah.

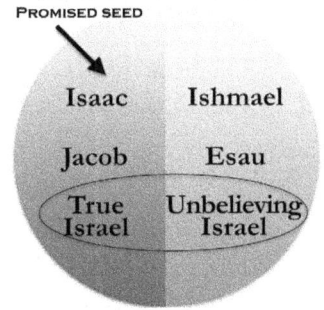

2. God is Selective (Rom 9:7-12)

Abraham had many descendants, but God chose to make a special covenant with Isaac's descendants rather than with all of Abraham's children. (This was difficult for Abraham to accept.) Other blessings, for example, would come to Abraham's other children, such as to Ishmael. He too would have many descendants. "And of the son of the maid I will make a nation also, because he is your descendant" (Gen 21:12-13), even from Isaac, He chose Jacob's descendants. Jesus Himself said, "I say to you that many will come from east and west, and recline at the table with Abraham, Isaac, and Jacob in the kingdom of heaven; but the sons of the kingdom will be cast out into the outer darkness; in that place there will be weeping and gnashing of teeth" (Mat 8:11-12).

Even before Isaac's twins were born, the LORD chose to bless (or love) Jacob rather than Esau. God did not choose people because of the good works that they would or could do; He chose them despite their bad works. Jacob's life of deceit testifies to this. Paul emphasizes this choice of God by quoting Malachi 1:2, "Just as it is written, 'Jacob I loved, but Esau I hated'" (Rom 9:13). Again this should convince us that we are not chosen because of our pious works, but simply because of God's gracious choice. His choice of us should humble us and cause us to delight in His awesome choice of us.

This discussion of God's choice will be discussed in greater length later on, but we need to understand some basic underlying assumptions, without which people might wrongly conclude that God shouldn't elect people.

- God has a sovereign right to do as He wishes.
- God's person defines holiness, justice, and righteousness; His works reveal them.
- Being fair would only leave us all unchosen, if indeed it was because of merit, because none of us seek God (Rom 3:9-18).
- A display of extra kindness and grace is not wrong but a choice and privilege.
- Assuming God has no higher purposes for not choosing everyone is rather arrogant.
- No one deserves God's choice. The clamor over unfairness should be shushed under the teaching that we all rightly deserve God's wrath.

Summary

Paul does not leave any loose arguments. His argument is clean. He does not give us the option of saying, "That is your interpretation. I believe God was not faithful to His promises to the Jews." Paul forcibly carries two arguments in these 13 verses. God is just and faithful.

Paul knew the questions that would arise upon his proper presentation of the truth of God. There are adequate answers and Paul explains them and is willing to take slight detours so not to altogether lose the opportunity of communicating these great truths of God. However, with regards to the situation with Israel, God is proven as faithful.

Romans 9:14-22

Questions About God's Elect

Questions regarding God's justice and fairness continue to the present day. Paul faced them too. In one sense, this is fortunate because we gain Paul's capable defense, if God indeed needs any. Paul brings up the objection right from the start.

A. God's Mercy and Justice (Rom 9:14-18)

14 What shall we say then? There is no injustice with God, is there? May it never be! 15 For He says to Moses, "I will have mercy on whom I have mercy, and I will have compassion on whom I have compassion." 16 So then it does not depend on the man who wills or the man who runs, but on God who has mercy. 17 For the Scripture says to Pharaoh, "For this very purpose I raised you up, to demonstrate My power in you, and that My Name might be proclaimed throughout the whole earth." 18 So then He has mercy on whom He desires, and He hardens whom He desires (Rom 9:14-18).

It is simply impossible that God would be unjust–even for a minute. He might look as if He is unjust, but that is simply not the case. Do not even start questioning God's justice. Be honest. We might not quite understand His whole plan, and we might misunderstand parts of it. God, however, is just. The Lord defines Himself as full of compassion and just (c.f. Ex 34:6-7). To allege God is any different from what He reveals Himself to be shows a problem in our understanding of His glorious person.

Why does man so quickly react against God's free choice? If we deny God's freedom to choose to bless certain people, then we are in fact denying the core of the gospel. We are saved by God's grace, not through our works. Paul defends God's prerogative of election and grace by selecting numerous cases wherein God had earlier stated His choice.

In the prior verse (9:13), He spoke of Isaac's son Jacob. "Jacob I loved, but Esau I hated." There are a number of commentators who wish to replace "loved" with "loved less" and "hated" with "not loved so much." This undermines God's point. He chose to pour out His blessing and love upon Jacob rather than upon Esau. God's wrath would too have rested on Jacob had the Lord not elected to love him and his descendants.

In verse 9:15, Paul highlights God's privilege to choose to bless whom He wishes. "I will have mercy on whom I have mercy, and I will have compassion on whom I have compassion." This was spoken to Moses after he asked to see God's glory (Ex 33:18-23). God's statement might be otherwise written, "I am God and I can do what I want! If I choose to be merciful to someone, then I will be merciful to them."

Man is very unwilling to listen to such statements, "It does not depend upon the man who wills or runs." This is especially true of modern man who is clothed in the religion of humanism. Man insists on boasting in his own choice, blindly thinking he can control his future, even if it includes the manipulation of God or gods to accomplish what he desires. At this point Paul quotes again from the Old Testament, this time with words to Pharaoh.

> For this very purpose I raised you up, to demonstrate my power in you, and that My Name might be proclaimed throughout the whole earth (17).

God can harden as well as soften hearts. In the case of Pharaoh, the Lord hardened Pharaoh's heart to exalt Himself and rebuke the king of the earth. If God does not bring mercy, then His judgment is poured forth upon individuals and nations alike. His mercy, like a shield, protects the people of the earth, sheltering them from His terrible wrath. One day, however, if refuge in Christ is not found, each of us will bear the brunt of His wrath when that shield of mercy is withdrawn.

"So then He has mercy on whom He desires, and He hardens whom He desires" (Rom 9:18).

Judgment hovers just over our heads like low, dark clouds, threatening to fulfill the beckoning curse. God delays it in His general good purpose, but it could be sped up. He reaches out and exerts His mercy to withhold the effects of His judgment. There is no clearer demonstration of this than in the cross. Justice was fully satisfied when Christ took His people's judgment on Himself. God had mercy by choosing to execute His judgment on His Son for the elect.

Those, however, who do not seek Christ only have God's judgment coming. His wrath is just and good.

B. God's Choice (Rom 9:19-22)

> [19] You will say to me then, "Why does He still find fault? For who resists His will?" [20] On the contrary, who are you, O man, who answers back to God? The thing molded will not say to the molder, "Why did you make me like this," will it? [21] Or does not the potter have a right over the clay, to make from the same lump one vessel for honorable use, and another for common use? [22] What if God, although willing to demonstrate His wrath and to make His power known, endured with much patience vessels of wrath prepared for destruction? (Rom 9:19-22)

Paul asks another question here in 9:19, "Why does He still find fault? For who resists His will?" (Rom 9:19) God is not liable for man's sin despite His choice of extending His grace and favor.

This question of fault targets those who wrongly conclude that God's sovereign hand in salvation means sin is God's fault and therefore people are not responsible for their own sin. They suggest that if it is God who hardens and softens, then He is the One responsible for their sins. This is wrong! Paul does not allow for this argument.

Through the illustration of the potter (i.e. the Lord) and the pots (i.e. human beings), we observe that God commits no folly when He designs various vessels, some for common use while others for honorable. This is God's prerogative. We dare not conclude that man is irresponsible by blaming our sinful choices on God. God created man holy. It was man who chose to disobey God (5:12-21). One of God's great purposes in all of this is to demonstrate His great wrath. He did it with Pharaoh, and He will again display his wrath in a grander way among those who choose to disobey the King of Kings. May we not be the ones upon whom God's mighty and just wrath falls!

Romans 9:23-33

Grace and Election

After establishing God's right to determine whom He calls to experience His grace, Paul addresses two major questions about this elect people. First, he defends the inclusion of Gentiles into the people of God, and second he excludes many of the Jews from belonging to the elect of God.

A. Calling by God's Grace (Rom 9:23-24)

> 23 And He did so in order that He might make known the riches of His glory upon vessels of mercy, which He prepared beforehand for glory, 24 even us, whom He also called, not from among Jews only, but also from among Gentiles (9:23-24).

This verse no doubt reveals one of the most powerful truths in scripture, namely, that God's whole redemptive program is carried out to display the wonders of His mercy. God was patient with sinners (see 9:22) so that He could in His own time display the wonders of His mercy. Otherwise angels and people alike would never know the depths of His mercy.

It is unfortunate that there are so many misunderstandings of this mercy. Satan no doubt realizes the power of God's people when they understand the awesome revelation of God's mercy. These teachings promote a genuine humility and love for God rather than a judgmental and critical spirit.

There are two kinds of abusive responses. One group decries election and grace by affirming their power of choice and free will. They do not realize how this claim distracts from bringing glory to the Lord. They are self-dependent rather than God-dependent.

The other group, full of pride regarding their knowledge of grace, misunderstand how God's mercy champions the doctrines of election and grace. They forget or ignore the implications of the grace that they boast of.

The proper response to election is characterized by those who are greatly humbled by their sinful condition and become grateful for God who intervened to save them and others. Upon realizing how God has saved them, they, in response, become very gracious to others.

> **The more we understand the depth of His grace and mercy, the more we experience the wonderful touch of His love and grace in Christ.**

Paul defends grace by identifying three misconceptions of grace and exposing their weaknesses.

1. Mistaken Notion #1: God is unfair when He doesn't save everyone.

God does not need to save anyone. He is just because His character is just (Rom 3:5-6). He cannot be otherwise. His justice and ensuing wrath are good things. They are not deficiencies in His character. This practically means that He must judge the sinner and not the innocent, but because we are all sinners (cf. Romans 1-3), all of us will suffer judgment. Even in salvation, judgment of sin is never overlooked. God fully dealt with our sin through Christ, who suffered on our behalf. God's obligation to justice stops with the satisfaction of His wrath (cf. Rom 3:25).

God is not obligated to mercifully love any of us.[45] If He was obligated, then there would be no such thing as grace. Grace and mercy ring with the sound of extraordinary compassion. No one, however, can demand grace or it is no longer grace. God is not obligated to give grace or mercy. He provides grace according to His pleasure.

2. Mistaken Notion #2: Everyone on earth is considered God's child.

Our second misconception is that everyone on earth is considered God's child. These individuals and groups pronounce that all those who God created are also God's children. The teaching on redemption in Romans (e.g. chapters 3, 4, 8) clearly rebuts this viewpoint. The children of God are carefully

---

[45] Once He commits to saving the elect, He then must save the elect. The Lord, though He be gracious, is not obligated to step into this commitment.

described as a group of individuals who have come out in allegiance to God by His grace.

3. Mistaken Notion #3: God is indebted to certain kinds of people.

The third misconception alleges that God is especially indebted to certain kinds of people. But in fact, we are instructed not to make any distinction between the Jew and the Gentile (c.f. 3:9). The Jew as well as the Gentile are equally judged or saved by grace through faith. Whenever we presume upon God's grace, we have taken a wrong turn. One simply cannot demand grace, for then grace would not be grace.

B. Calling Cannot be Taken for Granted (Ro 9:25-33)

> 25 As He says also in Hosea, "I will call those who were not by people, 'My people,' and her who was not beloved, 'Beloved.'" 26 "And it shall be that in the place where it was said to them, 'You are not My people,' there they shall be called sons of the Living God" (9:25-26).

Depending on our background and cultural prejudices, we might be surprised to find that God's election might include people we did not expect to find. The early church was surprised to find it included people like the Gentiles (non-Jews) and excluded those they thought would be included, such as the Jews. Paul carefully supports his position from the Old Testament scriptures, proving that God is saving people from the pagan nations (i.e. Gentiles) in the last verses of chapter 9.

Romans 9:25-33 articulates three theologies: remnant theology, grace theology, and faith theology. They are all pertinent to the teaching visualized by the diagram below; God has called His people from both the Gentiles and the Jews.

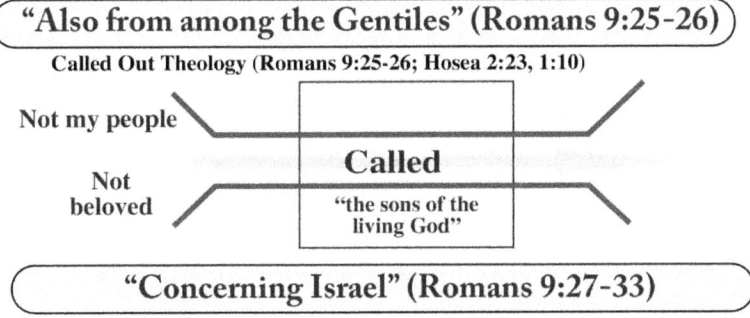

1. Remnant Theology (Rom 9:27-28; Is 10:22-23)

> ²⁷ And Isaiah cries out concerning Israel, "Though the number of the sons of Israel be as the sand of he sea, it is the remnant that will be saved; ²⁸For the Lord will execute His word upon the earth, thoroughly and quickly" (Rom 9:27-28).

God's promise are true; God is faithful. No matter what the media or various theology books state, the great news on earth is that God is saving a large remnant of people. The term remnant usually refers to the leftovers, which are undesirable or small in number. God states three things about this remnant, which will be unlike any other remnant:

a) The remnant will be a great number, "The sons of Israel be as the sand of the sea" (Is 10:22; Gen 22:17).

> Gentiles did not obtain it because of good works.
>
> Israel did not obtain it because of good works.
>
> Fair? Yes, the object of faith remains the same. Salvation is not on the basis of works but of faith - has nothing to do with one's origins.

b) The remnant will be saved, that is, a group from the inclusive 'everyone.' "It is the remnant that will be saved" (Rom 9:27; 10:22)

c) God is sure to complete His purpose from across the earth. "The Lord will execute His will throughout the earth" (Rom 9:28; Is 10:23).

God moves across the earth, stirring this and that people group to find His great riches in Christ. Some of them have been in darkness for a long time, but already nations and tribes across the world have come to know and profess His Name. This forms part of the foundations for missions.

2. Grace Theology (Rom 9:29; Is 1:9)

> ²⁹ And just as Isaiah foretold, "Except the Lord of Sabaoth had left to us a posterity, we would have become as Sodom, and would have resembled Gomorrah" (9:29).

God expressed His grace on two levels:

- God kept the remnant pure and holy. They kept their faith by living differently from the majority of Israelites, and by staying away from the world.

- God graciously kept Israel from becoming like Sodom and Gomorrah in two ways. 1) in behavior and 2) in judgment. If His grace was not active, we all would have ended up like the depraved city that was reserved for judgment—indeed it looks like depraved could describe many a city today, awaiting sudden judgment.

3. Faith Theology (Rom 9:30-33; Is 8:14; 28:16)

> 30 What shall we say then? That Gentiles, who did not pursue righteousness, attained righteousness, even the righteousness which is by faith; 31 but Israel, pursuing a law of righteousness, did not arrive at that law. 32 Why? Because they did not pursue it by faith, but as though it were by works. They stumbled over the stumbling stone, 33 just as it is written, "Behold, I law in Zion a stone of stumbling and a rock of offense, and he who believes in Him will not be disappointed" (9:30-33).

Paul mentioned in Romans the phrase "by faith" eleven times: "From faith to faith" (1:17). We are saved by faith and live by faith ('even the righteousness which is by faith').

He explains why the pagan Gentiles found faith in Christ while the Jews, who had the Word of God, did not find God's favor. The Israelites as a group (there were some that believed) lived out a religion of works instead of faith, and therefore, we can see how they stumbled. The chosen ones are evident through their faith and response in Christ.

Summary

God's Word shapes our minds being conformed to what is true and right. Theology based on the scriptures attempts to build the right mindset for ourselves which can be properly communicated to others. Without the scriptures, our comments would be expressions stemming from arrogance. Paul, deep in waters, continues on exploring and expounding these marvelous truths of God to strengthen God's people and lead others to faith.

Romans 10:1-21
Sharing the Gospel

From passages like Romans 10, we can obtain a deeper understanding of the various aspects of salvation (i.e. soteriology - the study of salvation). In this passage, we will study the relationship between the sovereignty of God and evangelism.

Introduction: Be Careful!

We need to be careful how we draw our theological conclusions. If we are not cautious, we could end up making wrong conclusions and spending our time defending them! For example, not a few wrongly conclude that, since the all-powerful God does the saving, then all would be saved. This is not what happens.

Others wrongly surmise that God is not faithfully saving the Jews as promised. The teaching of election, however, presented in these chapters should not only comfort our souls but should also establish the faithfulness of God. Just because some are not saved it does not mean that God has failed in His purpose. He saves all He wills.

Still others in error determine that if God sovereignly saves, then man does not need to do anything to procure salvation (i.e. waiting for it to happen) or that we do not need to take a strong initiative in reaching the lost (evangelism and missions).

This is the main thrust before us in this chapter. How do we relate the sovereignty of God to the salvation process? Are evangelism and missions really necessary? This chapter provides some much needed insight into these matters. He helps us to draw right conclusions from strong theological teachings.

A. Paul's Responses to Salvation (Rom 10:6-7)

There are many ways people can respond to God's sovereign activity in the salvation process. Some think it is unfair. Others simply deny it by putting their confidence in their own good works. This is important to note because many denominations and sectors of Christianity have gone astray from scriptural teaching and practice by focusing only on one aspect.

The apostle reveals his own personal responses, shaped by the scriptures, in chapter ten. By observing Paul's responses, we can guard against unbiblical conclusions regarding God's sovereignty and salvation.

1. Sympathetic (Rom 10:1)

> ¹ Brethren, my heart's desire and my prayer to God for them is for their salvation (10:1).

Paul intensely cares for the Israelites. Add to this the care seen in Romans 9:1-2–"great sorry and unceasing grief". Do you care for those around you?

Has the teaching of election stifled the gospel? What should our proper response be to sharing the gospel? How did Paul respond to this? How does prayer relate to this teaching of election and grace?

2. Intercessor (Rom 10:1)

Paul prays for the Jews. Despite our views of the sovereignty of God, we must be a prayerful church seeking the lost. How often do you pray for the lost?

3. Conclusive (Rom 10:2-3)

> ² For I bear them witness that they have a zeal for God, but not in accordance with knowledge. ³ For not knowing about God's righteousness, and seeking to establish their own, they did not subject themselves to the righteousness of God (10:2-3).

Paul recognizes that religious people, including his kinsmen the Jews, who try to establish their own righteousness are lost. This personal assessment keeps people from the effects of the gospel. Do you dare admit the lostness of the religious people about you, even your family members?

4. Discerning (Rom 10:4-5)

> ⁴ For Christ is the end of the law for righteousness to everyone who believes. ⁵ For Moses writes that the man who practices the

righteousness which is based on law shall live by that righteousness (10:4-5).

Salvation is only for those who believe in Christ. Those who trust in their good works or feelings are as lost as the pagan who totally rejects the existence and power of God. Sometimes it is hard to assert that baptism does not save but belief in Christ because of one's care for someone that used to go to one's church.

5. Selective (Rom 10:6-9)

Salvation is for only for those who believe certain things about Christ. We need to be careful not to equate intellectual assent with belief. When we hear, "Oh, I believe in Christ," we should be willing to investigate a bit further as to what they believe about Christ. This is even more important in this era where people including many professing Christians have not read their Bibles!

6. Inclusive (Rom 10:10-11)

Salvation is for all kinds of people–whoever calls upon Him. No matter what we conclude about God's sovereign hand in salvation, we must make an open proclamation to all people of every land and language that they too can believe in Christ.

B. Faith Demanded (Rom 10:6-7)

> 6 But the righteousness based on faith speaks thus, "Do not say in your heart, 'Who will ascend into heaven?' (that is, to bring Christ down), 7 or 'Who will descend into the abyss?' (that is, to bring Christ up from the dead)" (10:6-7).

Interestingly, these verses are loosely translated from the Old Testament (Deut 30:12-14). The Hebrew word used for abyss is translated as "the sea." But Paul uses the term abyss, which has a double meaning in Greek, abyss or the very depths of the sea, and in this way reminds us of Christ's death and descent to Hades, the place of the dead. So what do these esoteric verses mean?

"For in it the righteousness of God is revealed from faith to faith; as it is written, but the righteous man shall live by faith" (Rom 1:17).

Paul is demanding that we move from 'what can be' to 'what is'. Salvation is not about what God can do but what He has done in Christ. Do we need a sign from heaven? A special prophet? No. We have Christ. Do we need a necromancer or some psychologist who studies people who have died and come back to life? No again, for Christ has died and come alive. We do not need to climb our way into heaven or somehow discover the secrets of future life. Jesus has been in heaven and has ascended out from the very grasp of death. He will care for us.

C. Faith Discovered (Rom 10:8)

> 8 But what does it say? "The word is near you, in your mouth and in your heart"--that is, the word of faith which we are preaching (10:8).

> But the word is very near you, in your mouth and in your heart, that you may observe it. (Deut 30:14).

Deuteronomy 30 shows how God revealed Himself to the Israelites and was near to them (Deut 30:14). They had the Word of God; no other people had this. Paul equivocates the Word of God with Christ Himself (who is the Word of God, John 1:1-3,14).

God dealt with the Israelites because God revealed His Word to them, but now that Christ has come to earth, salvation's door has opened to all. God, in Christ, has visited the whole earth. Jesus came into the world! Since God has drawn near to us (the world), we all, not just the Jews, should respond in faith.

These verses are 'faith' verses. We cannot scientifically prove (or disprove) Christ's resurrection–though there is much evidence for it, but we believe by faith that He has risen! This is the truth. Our salvation is not based on our works or on merit by which we have earned to secure God's favor, (e.g. I fast two times a week and have devotions three times a week). Our faith rests on what God has done for us in Christ. This is the message that we all hear, and is the message of faith that Paul proclaims so that all can believe.

D. Faith Delivered (Rom 10:9-10)

> 9 That if you confess with your mouth Jesus as Lord, and believe in your heart that God raised Him from the dead, you shall be saved; 10 for with the heart man believes, resulting in righteousness, and with the mouth he confesses, resulting in salvation (10:9-10).

Confession of Jesus as Lord

Here are some statements stemming from what it means to confess Jesus as Lord:

- Jesus as master (focusing on our servanthood)
- Jesus as lord over our lives (He is master and owner of all)
- Jesus as chief of deities (other gods were called lord)
- Jesus as king rather than Caesar (Christians died for their allegiance)
- Jesus is Yahweh (the Name of God revealed in OT)

Does this term 'Lord' here refer to Yahweh in the Old Testament. It seems so.

Support for translating 'Lord' as Yahweh[46]

- *Kurios* (the Greek word for Lord) is translated for YHWH in the Septuagint (Greek OT translation) 6000+ times.
- The OT usages quoted in the NT refer to Jesus (Rom 10:13, 1 Th 5:2; 2 Th 2:2).
- Jesus is so titled, "Therefore also God highly exalted Him, and bestowed on Him the name which is above every name ... that Jesus Christ is Lord..." (Philippians 2:9-11).
- Romans 10:13 instructs all people to call out to Jesus Christ in prayer, which would be heinous to a Jew who would only pray to God and call to Him for salvation (e.g. God warned the Israelites not to worship idols).
- Christ's common association with God, His power and source of grace (Rom 1:7; 1 Cor 1:3).

Summary

Our belief that God became man in the form of Christ Jesus, died, and (physically) rose from the dead and now reigns on high is an essential part of Christian doctrine. Salvation, then, is not based on works of righteousness but on our confession about who Christ is and our personal response to God by our faith in Christ. Since the instrument of salvation is focused on faith in Christ instead of works of the Law, then the Gentiles (non-Jews) can also be saved.

---

[46] *Romans: A Shorter Commentary* by Charles Cranfield, pp. 258-259.

E. Faith Developed (Rom 10:11-15)

11 For the Scripture says, "Whoever believes in Him will not be disappointed." 12 For there is no distinction between Jew and Greek; for the same Lord is Lord of all, abounding in riches for all who call upon Him; 13 for "Whoever will call upon the Name of the Lord will be saved."

14 How then shall they call upon Him in whom they have not believed? And how shall they believe in Him whom they have not heard? And how shall they hear without a preacher? 15 And how shall they preach unless they are sent? Just as it is written, "How beautiful are the feet of those who bring glad tidings of good things!" (Rom 10:11-15).

God broadcasts His glory by saving people in time and space. The process outlined here is critical because it keeps our perspective and priorities in proper balance. Paul presents the process by starting with the individual who believes. This presentation is the way most of us understand things best, that is, from our own perspective. But much has gone on behind the scenes to actually bring us to salvation. Let us discuss those things as Paul presents them and later come back to look at the whole process.

1. Personal Belief (10:11-12)

This is one of the most welcoming and wonderful promises offered to us. "Whoever believes in Him will not be disappointed." It is true not only for salvation but also for our personal growth. Faith (same as belief) helps the ways of God become integrated into our lives. The most basic faith is salvation belief. This faith is open to all people on the earth, which is expressed by the phrase 'Jew and Greek.' God not only tolerates us, but saves us. Do not underestimate the power of the phrase 'believe in.'

In verse 13 Paul quotes a similar phrase, "Whoever will call upon the Name of the Lord will be saved." The first phrase from verse 11 is from Isaiah 28:16 while this later one is from Joel 2:32. One is to call upon, rather than simply believe in, Christ; mere head knowledge is inadequate. This is a big problem in popular religions including Christianity. Intellectual assent or emotional response are masks for true faith, which requires the incorporation of the mind, heart, soul, and will.

- Preacher is sent
- Preacher speaks
- People hear the gospel
- People call upon the Lord
- People believe in Christ

What does "call upon" refer to? Compare Jesus' words: "Blessed are the poor in spirit… Blessed are those that mourn" (Matt 5:3-4). The seeker or believer, suddenly shocked at his or her sin and lack of righteousness, calls out to a Savior who says He would help. Christ excels in coming to rescue those in need.

2. Process of Belief (10:13-15)

This paragraph then begins a series of four questions, which are followed by a declaration. The power of this section's instruction comes from the way it connects one event to another; the whole process is brought before our eyes, much as Paul did in Romans 8:28-30.

> 14 How then shall they call upon Him in whom they have not believed?
> **believe > call**
>
> And how shall they believe in Him whom they have not heard?
> **hear > believe**
>
> And how shall they hear without a preacher?
> **preach > hear**
>
> 15 And how shall they preach unless they are sent?
> **sent > preach**

Sent → Preach → Hear → Believe → Call

A sovereign God works through the instruments of His people and because of this commitment, we should acknowledge several truths.

It is a horrendous to conclude that because of God's election, man does not need to take initiative in spreading the gospel or in actively seeking salvation. Quite the contrary! God empowers those who seriously take their part in this mission process. We the church are responsible to increase the quantity and quality of these preachers.

The message and work of Christ and His resurrection stands at the heart of this proclamation. Regardless of the issue of election, our mission should be all-comprehensive, proclaiming the gospel to all people, all the time.

Summary

Paul concludes the subject of shaping our thoughts with powerful teachings of election. The church holds the great responsibility to take her place in the proclamation of the gospel. This calling should impact our mission policies and cause the church to prioritize reaching out to all peoples.

Missions is essential to genuine growth and salvation. Unfortunately, short-sighted churches often starve missions and strategic evangelism for the sake of preserving the growth of the local church body. The Lord in Isaiah sent the preacher and so did Jesus. The 'white of harvest' still exists (John 4:35). Pray that the Lord of the harvest will send workers into the harvest.

In what way are you actively taking part in the spreading of God's Word to those near and distant around the world?[47]

F. Faith Rejected (Rom 10:16-21)

1. The Rejection of God's Word (Rom 10:16)

> [16] However, they did not all heed the glad tidings; for Isaiah says, "Lord, who has believed our report?" (10:16).

If the gospel is preached, people will believe, right? Wrong. Many will not respond with belief. Paul quotes Isaiah 53:1 to reinforce the idea that it is not the problem of the message but the problem of the hearer (also see John 12:38). Jesus equally faced this problem. We should not allow the rejection of the message lessen our commitment to proclaim His Word. Not all the Jews rejected God's Word. Acts 2-4 testifies to this. However, many did. Paul discusses this group here.

2. Hearing is Not Believing (Romans 10:17-18)

> [17] So faith comes from hearing, and hearing by the word of Christ. [18] But I say, surely they have never heard, have they? Indeed they have; "Their voice has gone out into all the earth, and their words to the ends of the world" (Rom 10:17-18).

If they do not all believe, then we do not have to preach to everyone, right? No. Just as God has continually sent His revelation out to the earth (c.f. Ps 19:4), so we are to consistently proclaim His Word.

> The universal revelation of God in nature, was a providential prediction of the universal proclamation of the gospel. If the former was not fortuitous, but founded in the nature of God, so must the latter be. The manifestation of God in nature, is, for all his creatures

---

[47] J. I. Packer's, *Evangelism & the Sovereignty of God* provides good discussion of this important issue.

to whom it is made, a pledge of their participation in the clearer and higher revelations."[48]

The way the apostle connects faith to the hearing of God is important. The way to increase the faith of God's people is to increase the amount of God's Word communicated. However, we must remember that sometimes people can hear the Word and yet not believe (see 10:16). When people desire and believe God's Word, their faith will grow.[49]

3. Knowledge is Not Belief (Romans 10:19-21)

> [19] But I say, surely Israel did not know, did they? At the first Moses says, "I will make you jealous by that which is not a nation, by a nation without understanding will I anger you." [20] And Isaiah is very bold and says, "I was found by those who sought Me not, I became manifest to those who did not ask for Me." [21] But as for Israel He says, "All day long I have stretched out my hands to a disobedient and obstinate people" (10:19-21).

Israel knew God's Word but rejected it. The usage of 'disobedient and obstinate' in verse 21 indicate that they knew but rejected God's Word. Having rejected it, God revealed His alternate plans, which were hidden far back during the time of Moses (c.f. Dt 32:21). The great prophet in Isaiah 65:1-2 revealed God's distaste for those who consistently rejected His gracious Word.

Reflection

- How is faith different from knowledge?
- How many in our own church know God's Word but do not respond in belief?
- Is there an area in your life you have knowledge but not belief?

---

[48] Romans by Charles Hodge, p. 349

[49] Revive your faith through God's Word!

Romans 11:1-36
Salvation's Great Plan

Romans 11:1-36 completes a major section of the Book of Romans, chapters 6-11. From chapter 6 onward, and perhaps even earlier, Paul clarifies what the gospel is not. He tried to keep them from making wrong conclusions about the gospel, which would in turn hide or distort the power of the gospel.[50]

> **OUTLINE OF ROMANS**
> - A simple outline -
> A. Declaration of the Gospel (Rom 1–5).
>   Paul declares and explains the gospel
> B. Clarification of the Gospel (Rom 6–11).
>   Paul clarifies the gospel so that the truths are not confused.
> C. Relevance of the Gospel (Rom 12–16).

Up to this point the apostle has focused on spiritual Israel (believing Jews and Gentiles). In chapter 11, however, he focuses on what happens to national Israel. What about all the promises given to Israel in the Old Testament? It reminds us a lot of the question the apostles asked Jesus, "Lord, is it at this time You are restoring the kingdom to Israel?" (Acts 1:6) It is here that we get a few glimpses of God's plan for the nation of Israel.

The apostle shows that, despite the rebellious nature of the Jewish people, God's plans can never be frustrated. God uses the disobedience of the

---

[50] Paul also clarifies misunderstandings in chapters 1-5, but they are in the context of rightly presenting the gospel which he finishes doing in chapter 5.

Jew and the Greek (11:32) to accomplish an even greater display of His glory and compassion.

Observe the major structure of Romans 11 as a whole. Both 11:1 and 11:11 include Paul's oft used phrase, "May it never be!" combined with a question. This is the 9th and 10th (the last time) that he uses this phrase in Romans. He outright rejects the thought that God has forgotten His promises toward Israel. Paul's progression of thought can be seen in this outline.

Summary of Romans chapters 9-11
1. Clarifying the identity of the true Israel (9:1-13)
2. The means Jews and Gentiles become part of true Israel (9:14-29)
3. Gentiles accept the Messiah; the Jews reject (9:30-10:21)
4. God's promises to Israel are not in vain (11:1-36)

Chapter 11 itself is divided into four sections.

- God's partial rejection of Israel (Rom 11:1-10)
- Greater blessings on all upon ethnic Israel's return (11:11-15)
- Gentiles are grafted into Israel's olive tree (11:16-24)
- Some Gentiles and Israelites will be saved (11:25-36)

Having spoken on faith and the need to preach the Word of God to the nations (i.e. Gentiles) earlier in chapter 10, the readers are wondering about the Jews who had God's Word but did not believe. Paul shows how God has not totally rejected all the Israelites even though the vast majority of Jews rejected the Word of God.

A. God's Partial Rejection of Israel (Rom 11:1-10)

God has not rejected the few chosen Israelites. Paul again (see Rom 6-7) uses this particular method of teaching, a question followed by "May it never be" (also see 11:11). He is very conscious of people's wrong conclusions, including the ones presented here.

1. God Still Saves Israelites (Rom 11:1-4)

> 1 I say then, God has not rejected His people, has He? May it never be! For I too am an Israelite, a descendant of Abraham, of the tribe of Benjamin. 2 God has not rejected His people whom He foreknew. Or do you not know what the Scripture says in the passage about Elijah, how he pleads with God against Israel? 3 "Lord, They have killed Thy prophets, they have torn down Thine altars, and I along am left, and

they are seeking my life." ₄ But what is the divine response to him? "I have kept for Myself seven thousand men who have not bowed the knee to Baal" (Rom 11:1-4).

Does God's rejection of the Israelites and expanded work among the heathen nations (Rom 10) mean that God has completely forgotten the Israelites? No!

The apostle, who is of the tribe of Benjamin, first gives himself as a clear example. Although he does not state it here, he had formerly rejected God, but the Lord graciously intervened in his life and saved him. God is, to some degree, working with the Israelites; Paul, formerly Saul, is a Jew. Clearly God knew He would save a certain number of Israelites and make their salvation sure. The word 'foreknew' was used earlier in Romans 8:29, and was there discussed in length.

The fact that God still saves Israelites is also seen from the conversation God had with Elijah after the contest with the Baal prophets. Elijah, in his despair, saw himself as the only prophet. Everyone seemed to have deserted the Lord. God quickly broke up this pity party by telling him that He had kept a great number, 7,000 people, to worship Him alone (1 Ki 19:18). God knew their numbers!

God has by no means completely rejected the Israelites. The nation of Israel was not completely rejected; there remains a faithful remnant. We should not be surprised to see many Jews with hardened hearts, nor should we conclude that there are no believing Jews.

2. God's Judgment on Unbelievers (Romans 11:5-10)

> ₅ In the same way then, there has also come to be at the present time a remnant according to God's gracious choice. ₆ But if it is by grace, it is no longer on the basis of works, otherwise grace is no longer grace. ₇ What then? That which Israel is seeking for, it has not obtained, but those who were chosen obtained it, and the rest were hardened; ₈ just as it is written, "God gave them a spirit of stupor, eyes to see not and ears to hear not, down to this very day." ₉ And David says, "Let their table become a snare and a trap, and a stumbling block and a retribution to them. ₁₀ "Let their eyes be darned to see not, and bend their backs forever" (Rom 11:5-10).

Paul restates that those who believe do so by the Lord's gracious choice. He hopes that the Jews wake up out of their stubborn belief that belonging to the Jewish race is enough to please God. It is not. God saves by grace, not by works or nationality; He wants us to boast in Him as Savior (6).

God makes sure that He saves some Jews, the remnant. God, however, reserves a harsh judgment for the rejection of His Word. They knew His Word first and still rejected it. God in turn rejected them (see Is 29:10; Ps 69:22-23).

Summary

Some people do not want to be helped by God. If contented with their lives, then they will not seek God's salvation. God, however, will judge those who reject His truth because they are accountable for their sin.

B. Greater Blessings on Israel's Return (Ro 11:11-15)

Paul provides several surprising facts about Israel in 11:11-15. He is still trying to prevent us from drawing wrong conclusions. Note the question in 11:11 that drives the words in the rest of this chapter.

1. Israel is a Key Player (Rom 11:11)

> 11 I say then, they did not stumble so as to fall, did they? May it never be! But by their transgression salvation has come to the Gentiles, to make them jealous (Rom 11:11).

Paul makes a difference between stumbling and falling. Stumbling is tripping; one can get up again. (Paul uses this wording to "prove" Israel as a nation will come back one day.) Israel only stumbled. During the duration of Israel's rejection of the Lord, the gospel freely went out to the nations. The falling would refer to those who upon their rejection of the gospel never come to the gospel.

2. God Ably Uses Israel's Disobedience (Rom 11:12)

> 12 Now if their transgression be riches for the world and their failure be riches for the Gentiles, how much more will their fulfillment be! (Rom 11:12).

"Their transgression" refers to the sin of Israel as a nation. Through their sin, the riches of God (eternal life in the gospel) were diverted to the world so that the world could believe. God's eternal plan is hardly frustrated by man's disobedience, even when it involves His key player, Israel. Paul, in essence, is giving us reason not to conclude Israel's departure as a mistake of God's. The Lord is unraveling a subtle but glorious salvation plan to reach to the whole world with the Gospel through His love.

When Israel as a nation does obey, the fulfillment of the Gospel in their life will lead to a much richer fulfillment. Paul alludes to a time in the future when Israel will turn back to the Lord; and at that time God will marvelously work through Israel. This hint helps weigh the interpretation of Romans 11:25-26 in favor of referring to national Israel, as it has that meaning here.

3. One Clear Message (Rom 11:13-14)

> 13 But I am speaking to you who are Gentiles. Inasmuch then as I am an apostle of Gentiles, I magnify my ministry, 14 if somehow I might move to jealousy my fellow countrymen and save some of them (Rom 11:13-14).

If the Jews could get prideful and insolent, then so can the believers from other nations! This is, in fact, the danger of what happens once the gospel penetrates a certain culture (Rev 2-3). Paul, anticipating the Gentile's own pride, shares God's larger salvation plan for the Jewish people. God is concerned with saving people not only from the nations but also from the one country of Israel. By preaching the gospel among the nations, Paul the apostle hopes to stir up a holy jealousy among the Jews so that they too might believe.

4. The Two-fold Plan (Rom 11:15)

> 15 For if their rejection be the reconciliation of the world, what will their acceptance be but life from the dead? (Rom 11:15)

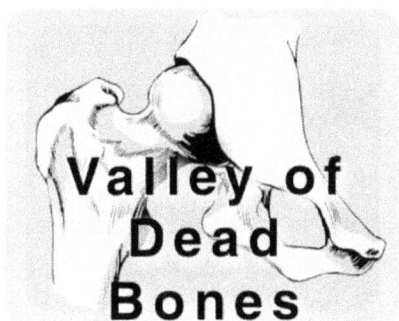

"For this son of mine was dead, and has come to life again; he was lost, and has been found.' And they began to be merry." (Lu 15:24).

Paul restates his former words by revealing two simple plans.

Plan #1: Through Israel's transgression, the reconciliation of the world comes about.

Plan #2: Through Israel's acceptance, the grand resurrection of the world comes about.

Throughout chapters 9-11 Paul has discussed Plan #1. This is the great mystery now revealed. Plan #2 and its use of the phrase "life from the dead" is only touched upon here, and probably refers to Ezekiel's vision of the valley of dead bones (Ez 37:1-14).

> ¹³Then you will know that I am the LORD, when I have opened your graves and caused you to come up out of your graves, My people. ¹⁴ "And I will put My Spirit within you, and you will come to life, and I will place you on your own land. Then you will know that I, the LORD, have spoken and done it," declares the LORD (Ez 37:13-14).

Once the Spirit softens Israel, more marvelous things will occur! As a nation, they will come alive, so to speak, (see 11:12 for a similar reference: "how much more will their fulfillment be!")

C. The Gentiles Grafted In (Rom 11:16-24)

Paul gives us a look at how this might happen through two illustrations.

1. Two Illustrations (dough and tree) (Rom 11:16)

"And if the first piece of dough be holy, the lump is also;	and if the root be holy, the **branches** are too"

A small piece of dough taken from the whole lump should provide a good representation of the whole batch. If the piece is holy, then the whole batch is holy. The same thing is true with a tree. If the roots from which the whole tree gains its life are holy, then the branches are holy.

In other words, no matter which way you look at it, we can rightly conclude that the original faith of the Israelites (e.g. Abraham, Isacc, Jacob, etc.) as being good, holy, and acceptable to God. The foundation is good enough to build upon, excluding the need to start anew.

2. Broken Off (Rom 11:17)

¹⁷ But if **some** of the branches were broken off (11:17a).

Many Jews were rejected from the covenant blessings because of their disobedience. This hardened state exists today. It does not speak of all the Jews, as can be seen from the word 'some' (see also 11:1).

3. Grafted In (Rom 1:17)

> ¹⁷ And you, being a wild olive, were grafted in among them and became partaker with them of the rich root of the olive tree (11:17b).

Paul, using the olive tree analogy, speaks of how the grafted branch (referring to the Gentiles) gains its life from the root of the tree. The branches are dependent upon the root, rather than the root upon the branch. This picture clarifies how the original community of God's people through Christ adopted the Gentile community into their community, rather than becoming something completely new.[51] Paul, in later chapters, will use this important theological construct to aid him in the portrayal of how the Jewish and Gentile believers are to act as one body (ch. 12:3-21).

Grafting a wild olive branch into a cultivated olive tree has two effects. First, the wild branch begins to produce good olives. Second, the old tree is newly invigorated by the severe pruning. This later point hints at Israel's renewed interest in Jesus Christ. Paul describes this root in Romans 9:1-5.

4. Be Careful! (Rom 11:18)

> ¹⁸ Do not be arrogant toward the branches; but if you are arrogant, remember that it is not you who supports the root, but the root supports you (Rom 11:18).

The Gentiles were evidently displaying some form of haughtiness over the Jewish believers. In the early church this Jew-Gentile tension was quite intense (cf. Galatians 2). There simply is no basis for this pride. As it has already been pointed out, all the branches are dependent upon the roots, not vice-a-versa. Though some branches might have been broken off so that these wild branches could be inserted, they likewise can be removed if they get prideful.

5. Broken Off (Rom 11:19)

> ¹⁹ You will say then, "Branches were broken off so that I might be grafted in" (11:19).

---

[51] This perspective is clearly taught in the Book of Acts, requiring each new work among non-Jews to be blessed by the Jewish apostles (e.g. Ac 10-11). This is also done by Paul's theological presentation of the Gospel in the earlier chapters of Romans, detailing how it equally saves both Jews and Gentiles by faith in Christ.

Paul accepts a greater plan encompassing the whole tree, all of God's people. Branches are not broken off without a reason or purpose. In God's economy, all things work together for His greater purpose. This connection between the Jews' rejection and the Gentiles' acceptance is seen in verses 11-14.

6. By Your Faith (Rom 11:20-21)

> [20] Quite right, they were broken off for their unbelief, but you stand by your faith. Do not be conceited, but fear; [21] for if God did not spare the natural branches, neither will He spare you (11:20-21).

In the spirit of chapters 3 and 4, Paul again affirms that we only belong to the community of God by faith in Jesus as Messiah. Neither the Jews nor the Gentiles can be attached to the tree of life without faith. They only belong because of their given faith.

This is a powerful statement against religiosity. The failure of Christian denominations to protect this faith in Christ leads whole segments of the Christian community away from the saving faith in Christ so they no longer belong to the tree. The religious community often looks at the broadening of their doctrinal statement to be more loving, but removal of the living faith and obedience to Christ is like extracting the heart or brain from the body. Absence of faith excludes the possibility of life.[52]

7. Kindness and severity (Rom 11:22)

> [22] Behold then the kindness and severity of God; to those who fell, severity, but to you, God's kindness, if you continue in His kindness; otherwise you also will be cut off (Rom 11:22).

We must not delude ourselves into thinking that God's love will enfold all sin into itself and be absorbed. Though the Lord is kind, He is also severe, which is illustrated in the description of His cutting of branches and judgment of people. Only a scanty understanding of God would attempt to separate these two fundamental qualities of God. Severity derives from God's holy wrath upon unbelievers. Was not Israel forbidden to enter the Promised Land until one generation perished (Numbers and Deuteronomy)? Did not Israel face several exiles? This was God's severe hand at work. Kindness is stored up for

---

[52] This does not teach the ability to lose one's salvation. This is an illustration that only speaks to God's general movement among the nations, not an individual's salvation. Nor is this meant to show that the general movement (cutting off Gentile or Jews) is exclusive but of God's general pattern. Paul retold, for instance, how God still saved him as a Jew even though many had rejected Christ.

those securely hidden in God's covenant through faith. Our faith in Christ assures us a place in that covenant (1 Co 11:23-27).

The blend of these seemingly incompatible attributes provide an awesome view of God's person, which can also be seen in Exodus 34:6-7 and John 1:14,16 where Jesus Christ is fully revealed in God's glory by being full of 'grace and truth'. Both attributes are fully blended in the Lord. Ignoring either inherent attribute of God will lead to horrible conclusions about salvation.

8. Do not continue (Rom 11:23)

²³ And they also, if they do not continue in their unbelief, will be grafted in; for God is able to graft them in again (11:23).

What about the security of faith? There are two sides to this.

(1) Those who taste God's kindness will be favored only if they hold onto their faith, whether Jew or Gentile (11:22).

Verse 23 asserts that if they do not continue in unbelief, then they can be joined back by faith. This leaves the door open for the unbelieving Jewish people to believe. This could also be applied to a person whose parents turned away from their faith in Christ.

We should not think of this revived Israel separate from a strong belief in Jesus as Messiah. Zionism, for example, is not this revival as it rejects faith in Jesus as the Christ. Faith must exceed the orthodoxy expressed by some Jews, basing their faith on Old Testament ceremonies. For those who insist on holding to the Old Testament ceremonies, as many Jewish people did in the early church, an affirmation of Jesus as Christ must also be present. Without faith, unbelief remains, which does not allow the branches to be regrafted in.

Application

- How should this passage shape our understanding of our own salvation?

Many of those who grew up in Christian homes or strongly influenced Christian communities will see problems develop around them that are similar to what the Jewish people faced. If God, in the end, scattered the unbelieving Israelites, then surely he will close down Christian churches that no longer hold to faith in Christ–the very thing we see happening around us.[53]

---

[53] It is not only liberals that have this problem. Fewer 'evangelical' believers now have confidence in God's Word or Christ's resurrection, which shows that they don't share this faith any longer.

We belong to Christ's body, not due to tradition, attendance, baptism; we belong only by faith. We cannot earn it or merely hope for it by being near to the church (cf. John 1:12-13). We must believe in Jesus the Messiah. Only in Him can we find forgiveness from our sins and restoration with God.

We should regularly affirm our faith and unabashedly live to protect that faith no matter what losses we might encounter: loss of job, reputation, loved ones, etc. Faith is the line between life and death. Wisdom demands that we protect that faith by an unswerving commitment to that belief. Did not God forbid Adam and Eve from entering the Garden again because of unbelief? This warning is repeated throughout the scriptures.

- Does this passage speak about losing one's salvation?

It is our faith that saves us. One is saved not because of what one believed in the past but on what one believes now. This constant faith is what characterizes a true believer. 1 John 2:19 describes those that left the faith as those who were never genuinely saved. The teaching of the perseverance of the saints instructs us that genuine belief is a persistent belief (see Heb 12).

What about our relationship with Jews and other religions and philosophies?

Though God's people are chosen, their salvation still only exists because of God's grace. We need to humbly accept His grace and yet urgently work, exhorting unbelievers of all sorts to come to faith in Christ while possible. At some point when the Jewish people believe upon Christ (cf. 11:12,15) salvation will greatly spread over the earth. Although God might move among the Jews in a particular way, there still remains no essential difference as to how the Jew or Gentile is saved for all are saved through faith in Christ.

Our perspective of the scriptures (i.e. hermeneutical framework)

Popular prophecy conferences and books have put a great focus on the future work of God among the Jewish people. There are several views that greatly shape one's interpretation of the Bible and, in turn, influence one's interpretation of God's treatment with the Jews.

In the chart below, each of the three main schools of thought on how God will work with the Jewish people as a nation are explained. Each system has inherent problems, some more serious, because they pursue their logic beyond the reach and purpose of the scriptures. These perspectives are being refined even now, the middle column itself being a modified view.

CLASSICAL DISPENSATIONALISM	PROGRESSIVE DISPENSATIONALISM	REFORMED COVENANTALISM
Scofield defined dispensation as "a period of time during which man is tested in respect of obedience to some specific revelation of the will of God." Traditional dispensationalism believes history can be broken up into usually 7 or 8 dispensations. They claim commitment to a literal interpretation of prophetic scripture and uniformly believe: 1) Distinction between prophecies of Israel in OT and the church in the NT. 2) They are premillennialists believing in a 1,000 year reign of Christ on earth. 3) Pre-tribulation rapture of the church. Two-stage return of Christ.	This revision of classical dispensationalism came about in 1980s. They part with the classicists by focusing on: 1) The "already" and the "not-yet" tension in eschatological promise. Christ for example has started His heavenly reign at the resurrection but not completely fulfilled until His return. 2) The church is not a parenthesis but like the Jews in the OT form a part of the one people of God. 3) The new covenant is being partly fulfilled by the church. 4) OT promises of Gentiles worshiping God is partly now being realized. They still agree with the classicists in that Israel will be restored, Christ's millennial return and pre-tribulation rapture.	The reformed group focuses on the two covenants (Old and New or the covenant of works and grace). They see God's work through the ages as a gradual unveiling of God's great plan. In this case they see no essential difference between the believing Jews and Gentiles. God is not working with them as a distinct people any more. There are of course modifications with this perspective as in dispensationalism.

D. Gentiles and Israelites Saved (Rom 11:25-36)

God's promises are important. If God was not faithful in His promises to Israel from the past, what confidence would we have toward His promises regarding salvation now? This passage shows how God's salvation plan is perfectly working on God's schedule, even fulfilling His promises to treacherous Israel.

1. Three Stages of Mercy (Rom 11:25-27)

25 For I do not want you, brethren, to be uninformed of this mystery, lest you be wise in your own estimation, that a partial hardening has happened to Israel until the fullness of the Gentiles has come in; 26 and thus all Israel will be saved; just as it is written, "The Deliverer will come from Zion, He will remove ungodliness from Jacob." 27

"And this is My covenant with them, when I take away their sins" (Rom 11:25-27).

Don't be "uninformed." This had been a problem, but with some instruction doesn't need to be. One must remain on constant guard against the danger of pride (11:18).

Discover God's mercy hidden in this now-revealed mystery (Greek: *musterion*). The Greek word for mystery, unlike the English, means 'former mystery' or mystery disclosed. The mystery has two sides to it, including both the partial hardening of Israel as well as the inclusion of the nations in the tree, as taught in the former section. The interpretation of these few verses is intriguing because of the many possible interpretations.

(1) Israel's Partial Hardening

²⁵ **A partial** hardening has happened to Israel (25).

"Partial hardening" refers to Israel's spiritual resistance and blindness to the Gospel, and is reflected in Israel's history, such as seen in Judges or later with the exile. The most obvious sign of this resistance is the way the Jews not only did not recognize their Messiah but put Him to death. The apostle frequently met up with this hardening for the Jews fiercely persecuted and opposed his work. Usually it was the Jews who mobilized the government or people to lock Paul up. This hardening is partial in that, though there are many Jews who do not believe, there are some that do–just what we find in the Book of Acts down to today.

The Lord graciously uses this stage of hardening to lead many non-Jews to come to faith in the Lord Jesus (Rom 11:11-12). A partial hardening has occurred to the nation of Israel so that the rest of the elect from among the nations would enter into the New Covenant. Following this time, the hardness of hearts will be replaced with softened hearts inclined to seek the Lord, and the nation of Israel will come to know her Lord. Do note that the Lord is not the agent of that hardening, though He sovereignly uses it for His greater purposes.

(2) Gentiles Saved

²⁵ **Until the fullness** of the Gentiles has come in (25).

The question that follows is, "For how long does this partial hardening occur?" The opening to the Gentile nations is but for a limited time. The flow of God's mercy is, for a time, diverted to the nations. The hardening of the Israelites became the means by which the Gentiles could be saved (32). (Paul, however, did not describe why the Jewish branches had to be broken off to allow the Gentiles to be implanted.)

The word 'until' signals that this period of this hardness has a limit. Jesus also refers to this Old Testament prophetic concept: "Until the times of the gentiles" in the gospels.

> And they will fall by the edge of the sword, and will be led captive into all the nations; and Jerusalem will be trampled under foot by the Gentiles (Greek: *ethnon*) **until the times of the Gentiles** (same: *ethnon*) are fulfilled (Luke 11:24).
>
> And this gospel of the kingdom shall be preached in the whole world for a witness to all the nations, and then the end shall come (Mt 24:14).

This opened door will continue only until all of those chosen from among the nations have entered into God's flock, along with all of the believing Israelites. There are some difference of opinion on whether the Gentiles will continue to enter God's kingdom once this hardening of the Jewish people ceases. They will, assuming that all the Gentiles have come in, or God will use the Jewish people to evangelize the nations, not through the hardening of the Jews, but through their belief (Rom 11:12)! The fullness, then, could refer to all the nations being reached (Mt 24:14) or to the "fulfillment" where the Jews would join in and finish the task (cf. 11:11-12).

(3) Israel Saved

²⁶ And **thus all** Israel will be saved (26).

The word 'thus' teaches a third chronological stage that follows the former two transitional stages (#1 only Jews saved; #2 Gentiles and some Jews saved). And so, Paul here shows how God will fulfill all His promises to Israel. The phrase "all Israel" probably refers to the whole olive tree (11:17) – all the chosen people of God, including both Jews and Gentiles (cf. Eph 3:1-13). This is most likely the case, though it is possible that it refers only to all the Jews He foreknew (truly believing Jews) or that at some point in the future when all the living Jews comprising Israel will believe in Christ as their Messiah. Isaiah 27:6 states, "In days to come Jacob shall take root, Israel shall blossom and put forth shoots and fill the whole world with fruit" (ESV). As one traces the influence of the Gospel through time, it appears that all the nations are being reached and that, through this word, Israel will be the last reached.

Before, all of this was a mystery but now it has been revealed, showing that the Israelites have been partially hardened until all those elected from different nations had entered into God's gracious kingdom. We should not, however, think that God has forsaken the Israelite people.

> When the Gentiles shall come in, the Jews also shall return from their defection to the obedience of faith; and thus shall be completed the salvation of the whole Israel of God, which must be gathered from both; and yet in such a way that the Jews shall obtain the first place, being as it were the first-born in God's family (Calvin, p. 437).[54]

Verses 26-27 confirm the above verses: "just as it is written" (11:26).

> And a Redeemer will come to Zion, and to those who turn from transgression in Jacob," declares the LORD. "And as for Me this is My covenant with them," says the Lord: "My Spirit which is upon you, and My words which I have put in your mouth, shall not depart from your mouth, nor from the mouth of your offspring, nor form the mouth of your offspring's offspring, from now and forever." (Is 59:20-21)

> O that the salvation of Israel would come out of Zion! When the Lord restores His captive people, Jacob will rejoice, Israel will be glad (Ps 14:7).

> Therefore through this Jacob's iniquity will be forgiven; and this will be the full price of the pardoning of his sin (Is 27:9).

> ... and I will forgive their iniquity, and their sin I will remember no more (Jer 31:34).

Several key points in these passages describe the full salvation experience: 1) the Deliverer (Redeemer), 2) God's dealing with His people, 3) The covenant through which sin is forgiven and restoration made.

2. Mercy Explained (Rom 11:28-32)

(a) The Calling of Israel (11:28-29)

> [28] From the standpoint of the gospel they are enemies for your sake, but from the standpoint of God's choice they are beloved for the sake of the fathers; [29] for the gifts and the calling of God are irrevocable (Rom 11:28-29).

---

[54] *Commentaries on The Epistle of Paul the Apostle to the Romans* by John Calvin. Trans. by John Owen, Eerdmans 1955, p. 437.

The Gentiles are profited by the Jews' antagonism toward the Lord, but God has not altogether forsaken the Jews. Both the gifts and the calling of God will not be retracted. The reference seems to clearly mark off the physical Jews from the people of God (the olive tree). In other words, the above verses state two things:

- The Gentiles have profited from the Jews stubbornness.
- The Jews are beloved and their promises of salvation will be fulfilled.

The view that believes that Paul refers only to spiritual Israel ignores the special plan for the nation of Israel, distinct from the Gentiles, though the believing Jews in fact are part of the whole church. John Calvin supports this interpretation that Israel means the spiritual people of God:

> But I extend the word Israel to all the people of God, according to the meaning, – When the Gentiles shall come in, the Jews also shall return from their defection to the obedience of faith; and thus shall be completed the salvation of the whole Israel of God, which must be gathered from both; and yet in such a way that the Jews shall obtain the first place, being as it were the first-born in God's family.[55]

Summary

Paul's whole argument asserts that God has not forsaken the Jew; God is faithful to His promises. One could, like Calvin, assume that the Jews are merely merged with the Gentiles into one new Israel (picture of one tree). However, Paul several times refers to the great blessing that will ensue when the Jewish people believe (11:12, 15). If he uses this approach to further his main argument, then it seems necessary to accept the viewpoint that God will do some future special work in Israel as a cultural people, just as the Lord has done with each nation around the world. This would demonstrate God's ultimate mercy and grace–not only by sparing the rebellious Jews but by greatly using them! Moses' words seem to confirm this, "When you are in distress and all these things have come upon you, in the latter days, you will return to the LORD your God and listen to His voice" (Deut 4:30).

Israel, then, will be the last nation that the Lord comes to visit with salvation before Messiah Jesus' return. It is likely that God will soften the heart of the Jews and mightily use them to finish the evangelism of the world or at least greatly strengthen the kingdom of God throughout the world.

---

[55] *Epistle to the Romans* by John Calvin, Eerdmans, p. 437.

(b) God's Spectacular Mercy (Rom 11:30-32)

> ³⁰ For just as you once were disobedient to God, but now have been shown mercy because of their disobedience, ³¹ so these also now have been disobedient, in order that because of the mercy shown to you they also may now be shown mercy. ³² For God has shut up all in disobedience that He might show mercy to all.

The same situation that brought blessings to the Gentiles through the stubbornness of the Jews is repeated, but in reverse. Now the disobedience of the Gentiles will ensure blessings to the Jews. This seems to indicate a coming spiritual revival of the Jews before Christ returns (all Israel refers to all the Jewish people 11:26), but it could refer to the remaining chosen Jews to believe along with the Gentiles (all Israel refers to all the chosen people of God pictured by the tree.) In either case, many Jewish people will come to know the Lord and all of God's promises will come to full fruition. God's faithfulness will be again demonstrated.

In either case, the disobedience and hardening of both Gentile and Jew will be evident at different times in history, further convincing all that none deserve salvation, only judgment. In this way everyone can see the manifest glory of God's mercy, that though none deserve to be saved, it is only God's grace that saves them.

Everyone is a debtor to God. We all need His salvation–whether Jew or Gentile. God's kingdom is not partial to race but all inclusive. God has loved the world and the major redemptive plot of the scriptures is revealed: God's amazing and undeserved love poured out to all the nations. As we gain a better appreciation of His love, our lives should more fully reflect God's love. This introduction of mercy introduces the following spectacular set of verses in 11:33-36.

3. Indescribable Wisdom (Rom 11:33-36)

What is it that we have learned about the Lord through His dealings with mankind?

> ³³ Oh, the depth of the riches both of the wisdom and knowledge of God! How unsearchable are His judgments and unfathomable His ways! ³⁴ For Who has known the mind of the Lord, or who became His counselor? ³⁵ Or Who has first given to Him that it might be paid back to Him again? ³⁶ For from Him and through Him and to Him are all things. To Him be the glory forever. Amen.

By referring to God's mercy in the previous verses, Paul starts declaring God's marvelous wonders. Although this paragraph might not seem related to chapters 9-11, Paul is defending God's faithfulness by carrying out His divine and awesome purposes. This redemptive plan for Israel and the nations might look accidental, guided by man's hardness, but stands as the key mystery of God's marvelous redemptive plan only being understood in Christ's work on the cross. Paul responds to this marvelous plan by declaring God's glorious person and ways.

The gospel displays God's mighty wisdom and mercy in the way that His salvation plan is carried out, even when the people God worked with resisted His ways. All the Lord's promises were true, and yet He was able to bring a proper judgment upon His people for their hardened hearts. In all of this we see the glorious wisdom and might of God.

If a person wants to understand the universe, he needs to know that all things were created for the Lord, exist through Him, and are ultimately designed to carry forth His purposes! Anyone standing against Him will ultimately be greatly frustrated. The more we affirm this purpose, the more the mighty Spirit of God will rise up through our lives no matter how great the evil of the world looms about us.

(a) God's Attributes (33-35)

God's wisdom, knowledge, judgments, and ways are all highlighted here. God is declared to be all wise in contrast to humans who are void of His insight further corrupted by their evil hearts clouding their minds. Mankind's criticism and rejection of (i.e. hardening) of God's plan is absolute folly. Rejection of God's wisdom brings judgment, while those who seek Him find His mercy and wonderful help.

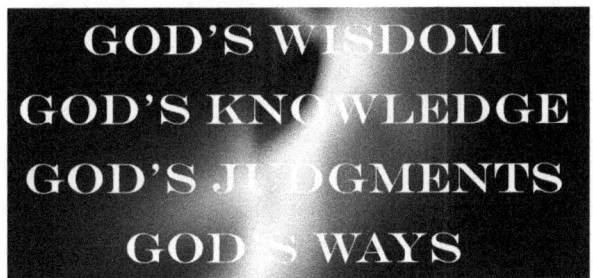

- Are there situations that confound the Lord?

- Is it right to ever blame God?
- Can we really understand God?
- Can our Christian growth ever max out?
- Is any problem too hard for the Lord to solve?
- Is it ever right to think that God owes us something?

All the answers to the above questions are, of course, 'no'. God is so far lifted from the earth's scene to compromise His character as some of us would charge.

(b) God's Sovereignty (36a)

³⁶ For from Him and through Him and to Him are all things (36).

Paul ends up refuting the Jew's dismissal of God's appointed Messiah and those who say, "It doesn't make sense..." by revealing how everything in the universe, whether spiritual or matter, submits to God's greater purposes.

"From Him" speaks of the source; "through Him" the means; and "to Him" the extended purpose for everything. Physicists should stop fooling themselves with their dogmatic assumptions that state that the universe holds no spiritual components. God, spirit Himself, has wrapped all things, seen and unseen, together through His vast wisdom and power.

Modern man's emptiness increases as he departs from this theocentric worldview. Instead of delighting in the way the Lord invested Himself in our lives (from Him), we end up feeling lonely. When separated from faith in God's careful working in our lives (through Him), we feel powerless, living as a wild atom let loose in a huge world. Ignorant of God's purpose for our lives (to Him), we devote ourselves to hedonism and extreme causes, never even being aware of the great and divine purposes for which God means to use us.

(c) God's Attributes (36b)

³⁶ To Him be the glory forever. Amen (36).

It is easy to forget the context and simply relish in the comprehensive purpose for which all things were made. While true, Paul still keeps our focus on the gospel which displays God's mighty wisdom through the implementation of His redemptive plan. Anyone who sides against Him will ultimately be greatly frustrated since, in His wisdom, He incorporates their hardened choices to fully exercise His purposes. Mankind's most brazen stubborn acts will all bow down to God's supreme purposes. Though the Lord brought proper judgment upon His people for their hardened hearts, all His promises and His greater redemptive plan come to fruition.

The disillusionment of pride can be easily struck down when it's viewed in light of the truth that all that we have is from Him, all the power we have to be and exert ourselves is through Him, and God has carefully equipped and placed us to fill the role He planned for us. A sense of accomplishment is good when we sense God's work in our lives to fulfill that part of His great plan.

As we affirm God's person and purposes, our faith is built up, and the mighty Spirit of God rises up through our lives, no matter how great the swirling clouds of evil loom about us.

Summary

Like the end of Job, a bright blast of God's glory shines into our confusion, keeping us from quickly dismissing His promises as impossible, and subduing our doubts regarding His good purposes for our lives.

Application

- It is inadequate that we rely on our past faith. If we have put our faith aside, we should immediately repent and return to the Lord where mercy can be found.

- Regularly affirm your faith. Just state it aloud. Affirm that you believe in Him no matter what happens. This is our life, our faith in Christ. When we are unclear of our faith, then the evil one can more easily confuse us.

- Refuse to place your faith in your Christian activities or traditions, or in any religious or humanistic activity. Only faith in Christ makes the saving difference that keeps us from judgment.

- Earnestly pray for the Jewish people to be saved.

- Reject any notion that the Jews in the future will be saved by restoration of their old sacrifices, temple, and so forth. This is clearly an unbiblical teaching. Jews can find saving faith in Christ.

Romans 12:1-8

Our Heart Responses

With the believer's relationship with God being restored (chapters 1-11), the apostle continues on, directing the believer to right living (chapters 12-16). In verses 1-2, Paul exhorts us to dedicate our lives to the Lord. Later, he identifies the right approach to care for our brothers and sisters in the church.

In contrast to the attitude that the hardened Israelites had to the Word of God as seen in former verses, God's people are to seek and follow the Lord. In light of His great mercy and grace (11:33-36), we open wide our hearts to respond to such a magnificent and compassionate God.

A. Living on the Altar (Rom 12:1-2)

> ₁ I urge you therefore, brethren, by the **mercies of God**, to **present** your **bodies** a **living and holy** sacrifice, **acceptable to God**, which is your **spiritual service** of worship. ₂ And do not be conformed to this world, but be transformed by the renewing of your mind, that you may prove what the will of God is, that which is good and acceptable and perfect (Rom 12:1-2).

Romans 12:1-2

In order to seek His full blessing and live out God's holy will, Paul points out three necessary spiritual actions: dedication, turning from the world, and renewal through meditation on His word, which is connected to the affirmation of God's will. The first area focuses on our bodies, but this dedication does not endure unless the Word of God transforms our minds.

1. Dedication to God

"By the mercies of God"

When coming before the Lord at the altar, we come not in self confidence but humbly and by the mercy of God (11:31-32). Presumption before God, even if it is to do His holy work, is sin. Only God's mercy can sufficiently humble us before His throne so that we do not assume our ways can please Him.

May we forever put aside the qualifications we place on our service and time, and persistently reject the demands on the conditions of our service. Either we live in total dedication or we are feeding our flesh. It is sin to say 'no' to His commands as well as to presume that we are not able to do something He wishes under His empowerment. God's mercy enables sinners like us to lay ourselves on His altar lest we be burned up upon our approach.

There is unequivocally no better place to be than on the altar of God: consecrated, committed, and content. Indeed it is only by God's amazing love and grace in Christ that makes us presentable even for a slight moment not to mention being able to keep us there in service to His great Name.

"To present"

Some pretend that their decision to serve is not involved in consecration since God is sovereign over our lives. But these conclusions only reveal another shade of pride. Obedience to His commands require a resolve of our wills. We must respond, either in the affirmative or negative. In this case, God commands us to present our bodies as a living and holy sacrifice to Him. We will, by our own will, respond by saying "yes" or "no." We will either commit ourselves or not.

As for me, I find myself, if not once then many times a day, presenting myself as a sacrifice on His altar. There is no greater place to be than living in harmony with the Lord.

In light of the mercy of God, we humbly present our bodies before Him. We give to Him what He desires so that He can further shape and use us as He pleases. The pot offers itself back to the potter for service. My strength in service derives from the clarity by which I commit myself to Him and the persistence I use in fulfilling the tasks He assigns me. As I present myself to my Master, I see myself as a gift, wrapped up and lifted, through God's grace, to the Lord who needs nothing but desires my whole heart.

"Your bodies"

We perhaps are quite surprised that it is our bodies that is to be offered to our Lord. Our very bodies have been defiled through their participation in unholy behavior, and yet it is our bodies that the Lord wants presented to Himself. God rejects Gnosticism and other beliefs that state that the flesh is inherently evil. God has stated it is what we do with our bodies that makes them good or evil, but through the cross our bodies can be purified and made presentable before Him in Christ. He redeemed us and therefore asks that we now dedicate our bodies to His service. What used to say profane things is now can say good things. The hand that once struck others is now called to aid. The Lord wants control over our bodies. He wants us to use our bodies the way they should be used. I must use my mouth, my voice, my eyes, my hands, my feet, my sexual parts, my mind all to glorify God. I am not to think that the Lord will use me apart from my body but with my body. Our bodies must be constrained by His purpose if we would serve our mighty King.

"Living and holy sacrifice"

An altar requires a sacrifice, a dedicated and offered up object, to please the one who owns the altar. Once sacrificed, the object no longer belongs to the one who made the offering. Ownership transfers from his hands into the owner of the altar. When we offer our bodies to the Lord, we instantly lose ownership over them.

> For we who live are constantly being delivered over to death for Jesus' sake, that the life of Jesus also may be manifested in our mortal flesh (2 Co 4:11).

In this case we see that the offering is both "living and holy." The "living" sense encourages us to remember that when we offer up ourselves, we must not first have our life taken from our bodies. Despite being worthy of death, He wants us alive so that He can use us the way He sees fit.

The "holy" sacrifice reminds us that our bodies are to live in a manner that portrays the holy ways of God. He is holy and so we are to be like Him. The sacrifice must be both "living and holy." The Lord wants to consume us while we are alive. Holiness refers to the absolute penetration of God's plan and purpose into our own lives.

I am the Lord's. Since I am alive as I sacrifice myself to the Lord, I find that I must daily dedicate myself to my Master and let Him always and in any way rule my life. As someone has wisely observed, the problem with a living sacrifice is that he or she can get off the altar! It is our purpose to stay on that altar through full obedience.

"Acceptable to God"
We take great joy to think that what we do for Him each day to please Him. Our bodies are dedicated to God to carry out His purposes. These very acts of our body become instruments of praise. We must not think God only wants our minds and hearts but also our bodies so we can be holy vessels for His service.

A prayer
> I deeply thank you Lord that you were able and willing to change me. I know my old selfish person and marvel at your hand of change over my life. I dedicate my body to You so that I might glorify you today and each moment of my remaining minutes straight into eternity. It is my highest pleasure to please you with my body, even with my whole life.

"Your spiritual service of worship"
What we do with our bodies can be used as our spiritual service. Our bodies, when dedicated to the Lord and to His service, become a spiritual act of service. This service, in turn, becomes an act of worship, reminding us of Jesus' words, "If you love Me, you will keep My commandments" (John 14:15). Love is far more than a feeling. Genuine love commands our whole attention.

We can be confident of our worship when we obey His commands with our physical bodies, even as a servant helps and cares for others. As our bodies conform to the purpose and will of the Almighty God, then these acts– through His mercy, become worship. Worship occurs not only when we gather together to praise Him but when we constrain our bodies to do what He instructs us. Holding a baby or tenderly caring for my wife are acts of worship as much as leading songs at a worship service or proclaiming the gospel to the lost.

> **I urge you to present your bodies a living and holy sacrifice, acceptable to God.**
---

2. Rejecting the World

² And do not be conformed to this world... (Rom 12:2).

A key component to a strong spiritual life is the inner rejection of what the world offers. Our bodies might be constrained by our environment, church, a parent, or available cash, but if our minds are still desirous of the world's ways, then we will fall into temptation. Persistent godly living depends on identifying the world's temptations, observing how they are hostile to God's ways (1 Jo 2:15-17), and rejecting the notion that what the world offers is better than what God has promised. The world, in many cases, greatly cripples the lives of believers by subtly warping their minds and commitments. Evolution for example, one of many dangerous philosophies, denies the creation account and sin's origin, but it also creates a sinister doubt in the reliability of God's Word.

3. Renewing of the Mind and Affirming God's Will

> ² And do not be conformed to this world, but be transformed by the renewing of your mind, that you may prove what the will of God is, that which is good and acceptable and perfect (Rom 12:2).

The way to escape the influence of the world is to transform our thought process. This starts by rejecting the ways of the world. If we love the world, we will be influenced by it. This transformation comes through the renewing of our minds through the Word of God. Because of God's nature now at work in us, we desire the Word of God. If we do not allow God's Word to guide us, however, then we can be assured that the evil one has already ensured us in one or more temptations to steer us off God's path.[56]

"Renewing of your mind"
Renewal of our minds challenges what we believe and accept. What we say we believe in is often not what we really believe. We can better tell what we believe by carefully tracing our decisions. For example, do we doubt God's will as being the best? Do we question our Maker's purpose as being inferior to our own plans? Our resistance to conforming to God's holy ways reveals our inner doubts. Renewal of the mind takes God's Word deeper into our belief system, much like a light turned on in a darkroom. This brings about the transformation Paul mentions, where the penetration of His truth into our unbelieving minds changes our beliefs and enables us to more faithfully obey Him. It is in obeying God that we gain a wonderful appreciation for His will.

---

[56] This concept is expanded in our small book, Life Transformation. http://www.foundationsforfreedom.net/Help/Store/Intros/LIfe-Transformation.html

"The will of God"

The renewing of the mind is a process by which we increasingly become convinced that God's ways are supreme in every way. The maturing believer becomes keenly aware of the inferior ways of the world and how God's will is always good, acceptable, and perfect. Each of us, then, proves God's will by our obedience and observing the results of obedience in our daily lives.

God's people, however, often do not renew their mind, and therefore remain unconvinced that God's will is always the best. The renewing of the mind most often occurs through effective daily spiritual quiet (i.e. devotional) times where we seek God's will and way in His Word.

B. Properly Ministering to Others (Rom 12:3-8)

Before Paul goes on to provide many exhortations to God's people (9-21), he provides a general approach on how each believer ought to care for one another as members of the same body. It is important for God's people to realize the importance of rightly relating to one another. We are to love God by caring for the ones He loves.

1. Responsible to Build Up Others (12:3-5)

> ³ For through the grace given to me I say to every man among you not to think more highly of himself than he ought to think; but to think so as to have sound judgment, as God has allotted to each a measure of faith. ⁴ For just as we have many members in one body and all the members do not have the same function, ⁵ so we, who are many, are one body in Christ, and individually members one of another (Rom 12:3-5).

God's people were not given their resources so that they could be selfishly used. If God has given us our faith and gifts, then we ought to humble ourselves and realize that God wants us to utilize them. We are one body, not many. God's one body has many members, and each form an important part, like a segment of a circle. Together, we form a whole. Everyone's contribution is significant. Observing what God has given us is the first step in learning to use what we have for the sake of others. It helps us grasp how God wants to use our lives. If we belong to each other, then we should treat them just as we treat ourselves.

"God has allotted to each a measure of faith" can refer either to the gospel and its associated faith by which we enter and remain part of the body of Christ, or the particular measure of faith associated with the gift that is given. I prefer to consider the second interpretation due to the context, which is expanded below. The major point is that God has allotted what we have received along with our salvation, faith, and gifts–a grace package. In verses 6-8, Paul identifies numerous spiritual gifts.

2. Responsible for Our Spiritual Gifts (12:6-8)

> 6 And since we have gifts that differ according to the grace given to us, let each exercise them accordingly: if prophecy, according to the proportion of his faith; 7 if service, in his serving; or he who teaches, in his teaching; 8 or he who exhorts, in his exhortation; he who gives, with liberality; he who leads, with diligence; he who shows mercy, with cheerfulness (Rom 12:6-8).

The spiritual gifts that we receive will vary. These gifts differ in proportion as well as in combination. Each believer has at least one spiritual gift and ought to use this special grace from God to carry out good deeds through the power of the Spirit of God and to His glory. This responsibility to serve is seen in the two phrases: "since we have gifts" and "let each exercise." Paul sees the whole body working together. No one has the right to exclude themselves from God's special grace or limit whom they should minister.

The grace that our Lord imparts to us largely shapes our future work for Him and others. Since it is given to us, there leaves no room for pride; we should only have determination to meet the needs of others. Paul is thinking about the grace that God imparts to the church through each of our lives, but he is probably also sharpening the sensitivities of the Jews and Gentiles, who are attending the same local church, on how they should minister to each other. This whole section on God's Spirit anointing, equipping, and serving seems lifted from this Old Testament scene, "I will take of the Spirit who is upon you, and will put Him upon them; and they shall bear the burden of the people with you, so that you will not bear it all alone" (Nu 11:17).

There are four major lists of spiritual gifts including: Romans 12, 1 Corinthians 12, Ephesians 4 and 1 Peter 4. Ephesians 4, however, focuses on offices in the church, though they equally feature God's grace, empowerment and gifting. What is unique here in Romans, seen in the chart below, is Paul's exhortation to exercise their spiritual gift according to the grace given to them.

Spiritual gifts	"Exercise accordingly..."
Prophecy	According to the proportion of his faith
Service	In his serving
Teachers	In his teaching
Exhorts	In his exhortation
Gives	With liberality
Leads	With diligence
Mercy	With cheerfulness

Neglect is irresponsibility since it is God's grace that imparts the gift and enables us to use it. The phrase "according to the proportion" shows that, while two people might share the same gifting, the grace might show itself differently and to varying degrees; but the truth remains: all are used of God for the betterment of the people of God.

Do you know what your spiritual gift(s) is? The table above is not an exhaustive list, but it is a good list to start to understand how God largely defines our lives by the way He specially gifts each person He saves. The overall understanding of the way God imparts grace to us is more important than the list of specific gifts. Nevertheless, Paul has reason for enumerating the different graces that he has listed, perhaps to emphasize the need for them as he thinks about the different house churches in Rome. Just by mentioning them, people will begin to find out whether they have such gifts.

Paul starts by listing the gift of prophecy, no doubt the most difficult to understand, though interestingly, by simply mentioning it here (unlike in 1 Corinthians), Paul doesn't seem to suspect it to cause a problem like it has in the church. The Reformers equivocate prophesying with preaching, but there are others who believe that interpretation is unbiblical and biased, leading to weak churches that are insensitive to God because of the neglect of the prophetic gift.

While both the Old and New Testaments instruct us to test prophets and their prophecies, they greatly differ in advice. Due to trickery and false prophets, people appropriately ask, "How shall we know the word which the LORD has not spoken" (Deut 18:21)?

> When a prophet speaks in the name of the LORD, if the thing does not come about or come true, that is the thing which the LORD has not spoken. The prophet has spoken it presumptuously; you shall not be afraid of him (Deut 18:22).

In the Old Testament the prophet that speaks falsely should be killed (Deut 18:20), but the New Testament, and this is where the confusion for us comes in, instructs us to carefully judge the prophecies of others. "And let two or three prophets speak, and let the others pass judgment" (1 Cor 14:29).

In the New Testament there is no longer severe judgment as is found in the Old Testament, perhaps because the prophecies no longer have to do with identifying the True Prophet, the Messiah (Deut 18:15). Jesus is the true Prophet. The New Testament only wants us to make sure the message is consistent with the Word of God, dismissing unbiblical statements. People can prophesy without being a Prophet. So indeed, Paul is encouraging prophecy among the local churches.[57]

The other gifts are relatively self-explanatory; each needs to be identified and developed in one's context. Note that these gifts are given to free God's people to do His will. They give us a wonderful sense of how the body of Christ is to minister to each other.

Notice that each is responsible to use the spiritual gift(s) God has given him or her. For example, God is not only pleased that a believer would give, but expects that that giving be done liberally. Faith is needed for a person to trust God to adequately give to him so that he can be a vessel through which God works. Those who lead must not just head up a group of individuals on some certain task but be diligent to carry out oversight over them, pitching in when needed, guiding everyone to use their gifts for the common good. The person with mercy gifts needs to serve with a sense of cheerfulness, not begrudging their opportunity and responsibility. The special admonition with each gift reminds us that the way we carry out our task is just as important as doing it.

Summary

God has graced our lives so that we can uniquely serve Him and others. In this way we expand His kingdom by further extending His grace into the lives of our fellow believers. Our spiritual gifts often becomes the area where we find

---

[57] Some take this to mean that until the canon has been fully produced, that prophecy, distinct from preaching, would be a common gift. Others assume this passage teaches, along with Eph 4, that prophecy is a common gift that has largely been ignored in many churches.

the greatest joy in serving, largely because God's Spirit has specifically anointed us in those areas. We observe certain needs and step in. Remember, although these are gifts, we improve as we regularly use those spiritual gifts.

Application
- What spiritual gift(s) is yours?
- When do you carry out that spiritual gift? How regularly?
- With what kind of attitude do you carry it out?

Romans 12:9-21
Principles of Christian Growth

Verses 9-21 form an extension of the first verses of the chapter. After the first two verses on dedication, "present your bodies a living and holy sacrifice," we are charged to commit ourselves to the body of Christ, the church. Our commitment to serving each other, the body of Christ, directly affects our love for Jesus Christ, the head of the body.

People are made in the image of God, so the way we treat others reflects how we treat God. Before enumerating the many exhortations, Paul shares how we as believers are spiritually integrated in the lives of those around us through our service toward them shown through our spiritual gifts (3-8). Christ is committed, as Head, to determine how we help and minister to others by giving us these spiritual gifts through the Holy Spirit. This works in reverse too, when we are ministered to by others so that we, as a whole, are strong and healthy.

> **EXHORTATIONS**
>
> Each instruction reveals weaknesses we need to stand guard against.
>
> The truth is a restatement of what ought to be true in our lives.
>
> The exhortation challenges us to extend our faith further in God to carry out what He deems to be important.
>
> Our resolve to obey helps us to target the changes that we need to make in our lives, often including a change in our attitudes and values.

The apostle, starting in verse 9, provides 25 exhortations to guide believers on how they are to live out their Christian lives. These terse 'tweets' on living righteous lives should stimulate the whole body of Christ to act properly toward one another.

Residing deep below the surface of each of the following exhortations lies a set of values and assumptions. Simple obedience will radically improve our lives, but they usually only affect us when they are on our minds. Each exhortation guides us a bit deeper in our thinking to reevaluate our thoughts and values, which in turn results in better decisions. This process was earlier referred to as "renewing your mind" (Rom 12:2).

For each command, I will list an objection to further stimulate your thinking regarding the exhortation. Each objection reveals one 'counter' thought and value that urge you to dismiss the exhortation as being irrelevant or unhelpful. Evaluate your own life and conform, for this is God's will for each of us: that we would live holy and godly lives.

A. The Exhortations

Let love be without hypocrisy. (Rom 12:9)

Objection: "But what if I don't really love them?"

This pretentious love hints at our willingness to present a false view of ourselves to others. We are forced to ask, "Can genuine love be companions with hypocrisy?" Genuine love is powerful because there are no secret motives. Love is an authentic concern that supersedes one's preoccupation with self and focuses on meeting the needs of others.

Abhor what is evil. (Rom 12:9)

Objection: "But then I can't watch my programs!"

This injunction to hate evil reveals our casual relationship with evil. Hate is more than avoidance; it is an intense dislike for something. Hate does not allow for compromise. Our lives are protected when our heart dislikes any shade of wrong. With the Spirit's help we need to understand what evil is and how to detest it.

Cling to what is good. (Rom 12:9)

Objection: "But I only sometimes meet with God and have devotions."

The instruction implies that we often set our hearts on evil and inferior things. 'Cling' reveals a strong response to what we treasure and consider most important. 'Good' includes all the wholesome plans, resources, and relationships that are appointed by God for our lives. The word 'cling' demands our whole grip, requiring that we release other loves. What God has stored up for us to possess is infinitely better than the vapors that the world offers.

Be devoted to one another in brotherly love. (Rom 12:10)

Objection: "But can't I just be nice?"

The command to be devoted to loving one another provides insight into how easy it is to trivialize this primary command, relegating loving acts toward others as less important than meeting the concerns for our lives. Brotherly love is the kind and expected treatment of others, as if they are family members. The word 'devoted' can be more literally translated 'be kindly affectionate.' Set aside any inclination to underrate the high calling to be kind to your fellow Christian.

Give preference to one another in honor. (Rom 12:10)

Objection: "But I like to be noticed."

This instruction to prefer others over ourselves connects our treatment of others with our attitudes toward them. 'Give preference' refers to focusing on the needs of those around us while the word 'honor' speaks of their importance. They are important because they have been called by the Lord, and therefore we must pay due care to their needs, as though they are honored guests. As we realize and respond to our privilege to prefer those around us, the 'me' instinct starts fading away.

Not lagging behind in diligence. (Rom 12:11)

Objection: "But I am used to just getting by."

This warning of lagging behind in diligence hints at how we put off what is important and compromise excellence. 'Not lagging' suggests laziness or a shifting of responsibilities. 'Diligence' focuses on the persistence in doing what is right and makes up for our imperfections. The Lord's calling sets us in the path to fulfilling His 'good works' for our lives (Eph 2:10), and so we give our time and energy to properly complete His assignments.

Fervent in spirit. (Rom 12:11)

Objection: "But I must not get carried away!"

This exhortation to fervency reminds us that it is easy to 'just get things done.' God is not only interested in the completion of certain tasks but in the way they should be completed. 'Fervent' is an eager and zealous push to even get the tough jobs done in the right way. 'In spirit' refers not to our bodies but our inner persons and attitudes, though our bodies will often be commandeered by this spirit. God's calling is a high calling and therefore requires everything we do to be done in a proper spirit.

Serving the Lord. (Rom 12:11)

Objection: "But I am very busy."

This instruction to serve the Lord, though seemingly so obvious, reveals how often we divorce our lives from our duties to complete our Master's wishes. 'Serving' is the wrestling of our will to complete the desire of another, in this case, the Lord Jesus' will. His plan and purpose for us is largely revealed by these many exhortations. We gain further confidence that what God wills is always best and perfect by carrying out what He asks (cf. Rom 12:2). All what we do must be connected to the purpose of accomplishing what our Lord desires. As His servants, everything we do should be in service to Him.

Rejoicing in hope. (Rom 12:12)

Objection: "But you don't know what I'm facing!"

This surprising exhortation to rejoice in hope reminds us that, at times, we might be tempted to dismiss hope and thus miss out on the bright joy that is ours. 'Hope' is the vibrant anticipatory stare that keeps us pursuing God's promises and love. 'Rejoicing' is an exuberant thrill over what God will do in time, even though we might be experiencing dark circumstances. We need hope to destroy all our doubts so that the seeds of hope in God can be planted in our hearts to strengthen our spirit.

Persevering in tribulation. (Rom 12:12)

Objection: "But it's my nature to give up."

This exhortation to persevere in tribulation suggests that we need extra encouragement to face difficulties lest we pull back, especially when affliction persists. 'Tribulation' includes all sorts of difficulties that we might face when we purpose to follow the Lord. 'Persevering' is the unwavering confidence to persist in doing what is good and right despite the opposition faced. A surge of confidence in God's way of working through these difficult times enables us to accomplish His greater purposes. Paul wrote the last half of Romans 8 to build up our trust in God in preparation of difficult times, so that we might persevere.

Devoted to prayer. (Rom 12:12)

Objection: "But I'm just a new Christian!"

This call to prayer shows us how easy it is for us to forget to pray or to be content with religious prayers that are not fortified with any real faith. Prayer is a special communion with God wherein we make our praise, confessions, and needs known to God. The word 'devoted' differs from verse 10, as it speaks of that powerful drive to do something. God wants to raise our confidence in the power of prayer. Tiny prayer meetings in churches with large congregations often reflect a lack of faith, but God has called us to come before Him seeking His blessing like a mighty throng.

Contributing to the needs of the saints. (Rom 12:13)

Objection: "But I have my own needs to take care of."

This exhortation to give to the needs of God's people remind us how easy it is to forget the greater needs of those around us and our responsibility to help meet those needs. We tend to focus on what we don't have, but the Lord wants us to focus on our ability to meet the needs of others. 'Needs' is a catch-all word. The word 'contribution' interestingly has its root word in *koinonia* (i.e. fellowship) and becomes one place God uses the community and contributions–not just financial–to accomplish His greater purposes of building up the body of Christ. We should carefully consider the specific amounts and percentages of our income that we contribute.

Practicing hospitality. (Rom 12:13)

Objection: "But my place isn't good enough."

This injunction to practice hospitality hints at the possible neglect of putting up others as they travel nearby. Without hotels, hospitality fulfilled a big need for the traveling saints. The word 'practicing' tells us that it not good enough to think about how we would like to host people, but pushes us to actually take steps to host them. God is pleased when we go out of our way and share what we have with others.

Bless those who persecute you. Bless and curse not. (Rom 12:14)

Objection: "But I can't stand them."

This call to bless our persecutors reminds us of Jesus' words on the Sermon on the Mount (Matt 5:44). The action 'bless' is not how we typically respond to persecution; in most cases, we'd rather bring harm to our oppressors. The word 'bless' is used twice, emphasizing that we only have one response and it must be done in faith, entrusting ourselves and our loved ones to God's sovereign care. Instead of just enduring, tolerating, or withholding evil words, we step out in faith by blessing our persecutors.

Rejoice with those who rejoice. (Rom 12:15)

Objection: "But why should he or she get all the breaks?"

This reminder to rejoice with others should shake us from our petty jealousies and unholy competitions. Paul awakens us from our self-seeking lives and pushes us to get caught up in the joy of others. Passive attention is unsatisfactory in light of the excitement we should have for others as they see God actively moving in their lives.

Weep with those who weep. (Rom 12:15)

Objection: "But I have enough of my own problems."

His command to weep with others warns us not to focus on our own troubles but to get engaged in the lives of those around us. Others might state, "Don't get involved with others so that you don't have to deal with their problems," but this is not the mindset set before us here. We must be willing to grieve with others. We are to get so involved in the lives of others that we can sympathize with them. Lord, increase our sense of mercy!

Be of the same mind toward one another. (Rom 12:16)

Objection: "But I just get along with that person."

This caution to guide our attitudes toward others not only keeps us from pride but brings us deeper into the bond of love. When our biases and arrogance are stripped away, we will see each brother and sister as designed according to God's special design. God is shaping them into Christ's image just as He is doing with us. This faith strengthens our commitment to others.

Do not be haughty in mind but associate with the lowly. (Rom 12:16)

Objection: "But I am better than him."

Pride wrongly separates us from others and causes disunity rather than a strong and healthy body life. Instead of solely associating with the rich, connected, and intelligent, we are called to spend time caring for the average and lowly person. The church always has those who do not fit into society, but these individuals are very much part of the church. We should fellowship with those that others neglect.

Do not be wise in your estimation. (Rom 12:16)

Objection: "But I think I can do it."

This prohibition to think too much of our own opinion allows us to break down the walls of pride that might have developed in our lives. By esteeming our own views, practices, and thoughts, we exclude ourselves from seeking insight from God and others, which negatively affects our walk with the Lord. Instead, let us be quick to acknowledge our weaknesses, ignorance, and needs, seeking with others to grow in the likeness of Christ by loving one another.

Never pay back evil for evil to anyone. (Rom 12:17)

Objection: "But I am just giving back what he deserves."

This exhortation to not pay back evil for evil (also 12:19) is a powerful statement that interrupts our flesh's desire to wrong those who have hurt us. As followers of Christ, we must refuse to go along with Satan who wants to bring more evil into the world, but instead purpose ourselves to introduce the Lord's love to those around us. We are forbidden to enter any contemplation or action of hurting someone or getting back at them.

Respect what is right in the sight of all men. (Rom 12:17)

Objection: "But I don't have to bother with what others think, do I?"

This instruction to respect what is right leads us to accept God-instilled values wherever they are found around the globe. Sometimes people are brought up to have a mutual respect for each other because of the good values that are embedded into their culture's moral code. Note, however, that we are not to respect all the opinions and customs of the world but 'what is right' from the Lord's viewpoint. At times societies adopt imperfect behavior, bringing harm upon the people. Even now, evil people purposely strip out any sense of 'right' and make evil into being 'good' and accepted. This command, however, guides us into a proper respect of all the good things people do.

As far as it depends on you, be at peace with all men. (Rom 12:18)

Objection: "But I can't forgive him."

This particular instruction to be at peace with all calls us to be reconciliatory at heart. Peace is the absence of conflict, a place where tension of opposing opinions are gone. We can sacrifice our preferences to gain this peace but never our values. Whether it be a brother, spouse, or colleague, we should always take steps to secure the peace that can be found, never holding back on our efforts when we see others withhold their due part.

> **Never take your own revenge, but leave room for the wrath of God.... (Rom 12:19)**

Objection: "But someone has to teach him a lesson or two."

Again, as in verse 17, we are called not to take revenge. Paul elaborates on this by speaking about God's prerogative to judgment. Refusing revenge should not be seen as denying justice because God handles that. Our part is to forgive, make peace, and treat others kindly. Taking revenge upsets God's way of handling judgment.

> **If your enemy is hungry, feed him, and if he is thirsty, give him a drink. (Rom 12:20)**

Objection: "But I am only treating him as he treated me."

Not only are we called to be kind and to withhold evil from our unkind neighbor, but we are to go out of our way to graciously help him or her. If they are hungry, feed them. If thirsty, give them a drink. We treat our enemy as our friend, bestowing kind acts to fulfill their needs.

> **Do not be overcome by evil, but overcome evil with good. (Rom 12:21)**

Objection: "But I am just so upset with her."

The prohibition to give oneself into evil reminds us that, without God's grace, each of us would end up overpowered by evil. But as God's people, we have God's mighty hand leading us by equipping us to overcome the tendency to do evil by carrying out acts of goodness. What a blessing to be able to choose and do good!

B. Other Questions

1. Is this legalism?

Responding to these exhortations is not legalism. Legalism does not focus on carrying out God's commands but on doing things better than others so that they can gain acceptance before God. Legalists often compare themselves with others because they use their own standards to judge themselves. Because of this, they often think much of themselves and despise others.

2. Are they laws?

We should think of the above statements as exhortations to keep the law of love. By doing them, we in no way can gain the righteousness that is needed before God (Rom 3:9-10); that only comes through God's forgiveness through the cross. Since we have already failed God, even a perfect attempt to please God still produces a stained record worthy of death. Instead, daily delight with me in Jesus as our Savior!

Living out these exhortations will produce righteous living (living the right way). These commands are the ways that we retrain our mind (c.f. Rom 12:2) to think about others so that we can rightly allow the Spirit of God to mightily work through our lives.

Application

Look back over the list once more. Notice what areas of life Paul is calling us to improve upon. He wants us to rightly treat other people, especially other believers. Having been redeemed, what should our lives look like?

Romans 13:1-14
Living in the World

In chapter 12, after he challenged us to fully dedicate our lives to God, Paul went on to speak of our mutual obligations to other believers. But those believers, like us, live in a real world that presents many obstacles that can prevent us from carrying out God's commands and exhortation. In Romans 13, Paul clearly states how to live rightly with those we have contact with–no matter who they are. He discusses our relationship with the government (13:1-7) as well as with the world in general (13:8-14).

A. Subject to Governing Authorities (13:1-7)
1. God's Establishment of Governing Authorities (Rom 13:1)

> ¹ Let every person be in subjection to the governing authorities. For there is no authority except from God, and those which exist are established by God (13:1).

Romans 13:1 powerfully calls all believers (and indeed everyone) to be subject to their governing authorities. God has established these authorities and is therefore in full control of them. Each believer must accept the government over them as God's instrument and respectfully subject himself to it,[58] though we should not conclude that God approves of what the governments does. He does hold them responsible, however.

2. Need to Subject Oneself (13:2-5)

> ² Therefore he who resists authority has opposed the ordinance of God; and they who have opposed will receive condemnation upon themselves. ³ For rulers are not a cause of fear for good behavior, but for evil. Do you want to have no fear of authority? Do what is good,

---

[58] This does not mean that we are not to get involved in the government. 1 Timothy 2:1-2 instructs us to pray for the government. How we pray and live impacts our government. The light and salt principles clearly bear on this (Mat 5:13-16).

and you will have praise from the same; 4 for it is a minister of God to you for good. But if you do what is evil, be afraid; for it does not bear the sword for nothing; for it is a minister of God, an avenger who brings wrath upon the one who practices evil. 5 Wherefore it is necessary to be in subjection, not only because of wrath, but also for conscience' sake (13:2-5).

Paul carefully shows how those who oppose or resist authority not only oppose the government but also God Himself. If we go against the government, then we are also going against God and will face severe consequences for our disobedience.

Practically speaking, the apostle wants us to come clean in our conscience. A person only fears the government when he hides wrong behavior.[59] He first summarizes this short section by reviewing the two reasons we ought to subject ourselves to the government: (1) avoid suffering severe consequences and (2) obtain clean consciences.

God works through the government to curb the evil of mankind. Some might question this, but in fact, these things appear to be much more difficult to believe in the ancient world of tyrants rather than in modern democracies. By sword it means that the government has every right to implement severe punishment to eliminate the evil and unruly. If we do evil, then God might just discipline us through the government. Paul is shaping the conduct of God's people to work along with God rather than against Him.

Subjection is a way of life. Righteous living not only avoids severe consequences, but enables one to live in the joy and freedom associated with a clean conscience. Inner joy is a wonderful byproduct of righteous service.

3. Paying Taxes (Rom 13:6-7)

6 For because of this you also pay taxes, for rulers are servants of God, devoting themselves to this very thing. 7 Render to all what is due them: tax to whom tax is due; custom to whom custom; fear to whom fear; honor to whom honor (13:6-7).

Some societies obligate its peoples to give very high taxes (socialistic societies demand over 50%). Whether we be rich or poor, paying taxes are God's means to provide for the rulers that He appoints over us to govern as they see

---

[59] The government sometimes commits unruly behavior and kills innocent citizens. Paul does not approve this, but asserts the government is responsible before God and will be held accountable. Paul will later be killed by this dictatorship that he tells us to honor.

fit. Yes, they might request more than we think is right or spend those tax dollars in ways that we object, but the government is responsible to God for their decisions. While entrusting them to God for judgment, we are exhorted to faithfully pay our taxes. Avoiding the payment of our due taxes with dishonesty is not a way to get more money for God! (Legal ways to lessen one's tax load is acceptable.) A proper attitude toward our government comes from understanding the government's role over us.

At the end of verse 7, the apostle starts mentioning other areas of concern, "Render to all what is due them: tax to whom tax is due; custom to whom custom; fear to whom fear; honor to whom honor" (13:7).

Paul had time to think about these matters when he was imprisoned by his persecutors. He saw benefits and abuses, but the fact that the government is God's appointed steward steers us away from any bitterness and should cause us to pray for those in authority. Poor laws need, if possible, to be contested before implementation, but if they become law, then we should obey–if indeed they do not blatantly force us into compliance with evil (Dan 6:10, Acts 4:18-19). People are called to respect their leaders, an example we are called to live out. The government is only one authority that we must reckon with, but whoever is in authority over us, must receive our due respect.

B. General Principles for Living (13:8-14)

1. Love Summarizes the Law (13:8-10)

> 8 Owe nothing to anyone except to love one another; for he who loves his neighbor has fulfilled the law. 9 For this, "YOU SHALL NOT COMMIT ADULTERY, YOU SHALL NOT MURDER, YOU SHALL NOT STEAL, YOU SHALL NOT COVET," and if there is any other commandment, it is summed up in this saying, "YOU SHALL LOVE YOUR NEIGHBOR AS YOURSELF." 10 Love does no wrong to a neighbor; love therefore is the fulfillment of the law (Rom 13:8-10).

These verses are a continuation from verse 7 and therefore provide two possible ways of understanding the word, 'owe'. The phrase, "Owe nothing to anyone" (8) is composed of very strong negatives in the original Greek, "Never for no reason owe...." Some understand this as an exhortation against taking loans (the OT speaks about usury) while others understand it to mean that we should not have outstanding debts like taxes.

(1) The word 'owe' is in the context of money (speaking of taxes) and therefore is to be understood as a charge not to borrow or owe people things. By refusing to borrow, we will not owe others. We are to be content with what God gives us.

(2) The second interpretation links the word 'owe' to our general obligations mentioned in 13:7, 'custom to whom custom, fear to whom fear; honor to honor.' We are not to come short on the proper treatment of others. A snobbish or rebellious attitude falls short of love's duty and therefore we 'owe' them.

Both interpretations are contextually possible. Even if we understand this exhortation to not solely focus on owing people money, we should be careful to include money as part of second interpretation and not to owe people anything. We are under obligation to love one another. As long as we borrow from others, we cannot easily live out righteous lives. Paul elsewhere instructed us work hard to give rather than spend (Eph 4:28). We are to be content with what we have. Our society's attitudes certainly challenges us as it applauds debt as a wise means of getting ahead.

He goes on and mentions the ten commandments. People say that we are not under the Law (which is true). Does this mean we are not to obey these commandments? We need to clarify what the Bible says in regard to this. The commands not to steal, murder, and commit adultery are still prohibitions for us. "Summed up" means that by focusing on properly caring for others, we will necessarily keep these other laws. If we do not covet, then we will not spend more than we have. We will not 'owe others' and take loans. We will not lust after others. "Love therefore is the fulfillment of the law" (10).

2. Love Supersedes Impurity (13:11-14)

> 11 And this do, knowing the time, that it is already the hour for you to awaken from sleep; for now salvation is nearer to us than when we believed. 12 The night is almost gone, and the day is at hand. 13 Let us therefore lay aside the deeds of darkness and put on the armor of light. Let us behave properly as in the day, not in carousing and drunkenness, not in sexual promiscuity and sensuality, not in strife and jealousy. 14 But put on the Lord Jesus Christ, and make no provision for the flesh in regard to its lusts (Rom 13:11-14).

Paul is not instructing us on the way we are to avoid association with people in general (1 Cor 5:10), but for the believer to not walk in the company of the seductive world. The believer must stay awake, preserving due vigilance, so as not to be caught unaware and fall asleep (be lured by adopting the world's values and ways). By salvation, he is not referring to the time believers were saved but the final glorification that takes place upon Christ's return.

The believer is to make sure that he does not partake in any deeds of darkness. Instead he is to put on the armor of light. The light is obedience (Eph 5:9), rightly responding to God's example of love and graciousness. Light in this case becomes a protective armor. If one indulges in his lusts, his shield is taken down, and he becomes susceptible to the attacks of the evil one. Strife or jealousy are not lesser sins then drunkenness or sensuality. Each strips off the armor and makes a person vulnerable to the enemy's attack.

The imagery of putting on a set of clothes or armor is conveyed by the phrase 'putting on the Lord Jesus Christ' (Eph 6:10-15). The believer needs to accommodate Jesus' holy ways, of living a life of love. Making 'no provision for the flesh' points to a certain weakness that is tolerated and protected in one's life. It allows an angry person to justify his anger ("He deserved it.") A 'repentant' adulterer might keep the girl or guy's number handy. The provision would keep the loan officer's card around just in case he changes his mind. We are forbidden to grant a place for evil to lie dormant where it can later subtly dangle sin in front of us, for in our weakness, we will again embrace these sins. Instead, may Christ lead us to rightly care for others, and to seek out special opportunities to love others.

Summary

Our relationships to others oftentimes extends beyond our family and church contacts into the world. These short treatments on how to relate to governing authorities and people in general benefit everyone. Living in light of the soon appearing of Jesus Christ enables us to persistently keep God's principles as guiding points for our lives.

Romans 14:1-23
Judge Not Others

In Romans 14 the apostle begins to address specific issues that have come up as a thorn between the Jewish and Gentile Christians. If they have equally been saved through faith in Christ, then they form one body of believers. Believers from varying backgrounds regularly meet up with each other and learn how to work together for the unity and proper functioning of the church. How are they going to handle these differences? If not properly dealt with, such issues will eventually lead to entangled relationships and a dysfunctional church. Rather than being filled with God's Spirit, they are consumed with prideful thoughts and bitterness.

These same potential troubles still occur in our churches today. How should we handle them? Though set in a different cultural context from what most of us face today, this passage provides an abundance of relevant teaching that is meant to guide believers. General principles on how to relate to each other were given in chapters 12-13, but extra insight is needed, lest we end up doing evil when we think we are doing the right thing. This was the problem before the believers in Romans 14.

Paul risked a lot of misunderstanding as he approached the issue of Christian liberty. Even as he shows how to handle differences between varying groups, other misunderstandings can develop. These issues of judging others and determining standards will be dealt with later.

Romans 14 specifically provides instruction as to what love and humility look like in a context where believers are convinced that others are in the wrong. The context reminds us that this is not over a crucial doctrinal truth or clear command as stated earlier in Romans, but how to live out holy lives.

 JUDGING OTHERS

In this particular case one group of believers judged another group because they came to different conclusions as to what consists of good or bad 'Christian' behavior. From one group's perspective, certain traditional religious activities or notions are important to holy living. The other group believed that there is nothing wrong with what they are doing, even if it is contrary to what the other group believes.

A. The Conflict (Rom 14:1-6)

¹ Now <u>accept the one who is weak</u> in faith, but not for the purpose of passing judgment on his opinions. ² One man has faith that he may eat all things, but he who is weak eats vegetables only. ³ <u>Let not him who eats regard with contempt</u> him who does not eat, and <u>let not him who does not eat <u>judge</u></u> him who eats, for God has accepted him. ⁴ Who are you to judge the servant of another? To his own master he stands or falls; and stand he will, for the Lord is able to make him stand. ⁵ One man regards one day above another, another regards every day alike. <u>Let each man be fully convinced</u> in his own mind. ⁶ He who observes the day, observes it for the Lord, and he who eats, does so for the Lord, for he gives thanks to God; and he who eats not, for the Lord he does not eat, and gives thanks to God (Rom 14:1-6).

Not only is this first section, verses 1-6, shaped by the command in verse 1, but the whole chapter is: "Accept the one who is weak in faith." There are three commands mentioned in verses 1-6.⁶⁰ They set the foundation for what Paul says in Romans 14.

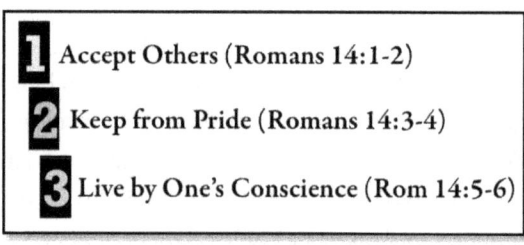

(1) Accept those who are weak in faith (14:1-2)

(2) Not regard those who eat with contempt (14:3-4)

---

⁶⁰ There are actually four if we count 'Do not judge' but we have categorized this one with the second.

(3) Be fully convinced in his own mind (14:5-6)

Paul defines, expands, and defends how the 'strong' are to accept the 'weak' in faith. The person who finds freedom in his conscience to treat all food and days alike is 'strong' rather than 'weak'. This person must be careful to accept the weak in faith, though this does not allow one to despise or be critical of others.

Application

Attitudes are important. Many of us, however, have never learned to hold positive attitudes toward those with whom we differ. Because of this, we end up disdaining the ones we disagree with rather than praying for and building them up. Do you usually experience negative thoughts toward those who disagree with you? Explain.

1. Accept Others (14:1-2)

The word 'accept' speaks of gracious and kind treatment. Believers should not judge or despise those who in their eyes possess an inferior faith. Each person must be respected for his own faith. This statement is very liberating, especially for those coming from legalistic backgrounds where one is so preoccupied with criticizing others that there is little time for love.

The Weak

The 'weak,' in this case, are the ones who believe that it is proper and necessary to be vegetarian ("eats vegetables only" verse 2). They are not just thinking that it is a better diet but that it is morally proper. In their minds, the absence or presence of this activity will largely influence a person's spiritual life.

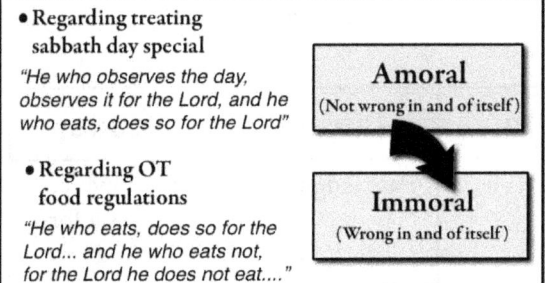

- Regarding treating sabbath day special
  "He who observes the day, observes it for the Lord, and he who eats, does so for the Lord"

- Regarding OT food regulations
  "He who eats, does so for the Lord... and he who eats not, for the Lord he does not eat...."

The weak in faith is the one who is bound in his mind from having complete freedom with regards to eating all food and keeping days (or similar amoral issues).

This includes the Jewish person who refuses to eat pork. He could eat pork but believes he is gravely displeasing the Lord by eating pork due to his upbringing with Old Testament traditions. In this case, it would be better for this person to not eat pork, even though he is free to do so.

Others consider those who eat meat to not be living holy lives. Perhaps they believe the meat that they eat is unholy, perhaps because it was offered to an idol. When teaching in India, believers would prepare both kinds of food, one for vegetarian and one for those who eat meat. This policy shows that they have come to respect both groups and their standards. Strict Hindus are brought up not eating meat for they believe the life in it is holy.

Paul tells those with such convictions that they are right to refrain from eating meat if they believe so deeply about the issue. As the diagram above shows, amoral issues, which are not really right or wrong, can become wrong to those when it counters their consciences.

This issue, no doubt, made this group content, but probably only in degree since they were described as 'weak'. They have not grown to full maturity in belief (though they probably think they have and wonder why the others have not caught up to them). They are to accept others who hold to different principles (verse 3).

The Strong

Paul, however, also reprimands the way the 'strong' might mistreat the 'weak'. The 'strong' believe it is fine to eat all sorts of food, and thus need to refrain from looking down on those who do not think it is proper to eat all things (those things probably being those not permissible according to the Old Testament law). The strong can actually get quite haughty and, if not careful, belittle the faith of those who do not accept their perspective.

Conflict	Faith	Attitudes	Needs
The strong	Can eat all	Pass judgment	Fully convinced he does it for God
The weak	eat what is holy	Judge others	Fully convinced he does it for God
Error in life is due to an error in perception.			

In Paul's mind, what one eats is not a moral issue, both are okay. They are different from the exhortations in Romans 12:9-21 which guide our attitudes and behaviors. Problems develop, however, when believers make these immoral issues into moral ones. For example, when I was a teen, many believers thought it immoral to watch any movie. How does one keep harmony with other believers when what you do is frowned upon as sin by others? Paul is instructing us on how some issues are different and our attitudes need to be carefully monitored.

Coming to Different Values

Although there is some debate regarding the circumstances that Paul was alluding to, it seems that there is a consensus that the apostle was addressing the problems between the Jews and Gentiles in the congregations in Rome. The church, being composed of many smaller congregations due to smaller buildings and less opportunity to travel across the city, necessarily were composed of believers from various backgrounds that lived in that vicinity. Some were raised with one set of customs while others another set. They even perhaps had different languages and foods.

The New Testament covenant had at that point only recently replaced the Old Testament covenant along with its dietary and sabbath laws. They were in effect for the Jewish believers up to the time when Christ with His blood initiated the New Covenant (see Book of Hebrews) but this defined their customs and ways. These Jewish and Gentile believers were worshipping with each other outside of Jerusalem, in Rome, in this case. They had mixed cultures and values and needed to work together as one (Eph 4:3-4).

Application

- What are some issues in life that would be considered irrelevant (amoral) by some in your churches and very important (moral) by others?
- How have 'strong' and 'weak' perspectives affected churches in your area?

Discerning between Amoral and Moral Issues

There is much confusion today about what moral and amoral issues are, or even when something that is not always wrong becomes wrong (e.g. medical ethics). But it is clear, just because Paul was clearly calling the believers not to judge one another, this does not mean every issue was to be tolerated.

Absolute Issues

We should recognize that Paul does say that many things people do are always wrong. For example, in Romans 1:24-32 he makes a long list of prohibitions. In Romans, starting in 12:9 right into chapter 13, is a whole list of things believers should observe. In other places such as 1 Timothy, Paul has added other items, along with Peter, James, etc., on how we talk, live, relate, worship, and dress.

Paul in Romans 12:2, says, "Do not be conformed to the world." We should not confuse Paul's warnings regarding immoral issues such as sexual immorality, greed, and drunkenness with amoral issues. Paul has already spoken against such matters and the church leadership is responsible to conduct church discipline to keep the church pure. "Trial marriage" is one clear immoral issue today because it furthers fornication.

Amoral Issues

On the other hand, Paul does help us recognize that when a certain habit or action is culturally based without any pertaining biblical instruction, then it is permissible (though perhaps not profitable).

However, we must always be careful to closely monitor our attitudes toward those who come to different conclusions than we do. It is here that we might judge others according to our own understanding or conscience. Paul states there are various ways to understand and live out one's faith.

In the adjacent chart identify where each item belongs: Always okay, sometimes okay, or always wrong?

Believers from around the world gathered in Rome, each with differing customs. Some might consider the placement of the Holy Scriptures on the ground to be sinful. We might not. If some consider our treatment of the Bible to be so significant, then how should their perspective affect the way we care for the Bible?

What about dancing? Stealing? What about a steamy movie? For some, 'steamy' might mean viewing a single kiss, while for another person a couple sharing a bed is okay. Let me share some personal comments on three different scenarios. Is it always wrong? Sometimes wrong? Never wrong?

> **You draw the line**
>
> Saying 'four letter' words
> Special sabbath rules Drinking alcohol
> Lying Styling hair
> Bible versions
> Stealing Women wearing pants
> Cosmetics
> Rock worship songs
> Eating pork Wear swimsuits
> Placing Bible on floor Premarital sex
> Watching steamy movies Dancing

Kissing

I remember wanting to show some photos from my second daughter's wedding while I was in India and was warned not to show the photo of the bridegroom kissing the bride. I took the photo out of the slideshow. They thought the public display of kissing between the newly married husband and wife to be wrong. Kissing is a sensual act and therefore should not be seen in public. I do not share that perspective, but greatly appreciated my brother mentioning it to me. It was important for me to be sensitive my brother's suggestion or I would have missed God's clue to avoiding offense among these people that I so love.

Modest clothing

Entertainment has redefined the essence of modesty by going as far as it can to cause further media attention. Where has this left our godly standards? One might not see anything wrong with wearing suggestive or revealing clothing, and it's common to hear a young person state, "What's wrong with it? Everyone wears this. Do you want me to dress out of fashion?" But there is a scriptural call to wear modest dress (1 Timothy 2:9). The question is not whether one's culture accepts that style of dress but whether it is considered modest. To understand this, we must use the scriptures to understand where this whole notion of modesty comes from.

Each individual must come to a standard and live consistently by it. In forming our opinion, we need to be very careful of what others think. For example, revealing clothing has many times forced me to close my eyes or look in different directions during worship services so that I would not have to struggle with temptation. This is improper. Modesty, for a woman, at a minimum, should mean that it does not cause a man to want to look twice in order to see more. And yes, this is my own conviction. I need to be gracious to women who, in my perspective, are wearing immodest clothing.

Drinking alcohol

Each believer must carefully study the scriptures on each controversial. Recently, we were discussing the standard of drinking alcohol during our family devotions. Another person joined us and shared how she used to think it was wrong to have even a little alcohol. Her church even had a 'fight' over one member keeping alcohol in the fridge. But she now believes a little alcohol is not wrong. The sin begins when the alcohol (or drug) affects a person (get tipsy, drunk). She also added that she would never drink alcohol if there was someone that would be hurt or tempted by it. Notice how her perspective changed over the years but continues to prioritize the scriptural admonitions ("do not get drunk") along with not becoming an offense to others.

The Christian life consists of growth in knowledge and practice. Hebrew 5:14 speaks of this process, "...The mature, who because of practice have their senses trained to discern good and evil." They see the dividing line and accordingly adjust their lives. Spiritual development is the process where believers gradually come to carefully discern these issues under the guidance of the scriptures. The other side of the issue is, however, to properly think and treat those who think differently from us. Paul speaks about this in verses 3-4.

2. Keep from Pride (Rom 14:3-4)

> ³<u>Let not him who eats regard with contempt</u> him who does not eat, and <u>let not</u> him who does not eat <u>judge</u> him who eats, for God has accepted him. ⁴ Who are you to judge the servant of another? To his own master he stands or falls; and stand he will, for the Lord is able to make him stand (Rom 14:3-4).

Paul spends a lot of time discussing attitudes. After all, it is not what they were doing regarding the days and food that really mattered. The major problem was the attitudes that affected the way they thought and treated each other. Monitoring attitudes is much easier said than done.

Put Away pride

First, each person should put away one's pride. Paul does not use the word 'pride' here in verses 3-4 but the phrases, "regard with contempt" and "Who are you to judge...", both carrying this meaning. The 'weak' tend to look down on those who, in their eyes, are insensitive to God's Word. The 'strong' can despise those with a weaker faith, those who do not eat (meat).

Pride always poisons. They are judging another as if they are responsible to judge them. This would be a grave mistake. Paul says that God is the judge. "To his own master he stands or falls; and stand he will, for the Lord is able to make him stand." God has accepted both groups. Neither group has the right to disdain or judge another.

Focus on One's Own Faith

Second, we should focus on our own faith before the Lord. We are not responsible to judge others, but we are responsible to consistently and faithfully live out our faith before the Lord.

There are many such issues in today's church including ordination of women, modest dress, the Lord's Day, foods, sports, etc. Instead of being prideful and regarding others with contempt, we need to double check whether we are rightly living before the Lord.

When we think of others, we need to accept their level of faith and help them grow in that faith–without a condemning spirit. This difference of lifestyle should not create conflict with each other but instead serve as an opportunity to prove our love. These tests will persist throughout our lives.

One example of this might be a church that respects the believers who do not eat pork (maybe from Muslim background). They, therefore, avoid using pork for a church luncheon. Another church, perhaps, joyfully prepares vegetarian meals (for those from Hindu or New Age background). Individual believers should go out of their way to regulate their standards for those 'weak' in faith.

But having said this, the 'weak' in faith should not assume everyone understands their convictions, nor should they judge those who would eat pork. It is important that the church as a whole is dictated by the consciences of all the weak. Moderation and wisdom is needed. Everyone is accountable to the Lord. Therefore we can focus on serving and loving each other. More specific treatment on this oft misunderstood phrase, "Judge not others" is below.

Issue: "Judge not Others"

The phrase 'judge not others' is often misunderstood because it is, interestingly so, often taken out of context to legitimize what is wrong. I have heard a number of believers say, "Don't judge me" as a defense mechanism for living in open disobedience to God's Word. The church is called to love and bring people to restoration in the Lord (Gal 6:1).

> Brethren, even if a man is caught in any trespass, you who are spiritual, restore such a one in a spirit of gentleness; each one looking to yourself, lest you too be tempted (Gal 6:1).

There is a place for correction, but it should be done from love (note the word 'restore'). The word trespass speaks of doing something that is clearly wrong (immoral). Where we fall short of a biblical standard, we need to repent from unholy choices. The same caution regarding pride given here is the same as in Romans 14. There is a whole different spirit here than that which is behind those groups in Romans 14.

Paul calls the church not to judge one another. The meaning arises from the context where one prideful group looks down upon another. 'Judge' in this sense means to criticize to a point of forming a judgment against another. When groups begin to judge each other, the church will struggle to focus on loving and serving one another. Paul clearly states that one believer should not usurp God's position as Judge. God is the judge, and as such, He will judge in His own time. When we set ourselves as the judge, then we take God's role as Judge.

As much as Paul speaks here about 'no one judging another', we should not conclude that there are no commands or standards. Love consists in living by standards (Rom 12).

Summary
- God does set standards, laws, commands (see Romans 12-13).
- God expects us to live by His standards (examine biblical usage of 'holy').
- God will judge us for not living by His standards (i.e. curse).
- God will reward us when we live by His standards (i.e. blessings).

Application
- Do you tend to look down on other believers? Why?
- Do you think that you are better than others?

- What areas do you tend to be most prideful in?

3. Live by One's Conscience (Rom 14:5-6)

⁵One man regards one day above another, another regards every day alike. <u>Let each man be fully convinced</u> in his own mind. ⁶ He who observes the day, observes it for the Lord, and he who eats, does so for the Lord, for he gives thanks to God; and he who eats not, for the Lord he does not eat, and gives thanks to God (Rom 14:5-6).

The church as a whole has not taught much regarding the importance of keeping a clean conscience. The term for 'clean conscience' is not used here, but this does not matter. The idea is clearly taught.

The phrase 'fully convinced in his own mind' helps each believer discern whether a given issue is proper always, sometimes, or never. Being 'fully convinced' speaks about what that person has come to believe through understanding the scriptures. It is important in one's own mind to come to grips with what God has to say about a certain issue. It protects the individual from adopting the values of others.

Our consciences have been affected by the fall. They need to be renewed by the Holy Spirit working through the scriptures (2 Tim 3:16-17). 'Fully convinced in his own mind' implies that there has been some wrestling with the issue. Because of this, different conclusions have arisen, each with their supporting evidence. Once a person has gone through this process, they can become fully convinced. This perspective, then, becomes one's upgraded conscience and one must consistently live according to it. It is superior to carefully consider the scriptures and form your own conclusions than to be influenced by the standards (or non-standards) of your friends.

The apostle brings the focus of the two groups to the same goal, that is, to please the Lord. When both have the same purpose, then the issues that could divide them further are minimized. But more than this, we begin to focus on the Lord. This is another Christian mindset that is often neglected. Our decisions are made in light of what the Lord wants for our lives, and so we carry out our decisions to please the Lord.

Application
- Have you become fully convinced about how you should conduct yourselves on certain practices? Which ones? From what scriptures do you base your conclusions?

- Which areas do you still need to be fully convinced in? List them out and start prayerfully studying one. Think of it as a journey where the Lord better trains you.
- Do you live unto the Lord? Think through two areas of your life and examine whether you live unto the Lord and what difference that perspective makes.

Summary of Romans 14:1-6

Many believers feel rather intense about these issues, but nonetheless, we are to accept or receive those 'weak' and 'strong' in faith. The biggest danger is pride; it can occur with both the strong and weak. Paul even mentions pride as a huge problem that develops with confrontation (Gal 6:1).

The danger is when one goes from discerning to judging: "He is wrong" or "I am better." Pride will never help us accomplish God's will. Pride is Satan's greatest assistant. We can be 'strong,' 'spiritual,' or even 'weak,' but pride is the chief danger. Once we start looking at 'the others' as on our side, then our attitudes toward them lead to acceptance, restoration, and reconciliation. Pride is eager to put down others while grace seeks the best for others. Pride is always the loser.

Summary illustration

Think of your latest family gathering. As the children play about, some of them are not doing or saying the right things. They need to be corrected. At the same time, however, notice how the adults exercise greater patience toward the little ones in those corrections. Although they don't like what the naughty children are doing, they continue to treat them as a member of the family because they *are* one family. This is the way the family of Christian believers needs to interact. We might need to correct one another, but we need to let that correction come from a place of love.

B. Personal Accountability (Rom 14:7-12)

In Romans 14:7-12, Paul further cautions us to focus on God's expectations of us rather than what we expect of others. This extends the lesson from the previous verses on what it means to please the Lord. Paul continues to remain in that same context of those who hold to different standards.

When we compare ourselves with others, pride easily enters. Paul speaks of a better way, that is, to capture every thought and action for the Lord. We live or die for the Lord. Christ is our Lord. The word "Lord" has many possible meanings (including Yahweh from the Old Testament), but Paul uses it in a way that causes us to focus on His great governing responsibility.

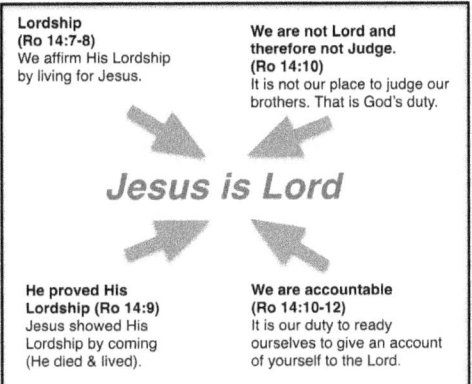

We are accountable directly to our Lord. If God is Judge, how can we dare act as judge? Should we go up to His seat, push Him off His throne, and dare to sit in it and judge others? We have enough to do just to ready ourselves before His judgment. Each of us must give an account for our lives before God. Notice the different aspects of Jesus' lordship.

1. Christ is Lord (14:7-8)

> 7 For not one of us lives for himself, and not one dies for himself; 8 for if we live, we live for the Lord, or if we die, we die for the Lord; therefore whether we live or die, we are the Lord's (14:7-8).

We do not live or die unto ourselves. We no longer belong to ourselves but to the Lord. If our lives rotate around what pleases the Lord, then truly all these discussions about how other brothers and sisters should properly treat others are really issues about what the Lord wants us to do.

2. Christ Proved His Lordship (14:9)

> 9 For to this end Christ died and lived again, that He might be Lord both of the dead and of the living (14:9).

Our devotion to serve the Lord with both our lives and death are only responses to God's overall plan. He is not Lord because we serve Him, but quite the contrary. He is Lord because of who He is. Christ humbly served that He might be Lord. Is Paul suggesting that when we live humbly among our brethren during this stage of life (as Christ did) then we likewise will be greatly rewarded in the future (Christ's reward - Mat 25:14-30)? Although

3. We are not Lord and Judge (14:10)

> ¹⁰ But you, why do you judge your brother? Or you again, why do you regard your brother with contempt? For we shall all stand before the judgment seat of God (14:10).

Paul leaves no room for judging the brethren here. He develops what was earlier stated in this chapter and concludes with yet stronger and stiffer statements with the clear intention of humbling us before the great mighty Lord. "For we shall all stand before the judgment seat of God!" (14:10).

4. We are Accountable (14:11-12)

> ¹¹ For it is written, "As I live, says the Lord, every knew shall bow to Me, and every tongue shall give praise to God." ¹² So then each one of us shall give account of himself to God (14:11-12).

Paul further supports his argument by quoting the Old Testament. (Part of this verse is also quoted in Philippians 2:10-11).

> I have sworn by Myself, The word has gone forth from My mouth in righteousness And will not turn back, That to Me every knee will bow, every tongue will swear allegiance (Isaiah 45:23).

If we dare judge another, we are usurping God's judgeship. This would be reprehensible. By such stern warnings, Paul is trying to bring about a real change in the attitudes of God's people. If God's people see their arrogance for what it is, then they will change, and restoration will follow. Stern speech is sometimes necessary.

Application
- What will your meeting before God be like? Will it go well?
- Can you identify any areas in your life that you try to keep hidden from God? Expose them now and seek to please the Lord in those areas.

C. Love's Greater Call (Rom 14:13-23)

> ¹³ Therefore let us not judge one another anymore, but rather determine this--not to put an obstacle or a stumbling block in a brother's way. ¹⁴ I know and am convinced in the Lord Jesus that nothing is unclean in itself; but to him who thinks anything to be unclean, to him it is unclean. ¹⁵ For if because of food your brother is hurt, you are no longer walking according to love. Do not destroy

with your food him for whom Christ died. ¹⁶ Therefore do not let what is for you a good thing be spoken of as evil; ¹⁷ for the kingdom of God is not eating and drinking, but righteousness and peace and joy in the Holy Spirit.

¹⁸ For he who in this way serves Christ is acceptable to God and approved by men. ¹⁹ So then let us pursue the things which make for peace and the building up of one another. ²⁰ Do not tear down the work of God for the sake of food. All things indeed are clean, but they are evil for the man who eats and gives offense. ²¹ It is good not to eat meat or to drink wine, or to do anything by which your brother stumbles. ²² The faith which you have, have as your own conviction before God. Happy is he who does not condemn himself in what he approves. ²³ But he who doubts is condemned if he eats, because his eating is not from faith; and whatever is not from faith is sin (Rom 14:13-23).

Paul's Wrap Up Call

Again, we are called not to judge one another but to love. Our attitudes can cause a brother or sister to fall (stumble). This is not what the Lord wants for us. A better way to live life is by sacrificing our preferences for the building up of others. We deliberately, and as regularly as needed, should defer from eating what we like or doing what we please, so that we will not cause another brother or sister to stumble.

The idea behind this is that when an individual sees you doing something that they think is wrong, sometimes they will go along with you, even though it goes against their conscience. So even though it is not sin in and of itself (we are still speaking of amoral issues rather than moral ones), when they join us in some activity such as watching (in their eyes) a questionable movie, they sin.

Paul knows there is nothing unclean, but this does not give him the freedom to do whatever he wants whenever he feels like it. Anytime we live for our own enjoyment at another's expense, we have missed the calling to follow Jesus. If Jesus died for them, then they belong to Him as we belong to Him. We are to treat with respect those to whom redemption has come.

If at any point we place food or personal preferences over gracious treatment of our brethren, we will have messed up. What we consider good can become evil. This is similar to how something amoral can become wrong (immoral - see discussion verses 1-2).

We work toward the expansion of God's kingdom on earth, "For the kingdom of God is not eating and drinking, but righteousness and peace and joy in the Holy Spirit."

Below are a number of 'love' commands that Paul lists. In other words, we are not to focus on judging one another but on how to love one another well. This way of loving is superior to seeking the opportunity to please ourselves (If only we could be persuaded of this!).

- Do not judge others (14:13).
- Do not be the cause of another's fall (14:14-16).
- Concentrate on doing what is acceptable to God (14:17-19).
- Don't destroy God's work for the sake of truth (14:20-21).
- Don't act in doubt (14:22). [Live by a good conscience.]
- Always act in faith (14:23).

A lot of Christians struggle with their conscience, but they need to resolve this by simply determining to live by conscience. If one person believes that he should or should not refrain from some particular activity (e.g. amoral action such as how he conducts himself on the Lord's Day), then he should live by his conscience.

It is so much better to live out a consistent life rather than struggling, falling into sin, finding cleansing through Christ's blood, and standing up again. Instead we live from 'faith to faith.' We are glad for Christ's forgiveness, but the struggle with sin is unnecessary and brings us away from the power of a Spirit-filled life.

By living with a clean conscience, we are deliberately making the choice to care for others. The result is a stronger, more vibrant life than the one caught in a struggle with the flesh. "Happy is he who does not condemn himself in what he approves" (14:22).[61]

Your companion might not believe the same thing as you, and may want you to dismiss your conscience and do what you feel is wrong. Your companion should be sensitive to your principles (you might need to speak up and tell him or her) and should not encourage you to break them even though, in his eyes, there is nothing wrong with them.

Paul gives the reason for this in 14:23: 'Whatever is not from faith is sin.' In other words, if I eat in doubt of whether it is proper, then I sin. Don't say to another, "Oh, that is okay. I have done it before." When you do that, you are encouraging your brother or sister to defile his or her conscience. Do not try to convince them; simply limit your own actions.

Self-examination
Reflect on your life and choices before the Lord in prayer. Seek Him regarding any area that you might have 'dirtied' your conscience. Where the Lord brings counsel, make sure you confess sin and present yourself ready to do His will.

Summary Romans 14
Paul cares about the church. In chapters 1-12, Paul spoke about the means God uses to bring a people to be His, while in these last chapters he focuses on how to maintain the unity within the church. In this case, the various groupings of believers in the church were divided by bitterness and pride. They wrongly judged others when they should have focused on loving them. Instead of insisting that their way was the right way, they should have adjusted their attitudes so as not to cause others to stumble. Paul's guidelines are clear and helpful in reminding us how to love others, even when they disagree with us. Our churches face many of these unclear issues. Believers need to train themselves to be more sensitive and discerning as to what situations are always wrong or sometimes wrong, but also how to best assist others in their spiritual growth.

- We are to be gracious as God is gracious (accepting).
- Grace enables us to transcend a judgmental spirit by accepting and embracing those different from us.

---

[61] The term 'good conscience' is used quite regularly throughout the NT (Ac 23:1; 1 Timothy 1:5, 1:19; Heb 13:18; 1 Pe 3:16, 3:21).

- Grace enables us to discern the real issues rather than being caught up in 'pride' wars.
- Grace enables a congregation to live out Spirit-filled lives as we live pure lives in a spirit of love.

Romans 15:1-13

Living for Others

Paul continues in the spirit of chapter 14 by stressing how love is to work itself out in strained relationships. The church in Rome experienced certain tensions, which mostly occurred between Jew and non-Jew.

Paul introduces certain positive actions that we can similarly take to relieve tension in difficult relationships. All the advice, in one way or another, returns to the foundational command to love one another, just as Jesus taught us. The word 'love' is not used, but it is this love that is being restated and reapplied for numerous situations.

A. Practice of Love (Rom 15:1)

> Now we who are strong ought to bear the weaknesses of those without strength and not just please ourselves (15:1).

"Strong" does not mean oppressive, but confident; living free from guilt in contrast to the weak in faith (14:1-2) who limit their freedom because of traditional religious concerns. The issue Paul focuses on is not who is right or wrong, but the need for harmonious living. And so, the strong subdues his pride over being right for the purpose of ministering and caring for the "weak."

The weak here are those who cannot share the freedom to eat meat dedicated to idols (14:2). Our chief purpose is to please the Lord, and therefore we must be willing to modify our choices for the Lord's greater purposes, living not to please ourselves but God, and to support the faith of other believers. This mode of prioritizing others should replicate itself in daily situations.

B. Instruction of Love (Rom 15:2)

> Let each of us please his neighbor for his good, to his edification (15:2).

Paul amplifies the first statement (v.1) by connecting it to Jesus' words to "love your neighbor as yourself" (Mk 12:31). The Golden Rule instructs us to edify (i.e. build up) others, working for their advantage. When we commit ourselves to support others, all sorts of good and fun ideas might come to our minds. Carry out the thoughts that the Spirit of the Lord brings to your mind through the strength that He provides.

C. The Basis for Love (Rom 15:3-4)

> ³ For even Christ did not please Himself; but as it is written, "The reproaches of those who reproached Thee fell upon me." ⁴ For whatever was written in earlier times was written for our instruction, that through perseverance and the encouragement of the Scriptures we might have hope (15:3-4).

The initial use of "for" identifies this explanatory note of the former conclusions made in verses 1 and 2. Some people avoid loving others because they might be hurt. It is a good thing Jesus did not go by the world's strategy, "Love those that are nice to you." Instead, from His  example, we love others no matter who they are or how they treat us. We do not treat people well because they deserve it but because the Lord calls us to live this way. This was clearly the policy Christ lived by, and it is the same for His disciples, both then and now.

The statement of "whatever was written in earlier times" refers to the Old Testament scriptures (note the many quotes Paul uses throughout Romans). The New Testament was still being written down–including this Epistle to the Romans! Today, we still use the Old Testament to encourage and direct us in our faith. Paul, for example, used the examples and words of David and Abraham in Romans 4 to establish that salvation is by faith rather than by works. The scriptures remain relevant and directive for our lives, though their truth is made clear by the New Testament and Christ's work on the cross. Paul might have stated this to give the Gentiles greater respect for the Old Testament, but in any case, we should carefully read the Old

Romans 15:1-13 Living for Others

Testament to build up our own faith so that we can carry out God's acts of love, even if it requires suffering.

D. The Result of Love (Rom 15:5-12)

> 5 Now may the God who gives perseverance and encouragement grant you to be of the same mind with one another according to Christ Jesus; 6 that with one accord you may with one voice glorify the God and Father of our Lord Jesus Christ. 7 Wherefore, accept one another, just as Christ also accepted us to the glory of God. 8 For I say that Christ has become a servant to the circumcision on behalf of the truth of God to confirm the promises given to the fathers (15:5-8).

Paul prays that we, the church, though sometimes tempted to fragmentation, will have the same mind toward each other. This was true for the groups within the Roman church experiencing tension, as well as for our churches today. The Lord's call to praise Him and serve one another rises high above our selfish concerns. We are to accept others even as Christ accepted us.

"Wherefore, accept one another, just as Christ also accepted us to the glory of God" (Rom 15:7).

"The glory of God" first refers to the honor that goes to God for Jesus' love toward us sinners when He died on the cross. The "just as" urges us to replicate this sacrificial love by accepting one another, so that we can have the privilege of bringing glory to God. If we have difficulty understanding the high calling of subjecting our wills to carry out God's law of love, all we need to do is look at how Jesus Christ the King became human, became a servant, and lived under the Law so that he could confirm the Old Testament promises and fulfill the Law. A commitment to love sets our lives in order to carry out God's will.

Verses 9-12 further supplies Old Testament 'proof' of the special calling of both Jews and Gentiles: "Praise the Lord all you Gentiles, and let all the peoples praise Him" (Rom 15:11). The greater vision for the Gentiles to serve along with the Jews was implanted right there in the Old Testament!

> 9 And for the Gentiles to glorify God for His mercy; as it is written, "Therefore I will give praise to Thee among the Gentiles, and I will sing to Thy Name." 10 And again he says, "Rejoice, O Gentiles with His people." 11 And again, "Praise the Lord all you Gentiles, and let all the peoples praise Him." 12 And again Isaiah says, "There shall come

the root of Jesse, and He who arises to rule over the Gentiles, in Him shall the Gentiles hope."

Verse nine originates from Psalm 18:49; verse 10 from Deuteronomy 32:43, verse 11 from Psalm 117:1 and verse 12 from Isaiah 11:10. Depending on the Bible version, the word 'Gentiles' is not often used in the Old Testament; rather its equivalent, 'nations' or 'peoples', is used to express the same idea. What we see happening is that every corner of the earth is turning to the Lord and giving Him praise. This is exactly what is happening right now in our generation. Praise the Lord!

E. The Power of Love (Rom 15:13; 15:5)

> [13] Now may the God of hope fill you with all joy and peace in believing, that you may abound in hope by the power of the Holy Spirit (15:13).

Interestingly, Paul engages another benediction (lit. good word) in verse 13. The first one was in 15:5. Paul closes his epistle to the Romans with a third blessing in 16:25. Other matters, evidently, kept coming to his mind so that after penning 15:13, he remembered that he had not explained the reason he had been so slow in reaching Rome.

Summary

Verses 14:1-15:13 provide special instructions on how two very different groups in the church are to live in harmony with each other and positively live out their lives in the spirit of Christ's love. Although the issues involved were not foundational to the faith, believers have the opportunity to mimic Christ's love and bring glory to God. After all, the Jews and Gentiles will be praising God forever in heaven. They might as well start now! The law of love provides us the opportunity to give praise to God through the loving acts that we carry out each day. What about those issues with which we disagree? Let God judge. Our responsibility is to live devoted to one another as Christ did for us. We are to busy ourselves finding opportunity to express our love for others, because in this Christ is glorified.

Romans 15:14-33
Our Will and God's Will

After the second benediction in 15:13, the apostle remembers one of the original reasons he wrote to the Romans. Early on in 1:10-11, Paul spoke about his hope to see them. (What a blessed detour this has been!)

> ¹⁰ Always in my prayers making request, if perhaps now at last by the will of God **I may succeed in coming to you.** For I long to see you in order that I may impart some spiritual gift to you, that you may be established (Rom 1:10-11).

Like any good novel, the elements of suspense and surprise are not only carefully hinted at in the beginning but cleverly revealed in the end. Paul wanted the Roman Christians to be able to understand the Lord's will in light of what God was doing around the world. God's special and wonderful redemptive program to adopt us into His spiritual family should directly impact our individual plans for today and tomorrow. God's mission program has everything to do with our plans and decisions. Even Paul's good and noble plans to go to Rome and Jerusalem to build up the Christian church was subjugated to God's desires to use Paul to further expand God's work around the world.

Paul explains his call to ministry (15:14-19) and shows why this call (15:20-25) had delayed him from visiting them (15:26-33). Despite the setbacks, he hoped he would be able to visit them as he carried out the ministry that God had given him. This passage's outline, providing insight into discerning God's will, will focus on God's will.

A. The Basics of God's Will (Rom 15:14-16)

What is it that God wants for our lives? He wants to totally affect each part of our heart, mind, and soul so that we would fully carry out His "good and acceptable and perfect" will (Rom 12:2). Paul mentions various aspects of God's general will here.

1. Developing Faith for Others (14)

> ¹⁴ And concerning you, my brethren, I myself also am convinced that you yourselves are full of goodness, filled with all knowledge, and able also to admonish one another (15:14).

Proper love and teaching shape our vision for others. Note the apostle's vibrant hope for people he has never met!

Regarding goodness (14)

"Full of goodness": When God enters our lives, we become "full of goodness." God's good plans are fulfilled in us, and we should be motivated to do good. God's will is good and our Lord insists on us to continue to carry out His good purposes as we relate to others. Goodness describes the essential, non-selfish, kind heart manifested toward others, which will lead to godly living. God is good and when we live out that goodness, we share God's nature.

Regarding Knowledge (14)

"Filled with all knowledge": Knowledge is based on fact, that which is real and true. If something is not factual, then it is not considered significant knowledge. True knowledge leads to a greater ability to discern what pleases God. In contrast to what the world says, God is pro-knowledge ('science' literally meaning 'knowledge'). When Christian organizations go to a country, it is not long before educational institutions are established. As in Romans 12:2, the mind serves an important part in the development of the believer.

Regarding Use of God's Word (14)

"Able also to admonish each other": Admonishment asserts certain doctrinal truths or behaviors against false ones and adds emphasis by revealing the consequences of the multiplicity of choices or belief. We must exhort one other, much as Paul has shown us through Romans. This can be exhortation concerning truth, that is, doctrines such as the justification of faith that he earlier addressed or God's worldwide redemptive plan that Paul wrote of in this chapter, or of the need to love others even when they hold different opinions.

God's people, then, are expected to admonish other believers by a thorough understanding of God's Word and will, and an application of it to their lives. This call to admonish others counters the spirit of independent Christians, going from congregation to congregation as they please, choosing to live and believe as they see appropriate. This ministry of admonishment doesn't stop with the apostles, but is expected from us too.

2. Affirming Gifts and Calling (15:15-16)

> 15 But I have written very boldly to you on some points, so as to remind you again, because of the grace that was given me from God, 16 to be a minister of Christ Jesus to the Gentiles, ministering as a priest the gospel of God, that my offering of the Gentiles might become acceptable, sanctified by the Holy Spirit (Rom 15:15-16).

Paul further bolsters his willingness to advocate certain teachings and conduct by referring to 'the grace' given to Him from God. Each of us have received some measure of this grace (i.e. gifting Romans 12:6). It is our duty, then, to connect that grace (15) with our life purpose(s). In Paul's case, this meant that he was to minister to the Gentiles in such a way that they become an acceptable offering to God.

Verse 16 stems from the later verses in Isaiah, again confirming God's purpose of reaching the nations (think Gentiles). In 66:18, the Lord says, "The time is coming to gather all nations and tongues. And they shall come and see My glory." He infers that these Gentiles, from all sorts of nations (cf. Acts 2) will join the Jewish brethren (Is 66:19), resulting in the powerful conclusion found in Isaiah 20-21, "Then they shall bring all your brethren from all the nations as a grain offering to the Lord... I will also take some for them for priest and for Levites," says the Lord" (Isaiah 66:21).

Paul alludes to his work of spreading the gospel among the Gentiles that their belief and service might become an offering to God. Perhaps he hopes that other Jewish believers will catch the vision of what God is doing, calling them to participate in the evangelization of the nations as well as the embrace of 'priests' (i.e. full-time ministers) from among the Gentile believers.

Summary and application

God extends His goodness and grace to Paul by making him a vehicle by which this vision is passed worldwide to all believers. The Jews and Gentiles in

Rome and around the world, however, are equally part of God's worldwide mission. Each of us has a part in this plan, which is what defines God's will for our lives. It is essential to understand the Lord's overarching purpose to extend His goodness to others by His involvement of our lives. Like the apostle, we must refuse to look at the topic of God's will in a selfish and narrow way. Instead, ask God how you might learn what He wants for your life so that you can better serve and help others know God and do His will.

B. Discover the Specifics of God's will (Ro 15:20-33)

When people think of God's will, they generally think of the specific will of God rather than God's general purpose for our lives. These general principles are important components, upwards of 95%, of the things a believer does. Without these general principles, one would not be able to carry out the specific directions of God's will. However, we should realize that when needed, God does specifically reveal details that we need to know to properly serve Him. Such was Paul's Macedonian call, which redirected the movement of Christianity into what we now know as Europe (Acts 16:9-10).

1) God's Will and Our Vision (15:20-22)

> [20] And thus I aspired to preach the gospel, not where Christ was already named, that I might not build upon another man's foundation; [21] but as it is written, "They who had no news of Him shall see, and they who have not heard shall understand." [22] For this reason I have often been hindered from coming to you (15:20-22).

Jesus specially called Paul, formerly Saul, to preach to the nations, but notice how he refined his goal or vision to focus on reaching those Gentiles who had not received the gospel, 'not where Christ was already named.' His focus of reaching the unreached fits well into God's overall purpose. Paul believes that the established church can, by God's grace, care for itself (Eph 4:10-13). Paul did not say that God told him to focus on that group, but it became his priority and chief burden. Paul was 'hindered' from going to Rome because of this refined goal. They already had a church there, and he sensed it more critical to go where there was no church (though this letter proves there were needs to be addressed in Rome).

If we are not devoted to the Old Testament scriptures, we should be! Paul gained clarity for God's will for his life through the Old Testament. The above quote comes from Isaiah 52:15, which is part of the great prophetic passage on Christ's suffering (Isaiah 53's message actually starts in 52:13). He doesn't quote the whole verse leaving out, "Thus He will sprinkle many **nations**" (cf. 1 Pet 1:1). Paul appropriately saw his life as we should see our own, as a glorious ongoing result of Christ's death on the cross. The Old Testament is not just for doctrinal perspicuity, but to direct and shape our conduct (15:4).

2) God's Permissive Will (15:23-25)

> 23 But now, with no further place for me in these regions, and since I have had for many years a longing to come to you 24 whenever I go to Spain--for I hope to see you in passing, and to be helped on my way there by you, when I have first enjoyed your company for a while-- 25 but now, I am going to Jerusalem serving the saints (Ro 15:23-25).

Within these refined goals, Paul found even more defined goals and purposes. First, we see his original plan fulfilled: "no further place for me in these regions." This opened up a new field of ministry. He was willing to visit them in Rome, though, only if it served the larger mission purpose. He reveals that his heart adopted the new field of Spain and would go by Rome to reach Spain. He conveniently adjusted his plans to visit Rome on his way to Spain. Paul's choice may not have been dictated by God's voice but it was certainly shaped by His larger purpose. The Spaniards were Gentiles. That was God's call. Were they reached yet? No.

Rome? Of course, Paul wanted to visit them–as is seen in this extensive letter to them. This visit, however, only became a consideration when, without much delay, he could reach his larger goal.

We always need to evaluate our calling and burden and keep the costs, time, and resources in mind. It is very interesting to observe how Paul saw his visit to Jerusalem fit into his larger set of plans, "be helped on my way there by you." Finding resources for ministry among God's people makes sense. Their supply, of course, forms a means by which they can be part of God's greater work.

3) God's Moral Directives (15:26-33)

Participation in missions is not only morally proper but foundational! Paul not only helped the church get established, but actually assisted the church to have a proper serving spirit. He encouraged the church at large to participate in two particular ways.

(1) Financial Participation (26-29)

> ²⁶ For Macedonia and Achaia have been pleased to make a contribution for the poor among the saints in Jerusalem. ²⁷ Yes, they were pleased to do so, and they are indebted to them. For if the Gentiles have shared in their spiritual things, they are indebted to minister to them also in material things. ²⁸ Therefore, when I have finished this, and have put my seal on this fruit of theirs, I will go on by way of you to Spain. ²⁹ And I know that when I come to you, I will come in the fulness of the blessing of Christ (Rom 15:26-33).

He invested his time and money (the cost of international travel was high back then) to help them express their love to Jerusalem, which was experiencing a famine. The apostle recognizes the need to materially reward those who spiritually benefitted by those in full-time service. He is showing how the Gentiles really have a heart for God's work. As they have received the Gospel, now they respond by giving material things. Paul sensed the need to accompany them to avoid any delay (2 Cor 8:11, 19-21).

(2) Prayer Participation (30-33)

> ³⁰ Now I urge you, brethren, by our Lord Jesus Christ and by the love of the Spirit, to strive together with me in your prayers to God for me. 31 that I may be delivered from those who are disobedient in Judea, and that my service for Jerusalem may prove acceptable to the saints; ³² so that I may come to you in joy by the will of God and find refreshing rest in your company. ³³ Now the God of peace be with you all. Amen (15:30-33).

Paul sought the church to join him in praying with him as he reached out to the Gentiles. I personally have similarly greatly depended on those who pray and give to my ministry. Again, Paul sees them working as a team, effectively makes it 'our' ministry.

"Our ministry" reveals a biblical ministry mindset. I once received this email from a friend who prays for our ministry: "I praise God. I consider myself part of this ministry, by being in prayer daily." This is the heart of God, to employ all of His people in His grand redemptive plan.

There seems to be a subtle reference to the purpose and drive of the three persons of God in verse 30. It is "by our Lord Jesus Christ" that we can go to God the Father to pray in His Name, empowered "by the love of the

Spirit" that characterizes the work of God, making it acceptable. From our perspective, the church and Paul both had a role in this and thus acted as priests (Paul seems to redefine prophets [12:6] and priests.)

More importantly, Paul identifies the Judaizers as a special prayer need and gathers prayer for them in their attempts to oppose God's will and mission. Paul had a heart to visit Israel, and he found the opportunity by encouraging the Gentiles to help the Jews find relief from the drought affecting Jerusalem. By praying, Paul seeks to visit them and find refreshment from them. Another benediction marks the end of chapter 15.

Summary

Our desire to conform to God's will should greatly influence our decision-making habits. We should notice different components of God's will:

(1) The call of God to direct a person's life,

(2) The general will of God to keep us within His will and focused on His good and healthy purposes, and

(3) Our individual burdens, gifts, and opportunities should direct us to appropriately work with others to make the right decisions in order to complete God's will.

Romans 16:1-27
Community Spirit

One would think that this theologian par excellence, this logician, master of argument, being both a miraculously called and driven man would be a little weak on the relational side of things. Paul the apostle, however, had a great affection and wonderful love for the Roman believers. He, like Jesus, was not carried away with His calling or devotion to teaching that he lost sight of the needs of the people to whom he ministered. Much can be observed from this passage about the Christian community there in Rome, as well as Paul's commitment to working together with them.

A. Remembering God's People (Rom 16:5,6,8, 10-11,13-16)

5 ... Greet Epaenetus, my beloved, who is the first convert to Christ from Asia. 6 Greet Mary, who has worked hard for you 8 Greet Ampliatus, my beloved in the Lord. 10 Greet Apelles, the approved in Christ. Greet those who are of the household of Aristobulus. 11 Greet Herodion, my kinsman. Greet those of the household of Narcissus, who are in the Lord. 13 Greet Rufus, a choice man in the Lord, also his mother and mine. 14 Greet Asyncritus, Phlegon, Hermes, Patrobas, Hermas and the brethren with them. 15 Greet Philologus and Julia, Nereus and his sister, and Olympas, and all the saints who are with them. 16 Greet one another with a holy kiss. (16:5,6,8, 10-11,13-16)

> **Paul and Women**
>
> Some suggest Paul looked down upon women. By just observing the comments he makes in chapter 16, how can we respond to them?
> - Phoebe Some(1)
> - Priscilla (3)
> - Mary (6)
> - Rufus' mother (13)

Paul was not attempting to mention all the names of the Christians in Rome in these verses nor even those he personally knew. The word "greet," mostly used at the beginning of the verse, is used seventeen times by Paul to address specific individuals at Rome (vv 3-16).

Although he had never been to Rome since his faith in Christ, he knew a lot of the people in the church there. Perhaps he met them on a missionary journey. The list includes the names of a great variety of people, perhaps representing different house churches. He reminded them of their common heritage in Christ with others in the church of God, even though they might differ on certain personal beliefs (Rom 14) or cultural backgrounds (e.g. Jew-Gentile).

B. Working with God's People (Ro 16:1-2, 3-5, 7, 9, 12)

> 1 I commend to you our sister Phoebe, who is a servant of the church which is at Cenchrea; 2 that you receive her in the Lord in a manner worthy of the saints, and that you help her in whatever matter she may have need of you; for she herself has also been a helper of many, and of myself as well. 3 Greet Prisca and Aquila, my **fellow workers** in Christ Jesus, 4 who for my life risked their own necks, to whom not only do I give thanks, but also all the churches of the Gentiles. Also greet the church that is in their house. 5 Greet Epaenetus, my beloved, who is the first convert to Christ from Asia… 7 Greet Andronicus and Junias, my kinsmen, and my fellow prisoners, who are outstanding **among the apostles**, who also were in Christ before me (Rom 16:1-5,7).

Throughout this long list of names, we should notice a strong sense of companionship. Paul was an apostle, but that position did not cause him to think of himself as better than others. Everyone had their part. They were "fellow workers in Christ Jesus" (3). He was quite willing to mention how others had special attributes such as 'outstanding apostles, who also were in Christ before me.'

There are two interpretations of 16:7. Some take it to mean "well-known among the apostles," while others interpret it as "outstanding among the disciples." The latter understanding is more probable, which would require the term 'apostle' to have a wider meaning than the original twelve (Acts 1:13,26) as in Acts 14:4, 14; 2 Cor 8:23; 1 Th 2:6.

Some suggest that Junias refers to a sister apostle. There is no other hint of female apostles anywhere in the scriptures. Jesus chose twelve men (nor should we be apologetic for this!). Clearly, Jesus had the opportunity to appoint women. Furthermore, the accentuation of Junias is with few exceptions clearly masculine. Junias is a shortened form of Junianus. The presence of female apostles would contradict passages like 1 Cor. 14:34-35. Paul did not think of woman as inferior since he highlights the giftedness of several sisters in this passage (16:1-3).

Because they had apostles in Rome, Paul had no 'need' to be there. Those apostles could help the church. He respected other leaders and worked along with them.

- Phoebe (1-2)
- Priscilla and Aquila (3-5)
- Andronicus and Junias (7)
- Urbanus (9)
- Tryphaena and Tryphosa (12)

What would it be like to meet in small groups and houses for worship? The erection of large places of worship was rare back then. More possibly, and clearly suggested here, is the presence of many churches in a certain locale. The verse, "Also greet the church that is in their house" (4) suggests this.

C. Sheltering God's People (Rom 16:17-20)

[17] Now I urge you, brethren, keep your eye on those who cause dissensions and hindrances contrary to the teaching which you learned, and turn away from them. [18] For such men are slaves, not of our Lord Christ but of their own appetites; and by their smooth and flattering speech they deceive the hearts of the unsuspecting. [19] For the report of your obedience has reached to all; therefore I am rejoicing over you, but I want you to be wise in what is good, and innocent in what is evil. [20] And the **God of peace** will soon crush Satan under your feet. The grace of our Lord Jesus be with you (16:17-20).

God's people are an oppressed people. Trouble dogs their path. Paul warns them of those who cause dissension and hinder the growth of the church. Whenever God's truth went into an area, so did false teachers. Things have not changed.

> Wise in what is good, and innocent in what is evil.

One source of this false teaching is the desire some have to satisfy their own appetites. For example, some pretended to be Christians but really were after money, sex, or praise. Paul encouraged genuine believers to be faithful to God's Word rather than to be influenced by those around them.

In contrast to those stressful experiences, Paul states that he wants the believers to be innocent in what is evil. It is not proper, wise, or good to primarily learn from experience. Just avoid what is evil and pursue that which is good.

"'God of peace" refers to how quarreling is sourced from His arch enemy, the evil one, Satan. "Soon crush" implies that Satan is still at large and able to hurt God's people, though only for a limited time. He alludes to Christ's return when the evil one will be fully judged. "Under your feet" refers to God's promise in Genesis where it speaks of Satan's head being crushed by the seed of the woman, which is Christ and His body, the church (Gen 3:15).

> **"And the God of peace will soon crush Satan under your feet!"**

D. Establishing God's People (Rom 16:21-27)

> ²¹ Timothy my fellow worker greets you, and so do Lucius and Jason and Sosipater, my kinsmen. ²² I, Tertius, who write this letter, greet you in the Lord. ²³ Gaius, host to me and to the whole church, greets you. Erastus, the city treasurer greets you, and Quartus, the brother. ²⁴ [The grace of our Lord Jesus Christ be with you all. Amen.] ²⁵ Now to Him who is able to establish you according to my gospel and the preaching of Jesus Christ, according to the revelation of the mystery which has been kept secret for long ages past, ²⁶ but now is manifested, and by the Scriptures of the prophets, according to the commandment of the eternal God, has been made known to all the nations, leading to obedience of faith; ²⁷ to the only wise God, through Jesus Christ, be the glory forever. Amen (Rom 16:21-27).

1. Introductory Comments (16:21-24)

Paul continues to greet those in Rome in verses 21-23 but this time on behalf of eight individuals. Paul dictated what has come to be known as the Book of Romans, but it was Tertius who actually wrote it down. Gaius was an important elder in the Corinthian church that baptized people in Corinth (1 Cor 1:14).

The phrase, "The grace of our Lord Jesus Christ" (24) is only found in some ancient manuscripts, but is typical of Paul's writing (2 Cor 8:9; Gal 6:18; 1 Th 5:28; 2 Th 3:18). Verses 25-27 are also excluded from other manuscripts, but appropriately summarize the book. This forms the last benediction, but even that turns into a mini-sermon! Note the expansion of this benediction below.

2. The Grand Purpose (16:25)

25 Now to Him ... to the only wise God,
 through Jesus Christ,
 be the glory forever. Amen

Paul is very concerned for God's glorification.[62] God's many good and manifold purposes, including redemption, are wrapped up in the ultimate purpose of bringing glory to His Name. This preoccupation with bringing extreme praise and honor to Himself for His works is proper and good. It is fitting and therefore demanded. Whenever the church loses its admiration of the Lord, she has lost the vision of what God is doing in His redemptive program.[63]

3. Being Established (16:25)

(25) Him who is able
 to establish you
 according to my gospel and
  the preaching of Jesus Christ

Paul identifies reasons to give praise to God, starting with stating what we have gained through His extraordinary grace. The only reason for a secure hope is that it was established through the gospel, the wonderful mystery that Paul has depicted throughout the Book of Romans.

There are two means by which God's people are established, though they appear to be very similar: "my gospel" and "preaching of Jesus Christ." "My gospel" refers to Paul's own message. There are unique aspects of it,

---

[62] Note that many doubt Paul ever wrote these concluding words in 25-27, because they were not part of certain manuscripts. They are, for example, excluded from Hodges and Farstad, "*The Greek New Testament According to the Majority Text*" but are in later, more complete, manuscripts: p61 ℵ B C D, etc. (*The Greek New Testament*, p. 577).

[63] The word 'glory' is appropriately used in fifteen verses of Romans: 1:23,2:7, 2:10, 3:7,3:23, 4:20, 5:2, 6:4, 8:18, 8:21, 9:4, 9:23, 11:36, 15:9,16:27.

including his own testimony on how God has saved him. But it only stands because it incorporates the preaching of Jesus. In both cases, it goes back to the heralding or preaching of God's gospel truths to the world, clearly emphasized in Romans 10:15-17. It is the sending out of the gospel rather than social works (which are natural results of the gospel) that become the awesome means by which God saves His people and manifests His glory. May we, like the apostle, become caught up in the extreme wisdom and love of God as seen in the gospel (Eph 3:9-11).

4. Revealing and Proclamation of the Gospel (16:25b-27)

> according to the revelation of the mystery
> > which has been kept secret for long ages past,
> > 26 but now is manifested,
> > > – and by the Scriptures of the prophets,
> > > – according to the commandment of the eternal God,
> > > > has been made known to all the nations,
> > > > leading to obedience of faith
> > 27 to the only wise God, through Jesus Christ, be the glory forever. Amen.

Further glory becomes apparent as we understand the full nature of the gospel, its hidden nature for millenniums and now its full revelation. All these aspects reveal the fullness of God's comprehensive salvation plan, which intentionally included both Jews and Gentiles.

And so Paul closes his lengthy letter by uniting the theme of obedience to His commandment to spread the gospel to the nations, including both Jews and Gentiles (i.e. everyone) with making manifest God's glory. At the same time, he defends his calling and ministry to the Gentiles as he goes to Spain, always hoping the Jews will catch a glimpse of God's greater program and themselves believe in the gospel of Jesus Christ.

Despite rejection by the Jews, God's ability to accomplish His plan unscathed–though with the pain of Christ's suffering–is a remarkable testimony of God's love, power, and wisdom that causes praise. Notice how Paul cannot stray from the theme of praise, as he brings it up in verse 25 by announcing the glory due God's great Name in verse 27. The declaration of the Gospel, then, exposes God's glorious person and brings glory to Him as the Name of Jesus is spread around the world.

Summary

Paul's famous message to the Romans ends here. This clear defense of faith in Christ has helped millions of believers over the years to grasp and preserve the glory of Christ's gospel. Having been strengthened by the clear knowledge of the gospel, ministers of the gospel have since been going to the ends of the world proclaiming God's powerful saving truth in Christ.

As God's people see His ultimate purpose of revealing His glorious person through redemption, they can, like the apostle, offer up an offering of good works to present to the Lord, not to gain salvation, but to humbly show their deep appreciation for welcoming them to join Him in declaring His grand redemption story in the gospel of Jesus Christ.

Appendix 1: Author's Information

Rev. Paul Bucknell teaches Christian leadership seminars around the world and has authored more than twenty books on topics including: Christian life, discipleship, godly living, biblical studies, call to ministry, marriage, parenting and anxiety. His blend of knowledge from different fields along with his deep care for training of God's people provide many new insights into this book. Paul and his wife, Linda, live in the USA and have eight children and five grandchildren. He is the founder and president of Biblical Foundations for Freedom[64], a web-based ministry that releases God's powerful, life-changing truths worldwide.

---

[64] www.foundationsforfreedom.net

www.ingramcontent.com/pod-product-compliance
Lightning Source LLC
Chambersburg PA
CBHW060458090426
42735CB00011B/2026